THE TWO AND

THE TWO AND THE ONE

MIRCEA ELIADE

Translated by
J. M. COHEN

The University of Chicago Press

This book was originally published in France
under the title of
Méphistophélès et l'Androgyne.

The University of Chicago Press, Chicago 60637
© 1962 Editions Gallimard
© 1965 in the English translation by Harvill Press, London,
and Harper & Row, Publishers, Inc., New York
All rights reserved. Published 1965
Phoenix Edition 1979
Printed in the United States of America

86 85 84 83 82 81 80 79   5 4 3 2 1

ISBN: 0-226-20389-1
LCN: 79-2268

Contents

Contents

Contents

Foreword

A. N. Whitehead has said that the history of western philosophy is no more than a series of footnotes to Plato. It is doubtful whether western thought can maintain itself any longer in this "splendid isolation". The modern epoch is too sharply distinguished from its predecessors to allow of that, being characterised by a confrontation with the "unknown", the "outsiders" and their unaccustomed and unfamiliar, exotic or archaic worlds. For the discoveries of depth psychology and the emergence into History of non-European ethnic groups truly amount to the invasion by "outsiders" of the once closed field of the western consciousness.

As has more than once been observed, the Western world is in process of radically modifying itself as a result of these discoveries and confrontations. Since the end of last century the researches of orientalists have progressively familiarized the West with the strange and fabulous elements in Asiatic societies and cultures. At the same time, modern ethnology was discovering dark and mysterious spiritual worlds which, if they were not, as Lévy-Bruhl at a certain moment believed, the product of a pre-logical mentality, were no less strangely different from the cultural landscapes familiar to Westerners.

But it is depth psychology that has revealed the most *terrae ignotae*, has caused the most dramatic confrontations. The discovery of the unconscious could be put on a level with the maritime discoveries of the Renaissance and the astronomical discoveries that followed the invention of the telescope. For each of these discoveries brought to light worlds whose existence was

9

not even suspected. Each, by shattering the traditional image of the world and revealing the structure of a hitherto unimaginable Universe, achieved a sort of "break-through". Now a break-through like this will inevitably have consequences. The astronomical and geographical discoveries of the Renaissance not only completely altered the picture of the Universe and the conception of space; they assured, for three centuries at least, the scientific, economic and political supremacy of the West, and at the same time opened the way that leads fatally to world unity.

Freud's discoveries constitute another "opening", but this time on worlds submerged in the unconscious. The psychoanalytical technique has inaugurated a new type of *descensus ad inferos*. When Jung revealed the existence of the collective unconscious, the exploration of these immemorial treasures—the myths, symbols and images of archaic humanity—began to approximate its techniques to those of the oceanographers and speleologists. Just as deep sea diving and cave exploration revealed elementary organisms that had long ago disappeared from the earth's surface, so analysis discovered forms of deep psychic life hitherto inaccessible to study. Speleology placed at the biologist's disposal tertiary and even secondary organisms, zoomorphic forms *that are not fossilizable*, that is to say forms that had disappeared without a trace from the surface of the earth. By the discovery of "living fossils", speleology has considerably advanced our knowledge of archaic forms of life. In the same way, archaic forms of psychical life, the "living fossils" buried in the darkness of the unconscious, now became accessible to study, thanks to techniques developed by the depth psychologists.

It is remarkable that the cultural flowering of psychoanalysis, as well as the growing interest in the study of symbols and myths, have coincided to a large extent with the emergence of Asia into History and, furthermore, with the spiritual and political awakening of the "primitive" peoples. After the Second World War, an encounter with the "others", with the "unknown", became for Westerners a historical inevitability. Now, for some years Westerners have not only felt with increasing sharpness what a confrontation with "outsiders" means; but have also realised that it is they who are being dominated. This does not necessarily imply that they will be enslaved or oppressed, but only that they will feel the pressure of a "foreign", non-Western spirituality. For the encounter—or shock—between civilizations is always, in the last resort, an encounter between spiritualities—between religions.

A true encounter implies a dialogue. In order to begin a valid dialogue with non-European cultures, it is indispensable to know and understand these cultures. Hermeneutics—the science of interpretation—is the Western man's reply—the only intelligent reply—to the demands of contemporary history, to the fact that the West is committed (one might be tempted to say "condemned") to a confrontation with the cultural values of the "others". Now in this present situation, hermeneutics will find its most valuable ally in the history of religions. When the history of religions has become the "complete discipline" that it should be, men will understand that the world of the "unconscious", like the strange worlds of the non-Westerners, can best be analysed on the plane of religious values and behaviour.

It has not yet been clearly realised that the "openings" effected by the discoveries of the psychologists and the explorers of archaic thought are homologous to the large-scale appearance of the non-European peoples in history; that it is not merely a question of the considerable enlargement of the scientific horizon (as was the case with the geographical and astronomical discoveries of the Renaissance), but also, and primarily, of experiencing an encounter with "the unknown". Now an encounter with the "totally other", whether conscious or unconscious, gives rise to an experience of a religious nature. It is not impossible that our age may go down to posterity as the first to rediscover those "diffuse religious experiences" which were destroyed by the triumph of Christianity. It is equally possible that the attraction of the unconscious and its activities, the interest in myths and symbols, the fascination of the exotic, the primitive, the archaic, and encounters with the "others", with all the ambivalent feelings they imply—that all this may one day appear as a new type of religious experience.

Now we may anticipate that all these elements are preparing for the growth of a new humanism, which will not be a replica of the old. For what principally concerns us now is to integrate the researches of the orientalists, ethnologists, depth psychologists, and historians of religion in order to arrive at a total knowledge of man. These scholars have untiringly revealed the human interest, the psychological "truth" and the spiritual value of all those symbols, myths, divine figures and practices to be found among the Asiatics and the "primitives". These human documents had hitherto been studied with the detachment and indifference that nineteenth-century naturalists brought to the study of insects. Today we are beginning to observe that they express typical human situations, that they form an integral part of the history of the spirit. Now, the proper frame of mind for discovering the meaning of a typical human situation is not the "objectivity" of the naturalist, but the intelligent sympathy of the exegetist, the interpreter. It is the *frame of mind* itself that has had to be changed. For the strangest, the most aberrant behaviour must be considered as a human fact; if considered as a zoological phenomenon or monstrosity it is not understood.

To approach a symbol, myth or archaic practice as the expression of an existential situation is already to recognize that it has human dignity and philosophical meaning. This attitude would have seemed laughably absurd to a nineteenth-century scholar. For him "savagery" or "primordial stupidity" could represent only an embryonic and consequently "a-cultural" phase of humanity.

But, as has been said, it is now important to relate and integrate the results of these researches, conducted in a very different spirit from that of the nineteenth century, and thus to arrive at a more exact knowledge of man. Very soon the West will not only have to know and understand the cultural Universes of the non-Westerners, but will have to value them as an integral part of the history of the human spirit and no longer consider them as infantile or aberrant episodes of an exemplary History of Man. Moreover, confrontation with the "others" helps Western man to know himself better. The effort spent on correctly understanding modes of thought foreign to the Western rationalist tradition, that is to say, in the first place on deciphering the meaning of myths and symbols, will be repaid by a considerable enrichening of the consciousness. Of course, the depth psychologists have begun to study the structure of symbols and the scenarios of myths in order to understand the power of the unconscious. But a confrontation with the non-Western cultures, governed by symbols and nourished by myths, must take place on a different plane; it is no longer a question of "analysing" these cultures, as one analyses a person's dreams, in order to "reduce" them to signs revealing certain modification in the deep psyche; henceforth we shall have to consider the cultures of non-Western peoples in their own right, and try to understand them with the same intellectual passion that we devote to understanding the Homeric world, the prophets of Israel, or the mystical philosophy of Meister Eckhardt. In other words, we must approach—and fortunately a beginning has already been made—Oceanic or African myths, symbols and rites with the same respect and the same desire to learn that we have hitherto devoted to the cultural creations of the West. Though these rites and myths sometimes display horrible or aberrant aspects, they nevertheless express prototypal situations of men belonging to societies of various types, and impelled by other historic forces than those that have shaped the history of the Western world.

The will properly to understand the "others" is rewarded, as we said, by an enrichment of the Western consciousness. The encounter might even lead to a renewal in the philosophical field, in the same way that the discovery of the exotic and primitive arts half a century ago opened up new perspectives for European art. A more profound study of the nature and function of symbols, for example, will probably stimulate Western philosophical thought and enlarge its horizons. It is striking that historians of religions have had to give prominence to the bold conceptions of the "primitives" and the East on the nature of human existence, on the Fall into Time, on the necessity of knowing "death" before attaining the world of the spirit. We recognize here ideas fairly close to those that are today central to Western philosophical inquiry. And when we find in archaic and oriental religious ideologies conceptions comparable to those of "classical" Western philosophy the confrontation is no less important, since these conceptions do not derive from the same premises. Thus, when Indian thought or certain "primitive" mythologies proclaim that the decisive act which determined the present condition of man took place in a primordial past, and that therefore the *essential precedes the actual human condition*, it would be highly interesting for the Western philosopher or theologian to learn how they arrived at this conception and for what reason.

If the discovery of the unconscious has driven Western man to a confrontation with his own secret and embryonic "history", the encounter with non-Western cultures will compel him to explore very deeply into the history of the human mind and perhaps to conclude that he must incorporate this history as an integral part of his own being. In fact, the problem which already presents itself, and which will present itself with increasingly dramatic urgency to investigators of the next generation, is this: By what means can we recover what is still recoverable of the spiritual history of humanity? And this for two reasons: (1) Western man will not be able to live indefinitely cut off from an important part of himself, a part that is made up of fragments of a spiritual history the significance and message of which he is incapable of deciphering; (2) sooner or later the dialogue with the "others"—the representatives of traditional Asiatic or "primitive" cultures—will have to be conducted, no longer in the empirical and utilitarian language of today (which is only capable of describing social, economic, political, medical, etc., circumstances) but in a cultural language capable of expressing human realities and spiritual values. Such a dialogue is inevitable; it is prescribed in the book of historical destiny, and it would be tragically naïve to imagine that it can be pursued indefinitely on the mental level at which it takes place today.

The studies gathered in this small book illustrate the progress of a historian of religions anxious to explain a certain number of the religious practices and spiritual values of non-Europeans. We have not hesitated to refer to familiar cultural facts founded on the Western tradition each time they have offered a standard of comparison capable of throwing light on our researches. Only by the use of such comparisons will the perspectives of a new humanism of the future be opened.

The first four chapters were read in the *Eranos* circle at Ascona, from 1957 to 1960; this explains their oral style. Although greatly tempted, we have not tried to rehandle or expand them on the occasion of their assembly in book form; each of these little essays would have run the risk of growing to the size of a book. We have confined ourselves to adding some references to recent publications.

MIRCEA ELIADE

University of Chicago
November 1960

Note

Reference is frequently made in the footnotes to earlier books by Mircea Eliade. The following have appeared in English:

The Myth of the Eternal Return, translated by Willard R. Trask (Routledge, London, and Pantheon Books, New York—Bollingen series XLVI—1954). French original, 1949.

Birth and Rebirth, translated by Willard R. Trask (Harvill Press, London, and Harper & Row, Inc., New York, 1961), a rehandling of the material in *Naissances mystiques. Essai sur quelques types d'initiation* (Paris, 1959).

Yoga: Immortality and Freedom, translated by Willard R. Trask (Routledge, London, and Pantheon Books, New York—Bollingen series LVI—1958). French original, 1948.

Myths, Dreams and Mysteries, translated by Philip Mairet (Harvill Press, London, and Harper & Row, Inc., New York, 1960). French original 1957.

Images and Symbols, translated by Philip Mairet (Harvill Press, London, and Sheed and Ward, New York, 1961). French original, 1952.

Shamanism: Archaic Techniques of Ecstasy, translated by Willard R. Trask (Routledge, London, and Pantheon Books, New York—Bollingen series LVI —1964). French original, 1951.

In addition, an important book in French not yet translated is *Traité d'Histoire des Religions* (Paris, 1959, 3rd edition 1959). A translation will be published by the Harvill Press.

Various shorter works and essays by the author are also cited, the earliest written in his native Rumanian.

I

Experiences of the Mystic Light

About the middle of last century an American merchant, aged thirty-two, had the following dream: "I was standing behind the counter of my shop in the middle of a bright, sunshiny afternoon, and instantly, in a flash, it became darker than the darkest night, darker than a mine; and the gentleman who was talking with me ran out into the street. Following him, although it was so dark, I could see hundreds and thousands of people pouring into the street, all wondering what had happened. Just then I noticed in the sky, in the far south-west, a bright light like a star, about the size of the palm of my hand, and in an instant it seemed to grow larger and larger and nearer and nearer, until it began to light up the darkness. When it got to the size of a man's hat, it divided itself into twelve smaller lights with a larger one in the centre, and then very rapidly it grew much larger, and instantly I knew that this was the coming of Christ and the twelve apostles. By this time it was lighter than the lightest day that could possibly be imagined, and as the shining host advanced towards the zenith, the friend with whom I was talking exclaimed: 'That is my Saviour!' and I thought he immediately left his body and ascended into the sky, and I thought I was not good enough to accompany him. Then I awoke."

For some days the man was so impressed that he could not tell his dream to anyone. At the end of a fortnight he told it to his family and afterwards to others. Three years later, someone well known for his profound religious life said to this gentleman's wife: "Your husband is born again and don't know it. He is a little spiritual baby with eyes not yet open, but he will know in a very short time." In fact, about three weeks afterwards, when he was walking with his wife in Second Avenue (N.Y.) he suddenly exclaimed: "A—, I have eternal life." He felt at that moment that Christ had just arisen in him and that he would remain in everlasting consciousness.

Three years after this event, whilst on a boat and in a crowd of people, he had a new spiritual and mental experience: it seemed to him that his whole soul, *and his body too*, were suffused with light. But in the autobiographical account that we have just given, he adds that these experiences in the waking state never made him forget the first, the experience he had known in dream.[1]

The principal reasons for my choosing to begin with this example of a spontaneous experience of the light are two: (1) it concerns a business man satisfied with his occupation and seemingly in no way prepared for a semi-mystical illumination; (2) his first experience of the light took place in a dream. He seems to have been deeply impressed by this experience, but he did not grasp its significance. He merely felt that something decisive had happened to him, something that concerned his soul's salvation. The idea that it was a spiritual rebirth only came to him when he heard what another person had said to his wife. Only after this indication from one with authority did he have the conscious experience of Christ's presence and, finally, three years afterwards, the experience of the supernatural light in which both his soul and his body were bathed.[2]

A psychologist would have many interesting things to say about the deep significance of this experience. For his part, the historian of religions will remark that the case of the American businessman admirably illustrates the situation of modern man,

---

[1]This autobiographical account was published by R. M. Bucke, *The Cosmic Consciousness*, Philadelphia, 1901, pp. 261-2. See other experiences of the light in dreams and their psychological interpretation in C. G. Jung, *Psychology and Alchemy*, New York and London, 1953, pp. 86, 89, 165, 177.
[2]Note the frequent recurrence of the number 3.

who believes himself—or wishes to be—without religion: the religious feeling for existence has in him been pushed back into, or has taken refuge in, the unconscious. Nowadays, as Professor C. G. Jung says, the unconscious is always religious. One could dilate at length on the apparent disappearance of religious feeling in modern man, or more exactly of its banishment to the deep levels of the psyche. But this is a problem outside my purpose.[1]

My intention is to produce a historico-religious commentary on the spontaneous experience of the inner light. The example I have just quoted brings us straight to the heart of the problem; we have just seen how a meeting with the light—even though it took place in a dream—ends by radically changing a human existence by opening it to the world of the Spirit. Now all experiences of the supernatural light present this common denominator: anyone receiving such an experience undergoes a change of being: he acquires another mode of being, which gives him access to the world of the spirit. The actual significance of the change in the individual's being, and of the spirit to which he has now access, constitute quite another problem, which will be discussed later. Let us dwell for the moment on this fact: even in a Far-Westerner of the nineteenth century, a meeting with the light indicates a spiritual rebirth.

This is not an isolated example; there are many similar cases and I shall have occasion to quote some of them. But I approach this subject as a historian of religions. First of all, therefore, it is necessary to know the significances of the interior or supernatural light in the different religious traditions. The subject is enormous; we must therefore observe limits. A satisfactory study of the religious values of the interior light would require not only a careful examination of all varieties of this experience, but also an explanation of the rituals and the different mythologies of the Light. For it is the religious ideologies that justify and, ultimately, give validity to mystical experiences. In so far as I can, I will try briefly to recall the ideological contexts of different

[1] See the present author's book *Das Heilige und das Profane*, "Rowohlt Deutsche Enzyklopädie", Hamburg, 1957.

experiences of the light in certain great religions. But numerous aspects will be omitted. I shall not speak of mythologies of the Light, nor of solar myths, nor of ritual lamps or fires. Nor shall I speak of the religious significance of the moon's light or of lightning, although all such manifestations of light have great importance for our subject.

QAUMANEQ

It is the mythology—or rather the metaphysics—of the lightning-flash that is of especial interest. The rapidity of spiritual illumination has been compared in many religions to lightning. Furthermore, the swift flash of lightning rending the darkness has been given the value of a *mysterium tremendum* which, by transfiguring the world, fills the soul with holy terror. Men killed by lightning are considered to have been snatched up into heaven by the storm gods, and their remains are worshipped as sacred relics. A man who survives being struck by lightning is completely changed; indeed he begins a new existence, he is a new man. A Yakout who was struck but not killed explained that God had come down from heaven, broken his body in pieces and then brought him back to life—but after this initiatory death and resurrection he became a shaman. "Now", he added, "I see everything that happens all around for a distance of thirty versts".[1] It is remarkable that in this example of instantaneous initiation, the familiar theme of death and resurrection is accompanied and completed by the motif of sudden illumination; the blinding flash of lightning causes the spiritual transformation by which man acquires the power of vision. "To see for a distance of thirty versts" is the traditional expression used by the Siberian shaman to indicate clairvoyance.

Now this kind of clairvoyance is, among the Esquimos, the result of a mystical experience called "lightning" or "illumination" (*qaumaneq*), and without it no one can become a shaman. Accord-

[1] C. W. Ksenofontov, *Legendy i raskazi o shamanach u jakutov, burjat i tungusov,* 2nd edition, Moscow, 1930, pp. 76ff.

ing to the statements of the Iglulik Esquimo shamans, gathered by Rasmussen, the *qaumaneq* consists of "a mysterious light which the shaman suddenly feels in his body, inside his head, within the brain, an inexplicable searchlight, a luminous fire, which enables him to see in the dark, both literally and metaphorically speaking, for he can now, even with closed eyes, see through darkness and perceive things and coming events which are hidden from others; thus they look into the future and into the secrets of others".[1] When the novice first experiences this mystic light "it is as if the house in which he is suddenly rises; he sees far ahead of him, through mountains, exactly as if the earth were one great plain, and his eyes could reach to the end of the earth. Nothing is hidden from him any longer; not only can he see things far, far away but he can also discover souls, stolen souls, which are either kept concealed in far, strange lands or have been taken up or down to the Land of the Dead".[2]

Let us note the essential points of this experience of mystical illumination: (a) it is the consequence of a long preparation, but it always occurs suddenly, like a "lightning-flash"; (b) it is a matter of inner light, felt throughout the body but principally in the head; (c) when a man feels it for the first time it is accompanied by the experience of ascension; (d) it involves vision into the distance and clairvoyance at the same time: the shaman sees everywhere and very far, but he also sees invisible entities (souls of the sick, spirits) and also sees future events.

Let us add that the *qaumaneq* is inseparable from another, specifically shamanistic spiritual exercise; the power to see one's own body reduced to the state of a skeleton. In other words, the shaman is capable of "seeing" what is at the time invisible. By this one can understand either that he sees through the flesh, in the manner of X-rays, or very far in the future, what will happen to his own body after death. In either case, this power too is a sort of clairvoyance, made possible by the illumination. On this

---

[1] Rasmussen, quoted in the present author's *Shamanism*, London and New York, 1964, pp. 60, 61.

[2] Rasmussen, quoted *op. cit.*, p. 61.

point one must insist: although experienced in the form of an inner light and felt as a luminous event, in the almost physical sense of the word, the illumination confers on an Esquimo shaman both paragnomic powers and knowledge of a mystical kind.

THE "LIGHT SOLIDIFIED"

It would be tempting to pass from shamanistic experience to study the Indian conception of interior light. We should find the same combination between experience of the light, gnosis and transcendence of the human state. But I wish to dwell for a moment on another group of facts concerned with primitive societies, and particularly on the initiation of Australian medicine-men. I know of no Australian examples comparable to the illumination of Iglulik shamans, but this lack is perhaps due to the fact that we do not know enough about Australian medicine-men. Nevertheless we are justified in comparing them with Siberian and Arctic shamans; not only have their respective initiations many features in common, but both have the reputation of possessing the same parapsychological powers: they walk on fire, they disappear and reappear at will, they are clairvoyant and capable of reading other men's thoughts, etc.[1]

Now the mystic light plays an important part in the initiation ceremonies of Australian medicine-men. The medicine-men imagine themselves to be Baiame, the master of the initiation, a being who resembles all other magicians "except for the light that shines from his eyes".[2] In other words, they feel that the state of a supernatural being is connected with a superabundance of light. Baiame performs the initiation of young aspirants by sprinkling them with "a sacred and powerful water", and this, according to the medicine-men, is a liquefied quartz.[3] Quartz plays an important part in the initiations. The aspirant is considered to have been killed by a supernatural being, cut in pieces

[1] See A. P. Elkin, *Aboriginal Men of High Degree*, Sydney, 1946, pp. 52ff.
[2] Elkin, *op. cit.*, p. 96.   [3] *Ibid.*, p. 96.

and filled with rock crystals; when he returns to life, he is able to see spirits, to read the thoughts of others, to fly up to Heaven, to make himself invisible, etc. Thanks to the rock crystals contained in his body, and particularly in his head, the medicine-man enjoys a different mode of existence from the rest of mortals. Quartz owes its extraordinary prestige to its celestial origin. Baiame's throne is made of crystal, and Baiame himself drops on to the earth fragments broken from his throne.[1] In other words, the crystals are supposed to have fallen from the vault of heaven; they are in a sense "solidified light."

Indeed, the Sea Dayaks call these crystals "light-stones".[2] The solidified light in the quartz is considered supernatural: it confers on medicine-men the power of seeing souls, even at a very great distance (for example when a sick man's soul has wandered into the scrub or has been seized by demons). Furthermore, thanks to these crystals, medicine-men are capable of flying up to Heaven— a belief also reported from North America.[3] To see into the very far distance, to ascend to Heaven, to see spirit beings (souls of the dead, demons, gods) means, in the final analysis, that the medicine-man is no longer confined to the Universe of profane man, that he shares the condition of superior Beings. He attains this condition thanks to an initiatory death, during which he is filled with substances considered to be solidified light: when he is mystically resurrected, he may be said to bathe in an interior, supernatural light.

Thus we find in Australian medicine-men the same identification between spiritual light, gnosis, ascension, clairvoyance and supercognitional faculties that we found in Esquimo shamans. But the element that interests us, spiritual light, is given quite a different value. The Australian aspirant is not believed to experience an illumination comparable to that of the Esquimo shaman: he receives the supernatural light directly in his body, in the form of rock crystals. This does not amount to a mystical experience of light—but to an initiatory death, during which the aspirant's body is filled with crystals, symbols of the divine

[1]See *Shamanism*, pp. 137, 138.   [2]*Ibid.*, p. 138.   [3]*Ibid.*, p. 138.

celestial light. Here we have a ritual of an ecstatic type; although "dead" and cut to pieces, the aspirant sees what happens to him: he sees the supernatural Beings fill his body with quartz and, on returning to life, possesses more or less the same powers that are attained by the Esquimo shaman as a consequence of his illumination. The accent falls on the ritual performed by supernatural Beings—whereas the illumination of an Esquimo shaman is an experience received in solitude and as a result of a long discipline. But, to repeat, the consequences of the two types of initiation can be described in the same terms: the Esquimo shaman, like the Australian medicine-man, is a new man who "sees", understands, has supernatural knowledge, and is capable of performing supernatural actions.

INDIA: THE LIGHT AND THE ATMAN

In Indian religions and philosophies, as might be expected, the mystique of the Light is much more complex. In the first place there is the basic idea that light is creative. "Light is procreation" (*jyotir prajanaman*) says the *Satapatha Brahmana* (VIII, 7, 2, 16-17). It "is the procreative power" (*Taittirya Samhita*, VIII, 1, 1, 1). Already the *Rig Veda* (I, 115, 1) affirmed that the Sun is the Life or the *atman*—the Self—of all things. The Upanishads particularly insist on this theme: that being manifests itself by the pure Light and that man receives knowledge of being by an experience of supernatural Light. Now, says the *Chandogya Upanishad* (III, 13, 7), the light that shines beyond this Sky, beyond all things, in the highest worlds beyond which there are none higher, is in fact the same light that shines within a man (*antah puruse*).

Consciousness of the identity between the interior light and the super-cosmic light is accompanied by two well-known phenomena of subtle physiology: a rise in the temperature of the body and the hearing of mystical sounds (*ibid.*, III, 13, 8). There are signs that the revelation of the *atman-brahman* in the form of Light is not simply an act of metaphysical cognition but a deeper experience to which a man commits his existential governance. The supreme gnosis brings a modification of his way of being. In the words of the *Bradaranyaka Upanishad* (I, 3, 28), "from non-being (*asat*) lead me to being (*sat*), from darkness lead me to the light (*tamaso ma jyotir gamaya*), from death lead me to immortality".

The light then is identical with being and immortality. The *Chandogya Upanishad* (III, 17, 7) cites two verses of the *Rig Veda* which speak of the contemplation of the "Light that shines above the Sky", and adds: "By contemplating (this) Very-high Light, beyond the Darkness, we attain the Sun, gods among the gods..." According to the famous expression of the *Bradaranyaka Upanishad* (IV, 3, 7) the *atman* is identified with the entity that is to be found at the heart of man, in the form of "a light in the heart" (*hrdy antarjyotih purusah*). "This calm being, rising from his body and reaching the highest light, appears in its own form (*svena rupenabhinispadyate*). It is the *atman*. It is the immortal, the fearless. It is Brahman. In fact the name of Brahman is *The True*" (*Chandogya Upanishad*, VIII, 3, 4).[1] At the moment of death, the *Chandogya Upanishad* (VIII, 6, 5) goes on to tell us, the soul rises upwards on the rays of the Sun. It approaches the Sun, "the Gate of the World". Those who know how can enter, but the Gate is closed for those who do not know.

We are concerned therefore with a science of a transcendental and initiatory character, for he who gains it not only gains knowledge but also, and principally, a new and superior way of being. The revelation is sudden; that is why it is compared to lightning—and we have analysed in another context the Indian symbolism of "instantaneous illumination".[2] The Buddha himself received his illumination in a moment outside time—when at dawn, after another night passed in meditation, he raised his eyes to the sky and suddenly perceived the morning star. In Mahayana philosophy the light of the sky at dawn, when there is no moon, has come to symbolise the "Clear Light named the

---

[1]Sankara interprets "rising from his body" (*sarirat samutthaya*) as "abandoning the notion of the identity of Self with body".

[2]See *Images and Symbols, Studies in Religious Symbolism*, pp. 75, 85.

Universal Void". In other words, the Buddha state, the condition of one who is free of all relativity, is symbolised by the Light that Gautama perceived at the moment of his illumination. This Light is described as "clear", "pure", that is to say not only without spot or shadow, but also colourless, and without qualities. For this reason it is called "the Universal Void", since the term void (*sunya*) exactly signifies that it is free of all attributes, of all differentiation: it is the *Urgrund*, the ultimate reality. Comprehension of the Universal Void, like the act of knowledge of the identity of brahman and atman in the Upanishads, is an instantaneous action, comparable to the lightning-flash. Just as nothing precedes the dazzling flash that suddenly rends the mass of darkness, nothing appears to precede the experience of illumination; it belongs to another contextual plane, there is no continuity between the time before it and the timeless moment in which it takes place.

YOGA AND THE "MYSTIC LIGHTS"

According to certain Indian schools, however, the change of level effected by illumination may be anticipated. The ascetic prepares himself by long meditations and Yoga, and in the course of his spiritual journey meets occasional signs warning him of the approach of the final revelations. Among these premonitory signs, the experience of different coloured lights is the most important. The *Shvetasvatara Upanishad* (II, 11) carefully notes the "preliminary forms (*rupani purassarani*) of Brahman" which reveal themselves during yogic practice in the form of luminous manifestations. These are mist, smoke, sun, fire, wind, phosphorescent insects, lightning, crystal and moon. The *Mandala Brahmana Upanishad* (II, 1) gives quite a different list: the form of a star, a diamond mirror, the orb of the full moon, the sun at midday, a circle of fire, a crystal, a dark circle, then a point (*bindu*), a finger (*kala*), a star (*naksatra*), and again the sun, a lamp, the eye, the radiance of the sun and of the nine jewels.[1]

[1]S. Radhakrishnan, *The Principal Upanishads*, London and New York, 1953,

As can be seen, there is no fixed rule for the sequence of experiences of light. Moreover, the order in which luminous manifestations are recorded does not correspond to a progressive increase of visual intensity. According to the *Shvetasvatara Upanishad* the light of the moon is perceived long after that of the sun. In the *Mandala Brahmana Upanishad* the succession of luminous manifestations is still more perplexing. This seems to me a further proof that we are not concerned with physical lights belonging to the natural world, but with experiences of a mystical nature.

The various schools of Yoga mention the manifestations of inner light. In commenting on the *Yoga Sutra* (I, 36), for instance, Vyasa speaks of "a concentration in the lotus of the heart" which leads one to an experience of pure light. In another context (III, 1) he mentions the "light of the head" as one of the objects on which the yogin should concentrate. Buddhist treatises insist on the potential importance of a luminous sign for the success of a meditation. "Do not let go of the sign of the light", one reads in the *Sravakabhumi*, "which may be that of a lamp, or the glow of a fire or the solar orb!"[1]

Needless to say, these luminous signs serve only as points of departure for the various yogic meditations. Yogavacara's treatise describes in detail the colour-succession of mystical lights experienced by the monk in the course of his discipline. The particular subject of the book is meditation on the cosmic elements; it sets out a considerable number of exercises, each one in three parts, and each part distinguished by the experience of a different coloured light. We have discussed elsewhere the

---

p. 721, reproduces a passage from the *Lankavatara Sutra*, according to which the Yogin sees, during his practice, the form of "the Sun or the Moon, or something like the lotus, or the underworld, or variable forms such as the sky fire and the like. When all these are put aside and there is a state of imagelessness . . . the Buddhas will come together from all their countries and with their shining hands will touch the head of the benefactor (Yogin)."

[1] ms cited by A. J. Wayman, *Notes on the Sanskrit term jnana*, ("Journal of the American Oriental Society", vol. 75, 1955, pp. 253-68), p. 261, note.

method of Yogavacara's treatise,[1] and there is no point in returning to the subject. Let us say only that penetration into the
ultimate structure of each cosmic element—penetration achieved
by means of Yoga meditation—is accompanied by the experience
of a different coloured light. We can understand the significance
and soteriological value of this immersion in the ultimate structure
of the cosmic substance if we recall that for the Mahayana the
cosmic elements—the *skandha* or *dhatu*—are identical with the
Tathagatas; the Yogin's meditation on the cosmic elements is in
fact a method of attaining a revelation of the very essence of
the Tathagatas, that is to say of advancing on the path of deliverance. Now the ultimate reality of the Tathagatas is the Light in
various colours. "All the Tathagatas are the five Lights", writes
Candrakirti.[2] The *dharmadhatu*, that is to say the transcendental
form of Vajradhara, is the Pure Light, the Light perfectly devoid
of colour. Candrakirti writes: "The *dharmadhatu* is the bright
Light—and yogic concentration is its perception".[3] This amounts
to saying that being can only be apprehended by an experience
of the mystical order—and that the apprehension of being is
accompanied by an experience of an absolute Light. One recalls
that in the Upanishads brahman or the atman are identified with
the Light.

We are dealing, therefore, with an all-Indian conception
which could be resumed in these terms: pure being, the ultimate
reality, can be known particularly through an experience of the
pure Light; the process of the cosmic revelation ultimately consists
of a series of luminous manifestations, and cosmic reabsorption
repeats the manifestations of these differently coloured lights.
According to a tradition conserved in the *Dighanikaya* (I, 2, 2),
after the destruction of the World there remained only radiant
beings named Abhassara: they had ethereal bodies, they flew in
the air, they gave out their own light and lived indefinitely. A

[1] See M. Eliade, *Yoga, Immortality and Freedom*, Paris, 1954, p. 194ff.
[2] Text quoted by G. Tucci, *Some Glosses upon Guhyasamaja* ("Mélanges
Bouddhiques et Chinoises", vol. III, 1935, pp. 339-53), p. 348.
[3] Tucci, *Ibid.*, p. 348.

reabsorption on the microcosmic scale also takes place at the moment of death—and as we shall soon see, the process of death consists in fact of a number of experiences of light.

Certain corollaries follow from the all-Indian metaphysic of the Light, particularly (1) that the most adequate revelation of divinity is effected by the Light; (2) that those who have reached a high stage of spirituality—that is to say, in Indian terms, have realised or at least approached the condition of a "liberated one" or Buddha—are also capable of giving out the Light; (3) finally, that the cosmogony is comparable to a photic revelation. Let us illustrate each of these corollaries by some examples.

LUMINOUS THEOPHANIES

As readers of the *Bhagavadgita* know, the exemplary theophany takes the form of a dazzling stream of light. Remember the famous 11th chapter in which Krishna reveals himself to Arjuna in his true form, which is essentially a form of fire:

> If the effulgence of a thousand suns were to shine at once in the sky, that might resemble the splendour of that great being. (v. 12)
> I see Thee with diadems, maces, discus, shiningly effulgent everywhere, blazing all around like the burning fire and the sun, dazzling to the sight and immeasurable. (v. 17)
> I see Thee without beginning, middle or end, with infinite power, with numberless arms, the sun and moon as Thine eyes, Thy mouth as the blazing fire, heating this universe with Thine own radiance. (v. 19)
> Seeing Thy mouths, terrible with long teeth, blazing like the fires of destruction I know not the four quarters, nor do I find any peace. (c. 24-5)
>
> *(Transl. Swami Paramananda)*

But this example is only the most celebrated of innumerable luminous theophanies in the *Mahabharata* and the *Puranas*. The *Harivamsha* tells of the voyage of Krishna, Arjuna and a brahmin to the northern ocean. Krishna commands the waves to retire, and the three cross the ocean between two walls of water. They arrive before the majestic mountains and at Krishna's command the mountains disappear. Then they come into a region of mist and the horses stop. Krishna strikes the mist with his *cakra* and disperses it—then Arjuna and the brahmin perceive an extremely bright light in which Krishna finally dissolves. Afterwards Krishna reveals to Arjuna that this Light is the true Self.[1]

In book XII of the *Mahabharata*, Vishnu reveals himself in a lightning flash as bright as the light of a thousand suns. And the text adds: "by penetrating this light mortals skilled in Yoga attain final deliverance".[2] The same XIIth book of the *Mahabharata* tells the story of three sages who, in the country to the north of Mount Meru, had for a thousand years practised a discipline in order to contemplate the true form of Narayana. A voice from the sky bade them go to the north of the Milky Ocean, to Shvetadvipa, the mysterious "White Island" of Indian mythology, the symbolism of which relates both to the metaphysics of the Light and to the soteriological gnosis. The sages arrive at Shvetadvipa, but on doing so are blinded by a light emanating from Narayana. They then practise their discipline for a hundred years longer, and begin to perceive men who are white as the moon. "The brightness of one of these men", the text states, "was as great as that of the Sun when the moment comes for the dissolution of the Universe". Suddenly the three sages perceive a light comparable to the radiance of a thousand suns. This is the manifestation of Narayana—and the entire population of Shvetadvipa runs to the light and worships it with genuflexions and prayers.[3]

This last example illustrates two points at once: that the Light is the very essence of the divinity, and also that mystically perfect

---

[1]*Harivamsha*, 169 (II, 186-8); cf. *Mahabharata*, XII, 333, 10; XIII, 14, 382-3. See also W. E. Clark, *Shakadvipa and Shvetadvipa* ("Journal of the American Oriental Society", vol. 39, 1919, pp. 202-42), pp. 226ff.

[2]*Mahabharata*, XII, 336, 39-40.

[3]*Mahabharata*, XII, 336; cf. W. E. Clark, *op. cit.*, pp. 233ff.

beings are radiant. The image of the Shvetadvipa[1] confirms the identity of the Light and spiritual perfection; this country is white because it is inhabited by perfect men. And one has only to mention the other "white islands" of the Indo-European tradition —Leuke, Avalon—to realise that the myth of transcendental regions, of countries that have no place in geography, is based on the mystical value accorded to the colour white as a symbol of transcendence, perfection and sanctity.

BUDDHISM

Similar ideas are to be found in Buddhism. Buddha himself says in the *Dighanikaya* that the precursory sign of the mani-festation of Brahma is "the light that rises and the glory that shines".[2] A Chinese sutra affirms that in the *Rupaloka*, thanks to the practice of contemplation and the absence of all unclean desires, the gods (Devas) reach the state of *samhadi* known as the "flash of fire" and their bodies become more radiant than the Sun and Moon. This extreme radiance is a result of their perfect purity of heart.[3] According to the *Abhidharmakosa*, gods of the Brahma class are white as silver, while those that belong to the Rupadhatu are yellow and white.[4] According to other Buddhist texts the eighteen classes of gods all have bodies that shine like silver and live in palaces as yellow as gold.[5]

A fortiori, the Buddha is pictured as radiant also. At Amaravati he is represented in the form of a column of fire. At the end of a discourse he relates: "I have become a flame and I have risen into the air to the height of seven palm trees" (*Dighanikaya*, III, 27). The two images that express transcendence of the human condition—a fiery brightness and ascension—are here used together. The Buddha's brightness becomes almost a cliché in the texts (*Divyavadana*, XLVI-VII, 75; *Dhammapada* XXVI,

---

[1]Concerning this matter, see *Shamanism*, p. 409; *Yoga*, p. 328.
[2]*Dighanikaya*, XIX, 15 ("Dialogues of the Buddha", II, p. 264).
[3]S. Beal, *A Catena of Buddhist Scriptures from the Chinese*, London, 1871, p. 87.
[4]Beal, *op. cit.*, p. 88.   [5]Beal, *op. cit.*, p. 97.

51, etc.). The statues of the Gandhara school show flames coming out of the Buddha's body, particularly from his shoulders.[1] Certain Buddhas are pictured flying in the air; which has given rise to a confusion between flames and wings.[2]

That this light is yogic in essence, that is to say the result of the experimental realisation of a transcendent unconditioned state, is affirmed by a number of texts. When Buddha is in *samadhi*, says the *Lalitavistara*, "a ray named the Ornament of the Light of Knowledge (*jnanalokalanakram nama rasmih*) rising from the cranial suture (*usnisa*) shines above the head".[3] This is why iconography represents the Buddha with a flame rising above his head. A. K. Coomaraswamy recalls this question from the *Saddharmapundarika* (p. 467); "On account of what knowledge (*jnana*) does the cranial protuberance of the Tathagata shine?"— and he finds the answer in a verse of the *Bhagavadgita* (xiv, 11): "When there is knowledge the light shines through the orifices of the body".[4] [The shining of the body is, therefore, a symptom of the transcendence of all conditioned states: gods, men and Buddhas shine when they are in *samadhi*, that is to say when they are one with the ultimate reality, Being. According to traditions elaborated by Chinese Buddhism, five lights shine at the birth of every Buddha—and a flame springs out of his corpse.[5]

[1] See B. Rowland, Jr., *The Iconography of the Flame Halo* ("The Bulletin of the Fogg Museum of Art", xi, 1949, pp. 10-16). See another Gandhara statue reproduced in the catalogue of the exhibition, *L'Arte del Gandhara in Pakistan*, Rome, 1958, pl. 3.

[2] In the iconography of Irano-Hellenistic syncretism, flames emanating from the shoulders were the characteristic of certain gods and the Kushana sovereigns. See Ugo Monneret De Villard, *Le monete dei Kushana e l'Impero romano* ("Orientalia", xvii, 1948), p. 217; A. C. Soper, *Aspects of Light Symbolism in Gandharan Sculpture* ("Artibus Asiae", xii, 1949), p. 269. This symbolism was probably applied by the Gandhara artists to Buddha as a plastic expression of his radiance. But the "fiery luminosity" of those who have transcended the human condition is an idea common to all India.

[3] *Lalitavistara*, i, ed. Lefmann, 1902, p. 3. See Ananda K. Coomaraswamy, *Lila* ("Journal of the American Oriental Society", 1941, pp. 98-101), p. 100.

[4] A. K. Coomaraswamy, *Lila*, p. 100.

[5] See E. J. Eitel, *Handbook of Chinese Buddhism*, 2nd edition, London, 1888, p. 136a, 138b.

And every Buddha can light the whole Universe with the tuft of hair which grows between his eyebrows.[1] It is well known that Amita, the Buddha of the Boundless Light, is the central figure of Amidism, the mystical school which attaches capital importance to the experience of the Light.[2]

Another mystical theme important for our researches is the Indra's visit to the Buddha when he was meditating in the cave (*Indrashailaguha*). According to this myth, Indra, accompanied by a crowd of gods, descended from the sky to Magadha, where Tathagata was meditating in a cave in the mountain Vediyaka. Roused from his meditation by a Gandharva's singing, Buddha magically widened the cave so that his guests could enter, and received them courteously. A bright light lit the cavern. According to *Dighanikaya* (Sakka Panha Sutta), the light emanated from the gods, but other sources (*Dirghanana-Sutra*, x, etc.) attribute it to the "fiery ecstasy" of the Buddha. Indra's visit is not mentioned in the classical biographies of the Buddha written in Pali and Sanskrit. But this episode occupies an important place in the art of Gandhara and Central Asia.[3] This mystical theme affords a parallel to the legend of Christ's Nativity in a cave and the visit of the Magi (see below, pp. 51ff.). As Monneret de Villard observed,[4] both legends relate how a King of the Gods (Indra) or "Kings, sons of Kings" enter a cave to pay homage to the Saviour, and in the course of their visit the cave is miraculously lit. This mythical theme is certainly older than Indo-Irano-Hellenistic syncretism; it is one with the

[1]See Eitel, *op. cit.*, p. 188b. Ashvagosha had already compared the Buddha's birth with the triumphal rising of the Sun, which lights the whole world (*Buddhacarita*, I, 28, etc.). On the solar symbolism in the Buddha legend, see B. Rowland, Jr., *Buddha and the Sun God* ("Zalmoxis", I, 1938, pp. 69-84).
[2]See T. Richards, *The New Testament of Higher Buddhism*, Edinburgh, 1910, pp. 55, 140ff., etc.; H de Lubac, *Amida*, Paris, 1955, *passim*.
[3]The problem has been amply studied by A. C. Soper, *Aspects of Light Symbolism in Ghandharan Sculpture* ("Artibus Asiae", XII, 1949, pp. 252-83, 314-30; XIII, 1950, pp. 63-85). The author suggests a Mithraic influence (pp. 259ff.).
[4]Ugo Monneret De Villard, *Le Leggendi Orientali sui Magi Evangelici* ("Studi e Testi", 163, Vatican City, 1952), pp. 59-60.

myth of the Sun God's victorious emergence from the Primordial
Cave.

We must now say something about the relations between the
cosmogony and the metaphysics of the light. We have seen
that the Mahayana identifies the Tathagatas with the cosmic
elements (*skandha*) and considers them luminous entities. This
is a bold ontology which only becomes really intelligible if we
take into account the whole history of Buddhist thought. But it
is possible that similar ideas, or at least presentiments of the grand
conception of the cosmogony as a manifestation of the Light,
had already been expressed in earlier times. Coomaraswamy
associates the Sanskrit word *lila*—meaning "play", especially
cosmic play—with the root *lelay*, "to flame", "to sparkle", "to
shine". This word *lelay* may convey notions of Fire, Light or
Spirit.[1] Indian thought seems then already to have found a
certain relationship between, on the one hand, cosmic creation
conceived as a divine game, and on the other, the play of flames,
the dancing of a well-fed fire. Clearly it was only possible to
relate the image of cosmic creation to that of dancing flames
because flame was already considered the exemplary manifestation of divinity. In view of the Indian evidence that we have
quoted, this conclusion seems to us to be established.[2] Flame
and light, then, symbolise in India the cosmic creation and the
very essence of the Cosmos, on account of the fact that the
Universe is conceived as a free manifestation of the divine or,
in the last analysis, its "play".

A parallel series of images and concepts, crystallised round
maya, reveal a similar vision: cosmic creation is a divine play, a
mirage, an illusion magically projected by the deity. One knows
how great an importance the notion of *maya* has had in the
development of Indian ontology and soteriology. Less stress has
been laid on this point: that to tear the veil of *maya* and pierce

[1] A. K. Coomaraswamy, *Lila*, p. 100.
[2] Coomaraswamy cites *Acts*, II, 3-4 (in which the Holy Ghost appears to the
Disciples in the form of tongues of fire) to show that this is not merely an
Indian conception (*op. cit.*, p. 101).

the secret of cosmic illusion amounts primarily to understanding its character as "play"—that is to say free, spontaneous activity of the divine—and consequently to imitating the divine action and attaining liberty. The paradox of Indian thought is that the idea of liberty is so concealed by the idea of *maya*—that is of illusion and slavery—that it takes a long detour to find it. It is enough, however, to discover the deep meaning of *maya*—divine "play"—to be already on the way to deliverance.

LIGHT AND THE BARDO

For Mahayana the Clear Light symbolises at once the ultimate reality and the *nirvana* consciousness. All men confront this Clear Light for some moments at the instant of death; yogins experience it during *samadhi* and the Buddhas experience it without interruption.[1] Death is a process of cosmic reabsorption, not in the sense that the flesh returns to the earth, but in the sense that the cosmic elements progressively dissolve into one another: the element Earth "sinks" into the element Water, Water into Fire, and so on. It is evident that each fusion of a cosmic element represents a new regression and that at the end of the process the Cosmos which formed living man is annihilated just as the Universes are annihilated at the end of the Great Cycles (*mahayuga*). Each regression is physiologically perceived by the initiate. For example when the element Earth dissolves into the element Water, the body loses its support (lit. its "prop"), that is to say, its power of cohesion;[2] it becomes loose, like a marionette. (See below, ch. IV.)

When the process of cosmic reabsorption is complete, the dying man perceives a light like that of the Moon, then like that of the Sun, then sinks deep into the darkness. He is suddenly

[1]See W. Y. Evans-Wentz, *Tibetan Yoga and Secret Doctrines*, Oxford, 1935, pp. 166, 223ff., etc.
[2]Evans-Wentz, *op. cit.*, p. 235.

awakened by a dazzling light;[1] this is his meeting with his real
Self, which, according to the doctrine of all India, is at the same
time the ultimate reality, Being. *The Tibetan Book of the Dead*
calls this Light the "Pure Truth", and describes it as "subtle,
sparkling, bright, dazzling, glorious and radiantly awesome".
The text enjoins the dead man: "Be not daunted thereby, nor
terrified, nor awed. That is the radiance of thine own true
nature. Recognise it!" At this moment from the heart of this
radiance bursts a sound reverberating like a thousand thunders
simultaneously sounding. "This is the natural sound of thine
own real Self", states the text, "Be not terrified . . . Since thou
hast not a material body of flesh and blood, whatever may come
—sounds, lights or rays—are, all three, unable to harm thee:
thou art incapable of dying. It is quite sufficient for thee to
know that these apparitions are thine own thought-forms.
Recognise this to be the *Bardo*".[2]

But, as is the case with the majority of humans, the dead
man cannot put this advice into practice. Conditioned by the
karmic situation, he lets himself be drawn into the cycle of
manifestations characteristic of the *Bardo* state. On the fourth
day after his death, he is warned that he will see radiances and
deities. "The whole Heavens will appear deep blue". He will
see the Bhagavan Vairochana, white in colour, then from its
heart the wisdom of Dharma-Dhatu, always blue in colour, will
shoot forth, shining, transparent, glorious with a light so radiant
that he will scarcely be able to look at it. "Along with it there
will also shine a dull white light from the *devas*, which will strike
against thy brow." Because of the power of bad *karma*, the soul
will be frightened of the bright light of the Dharma-Dhatu and
will become fond of the dull white light of the *devas*. But the
text advises the dead man not to attach himself to the light of
the *devas*, in order not to be drawn into the whirl of the six
Lokas, and to put his whole thought on Vairochana. Thus he

[1]*Ibid.*, p. 235; see also Evans-Wentz, *The Tibetan Book of the Dead*, Oxford,
1927, pp. 102ff.
[2]Evans-Wentz, *op. cit.*, p. 104.

will finally merge, in a halo of rainbow light, in the heart of Vairochana and obtain Buddhahood in the Central Realm of Sambhoga-Kaya.[1]

For six more days the dead man will have a chance of choosing between the pure Lights—representing liberation and identification with the essential Buddha—and the impure Lights, symbolising some form of after-life, in other words a return to Earth. After the white and blue Lights he will see yellow, red and green Lights and finally all the Lights together.[2]

It is impossible for us to comment on this extremely important text as fully as it deserves. We must confine ourselves to some remarks directly concerned with our inquiry. As we have seen, every man has his chance of deliverance at the moment of death; all that he needs for this is to recognise himself in the Clear Light that he meets at this moment. Considering the importance of karma in all Indian thought, which insists that a man reaps the fruits of his actions, this seems at first sight paradoxical. The actions of an individual who has lived in ignorance constitute a karmic inheritance that it is impossible to destroy at the moment of death. But in reality everything happens according to the law of karma: for the ignorant man's soul rejects the appeal of the Clear Light and allows himself to be attracted by the dull lights, which stand for the inferior modes of existence. On the other hand, those who have practised yoga during their lives are capable of recognising themselves in the Clear Light and consequently of dissolving in the essential Buddha.

The light met at the moment of death, therefore, is the same interior light that the Upanishads identify with the *atman*: during earthly existence this is only accessible to those spiritually prepared for it by the practice of yoga or by gnosis. If one looks closely one sees that the same situation repeats itself at the moment of death; the Light reveals itself to all but is only recognised —and accepted—by initiates. It is true that during the last

[1]Evans-Wentz, *op. cit.*, pp. 105ff.
[2]*Ibid.*, pp. 110-30; cf. also pp. 173-7, and *Tibetan Yoga and Secret Doctrines*, pp. 237ff.

moments and in the days immediately after death, *The Book of the Dead* is read by a lama for the dead man's benefit, and this reading aloud constitutes a final appeal; but it is always the dead man who decides his fate. It is he who must have the will to choose the Clear Light and the strength to resist the temptations of the after-life. In other words, death offers a new possibility of initiation, but this initiation involves, like any other, a series of tests that the neophyte must face and conquer. The experience of the Light *post mortem* constitutes the last, and perhaps the most difficult, initiatory test.

LIGHT AND *maithuna*

Tantricism knows another possibility of experiencing the interior Light, during *maithuna*, which is the ritual union with a young girl (*mudra*) who incarnates the Shakti. Let us observe that this is no profane action but a ceremonial which imitates the divine "play", for it must not end with an ejaculation of semen.[1] Commenting on one of the most important Tantric texts, the *Guhyasamaja Tantra*, Candrakirti and Ts'on Kapa insist on this detail: during the *maithuna* a mystical union (*samapatti*) is effected, as a result of which the couple obtain nirvanic consciousness. In the man this nirvanic consciousness, called *bodhicitta*, "Thought of Awakening", is manifested by and is in some sort identical with a drop, *bindu*, which descends from the top of the head and fills the sexual organs with a jet of five-fold light. Candrakirti directs: "During union he must meditate on the *vajra* and the *padma* considering them as filled within with five-fold light".[2]

The "drop" is identical with nirvanic consciousness and, as such, is supposed to form at the top of the head, the place where the interior light is generally experienced. The "drop", therefore, is the "Clear Light" of the nirvanic consciousness. But in

[1] On the ideology, techniques and history of the *maithuna*, see *Yoga*, pp. 259ff., 400ff.

[2] Text quoted by Tucci, *Some glosses upon Guhyasamaja*, p. 349.

Tantricism the *bodhicitta* is at the same time identified with the essence of the *semen virile*. To explain this subtle paradox more fully, we should have to enter into details of subtle Indian physiology. Let us remember at least this fact: the nirvanic consciousness is an experience of absolute light, but when it is obtained by means of *maithuna* it is capable of penetrating into the depths of organic life and discovering, there also, in the very essence of the *semen virile*, the divine light, the primordial splendour that created the World. For the Mahayana, this identification of the mystic light with the essence of the *semen virile* was not absurd—for the cosmic elements as well as the Tathagatas and, in the final analysis, the *Urgrund* of all existence and the modality of the awakened consciousness, all these are made up of the Primordial Light.

This metaphysic and soteriology of the light certainly agree with a long and ancient tradition of all India. Nevertheless, as Professor G. Tucci has shown, the *Guhyasamaja Tantra* and, even more, the commentaries of Candrakirti and Ts'on Kapa present similarities with Manicheism so obvious as to arouse an inevitable suspicion of a probably Iranian influence.[1] One thinks immediately of the five luminous elements that play an important role in the Manichaean cosmology and soteriology, and also of the fact that the divine part of man, the *bodhicitta*, is identified with the *semen*.

TIBETAN MYTHS OF MAN-AS-LIGHT

It is probable that Iranian influences have also affected some Tibetan myths concerning the origin of the world and of man. One of these relates how from the Primordial Void emanated a blue light which produced an egg, from which the Universe was formed. Another myth relates that the White Light gave birth to an egg, from which Primordial Man was hatched. Finally, a third myth gives the following version: from the

[1] G. Tucci, *op. cit.*, pp. 349ff.

void the Primordial Being was born, and from him shone the Light.[1]

As can be seen, according to these myths both the Cosmos and Primordial Man were born of the Light, and fundamentally, consist of Light. Another tradition explains how the transition from Man-as-Light to actual human beings took place. At the beginning men were asexual and without sexual desires; they had the Light within them and radiated it. The Sun and Moon did not exist. When the sexual instinct awoke, the sexual organs appeared—but then the Light was extinguished in man and the Sun and Moon appeared in the sky.[2] A Tibetan monk gave Father Mathias Hermanns these supplementary explanations: At the beginning men multiplied in the following way—the light emanating from the body of the male penetrated, lit and impregnated the womb of the female. The sexual instinct was satisfied by sight alone. But men degenerated and began to touch one another with their hands, and finally they discovered sexual union.[3]

According to these beliefs, the Light and Sexuality are two antagonistic principles; when one of them dominates, the other cannot manifest itself, and vice versa. Perhaps we have here an explanation of the Tantric rite that we analysed above: if the appearance of sexuality forces the light to disappear, the light

[1] See G. Tucci, *Tibetan Painted Scrolls*, Rome, 1949, vol. ii, appendix i, pp. 709ff.; Mathias Hermanns, *Mythen und Mysterien, Magie und Religion der Tibeter*, Cologne, 1956, pp. 14ff.

[2] M. Hermanns, *Schöpfungs—und Abstammungsmythen der Tibeter* ("Anthropos", 41-4, 1946-9), pp. 279ff.; Id., *Mythen und Mysterien*, p. 16.

[3] M. Hermanns, *Mythen und Mysterien*, p. 16. One finds similar ideas among the Mongols: the gods make love by embracing, by laughter or by taking hands. See A. Schiefer, *Mélanges asiatiques*, i, p. 396. But the origin of this idea seems to be Tibetan: cf. M. Hermanns, *op. cit.*, p. 29. On the Adam-Light in the Apochrypha of John and other Gnostic texts, cf. J. Doresse, *Les Livres secrets des gnostiques d'Égypte*, i, pp. 225ff., 88 (Bruce Codex), 190 (untitled *Revelation*, devoted particularly to the *Pistis Sophia*), 217 (Wisdom of Jesus); E. S. Drower, *The Secret Adam, A study of Nasoraean Gnosis*, Oxford, 1960, pp. 72, 75 *et passim*.

will inevitably be found hidden in the very essence of sexuality, the seed. So long as man practises the sexual act in instinctual blindness, that is to say like any other animal, the light remains hidden. But it is revealed—in a complex experience of illumination, gnosis and beatitude—if the union becomes a ritual or divine "game", that is to say if by checking the seminal ejaculation one defeats the biological purpose of the sexual act. Considered from this point of view the *maithuna* appears a desperate effort to recover the primordial situation, when men were luminous beings, reproducing themselves by the light.

No doubt the *Guhyasamaja Tantra*, as commented on by Candrakirti and Ts'on Kapa, does not consciously propose this end. The Light that is experienced during the *maithuna* is the Clear Light of the gnosis, of nirvanic consciousness—which is sufficient justification for this bold exercise. But a whole group of Indo-Tibetan beliefs, which agree both with the myth of Primordial Man as Light and with Tantric and alchemical ideologies and techniques, speak of certain yogins who have realised immortality in the body. These yogins do not die, they disappear into Heaven clothed in a body called the "rainbow-body", "celestial body", "spirit-body", "body of Pure Light" or "divine body".[1] One recognises here the idea of the astral body—that is a body made of Light—of Primordial Man.[2]

INDIAN EXPERIENCE OF THE MYSTIC LIGHT

Considered as a whole, the different experiences and appraisals of the interior Light advanced in India and in Indo-Tibetan Buddhism can be integrated into a perfectly consistent system. Experience of the Light signifies primarily a meeting with ultimate reality: that is why one discovers the interior Light when one becomes conscious of the Self (*atman*), or when one penetrates into the very essence of life and the cosmic elements, or, last of all, at one's death. Under all these conditions the veil of illusion and ignorance is torn. Suddenly a man is blinded by the

[1]See *Yoga*, pp. 282ff., 311ff. [2]See M. Hermanns, *Mythen und Mysterien*, p. 42.

Pure Light; he is plunged into being. From a certain point of view one may say that the profane world, the conditioned world, is transcended—and that the spirit breaks out on to the absolute plane, which is at once the plane of being and of the divine. Brahman, and the Buddha also, are at once a sign of the divine and of being, of the supreme reality. Indian thought identifies being, the divine and the mystic consciousness, the act by which one becomes conscious of reality. That is why one meets the Light both in meditating on being—the practice of the Upanishads and of Buddhism—and in trying to attain a revelation of the divine, the method followed in certain forms of yoga and the mystic schools. Since being is identical with the divine essence, divinities are necessarily luminous or reveal themselves to their worshippers in manifestations of light. But men also radiate light when they have destroyed the system of conditions under which worldly life is lived; that is to say when they have acquired supreme knowledge and attained the plane of liberty. In Indian thought, liberty is inseparable from knowledge; the man who knows, the man who has discovered the profane structures of being, is a man delivered in this life, he is no longer conditioned by cosmic laws. Henceforth he has immediate enjoyment of the divine, he no longer moves like a human automaton obedient to the laws of cause and effect, but "plays" like the gods—or like the flames of a fire.

To reach a conclusion: for Indian thought the Light mystically perceived denotes transcendence of this world, of profane and conditioned existence, and the attainment of another existential plane—that of pure being, of the divine, of supreme knowledge and absolute freedom. It is a certain sign of the revelation of ultimate reality—of reality devoid of all attributes. This is why it is experienced as a dazzling white Light, into which one gazes blinded and into which one finally disappears, dissolving and leaving no trace. For traces are linked with the personal history of the individual, with the memory, therefore, of transitory and, in the long run, unreal events—elements which have nothing at all to do with being. One who reaches the

Light and recognises himself in it reaches a mode of transcendent being beyond the reach of the imagination. All that we can understand is that he is finally dead to our world—and that he is dead also to all other possible worlds of after-death existence.

CHINESE TECHNIQUES

Turning to China, we find that there also the experience of the Light denotes passing beyond worldly consciousness. "Those whose hearts are in a state of repose", writes Chuang Tzu (ch. XXIII), "give forth a divine radiance by the light of which they see themselves as they are (the Real Self). And only by cultivating such repose can man attain to the constant" (transl., Giles). A meeting with the Light may be spontaneous or the result of a long discipline. Under the Ming dynasty (16th century) a disciple took up his dwelling beside a master who had been meditating for thirty years in a cave. One night, when going along a mountain path, the disciple "felt a light circulating inside his body, and heard a rumbling of thunder at the top of his head". The mountain, the stream, the world and his own self disappeared. This experience lasted "as long as it takes five pinches of incense to burn". Afterwards he felt that he had become an entirely different man and had been purified by his own Light. The master explained to him later that he had quite frequently had this experience during his thirty years of meditation, but that he had learnt to take no notice of it—he taught his pupil that even this mystic light must be put aside.[1]

In this instance the experience of the interior Light indicates a rupture of planes, but it does not necessarily signify—as in India—a meeting with ultimate reality. Certain psycho-physiological techniques, however, developed—or systematized—by neo-Taoism attach great importance to the experience of the various interior lights. A whole group of exercises, which present certain similarities with Yoga, aim at what was called the

[1] See Chung-Yuan Chang, *An Introduction to Taoist Yoga* ("Review of Religion", 1956, pp. 131-48), pp. 146-7.

absorption of the breath. They consist of meditation on each breath until one comes to see its colour—and at that moment to absorb it. One visualizes these breaths as if they came from the four points of the compass and the Centre—that is to say from the entire Universe—and one swallows them, forcing them to penetrate into the body. In this way cosmic energy—which is both the life essence and the seed of immortality—fills the inside of the body, lights it and transmutes it; for the Taoist's ideal is not deliverance but glorious and limitless Life, the blessing of an existence perfectly integrated with the cosmic rhythms.

This process of absorption of coloured breaths seems to derive from a more ancient technique, the aim of which was to absorb the breath of the Sun. This is how one should proceed, according to a neo-Taoist treatise:[1] "At dawn (three or five o'clock in the morning), at the moment when the sun rises, sitting or standing, (but) concentrating the attention, to grit the teeth nine times, to call from the depths of the heart on the *houen* of the sun which is shining like a pearl with green reflections that are turning to a red halo, a red youth, a mysteriously flaming image; then to close the eyes and keep them tight shut, and meditate on the fact that the five colours that are in the sun spread in a halo and all come to touch the body, reaching as low as the two feet and as high as the top of the head. Then to make a purple breath like the pupil of the eye arise at the centre of the bright cloud, etc."

One can obtain the same result by absorbing the Sun's image instead of its breath. One writes the hieroglyphic of the sun in a square or a circle, "and each morning, turning to the east and holding the paper in the right hand, one concentrates on it in such a way that it becomes the shining sun itself; one swallows it and brings it to rest in the heart".[2] Another method consists in meditating at midnight "on the idea of the sun's entering the

[1] Fragment translated by Henri Maspéro, *Les procédés de "Nourir le Principe vital" dans la religion taoïste* ("Journal Asiatique", 1937, pp. 177-252, 353-430), p. 374.
[2] H. Maspéro, *op. cit.*, p. 374.

heart by way of the mouth, and lighting the whole interior of the heart, so that the heart is as bright as the sun; one leaves heart and sun together for a certain time, and one feels the heart growing warm".[1] In this last instance the real sun no longer plays any part. Its image is internalized and projected into the heart in order to awake the interior light there. Another text adds a significant detail: after visualizing the solar disk—red and as large as a coin—which is to be found in the centre of the heart, one makes this image circulate through the whole body.[2]

THE SECRET OF THE GOLDEN FLOWER

This allusion to the circulation of an image within the body becomes more understandable if one turns to the methods followed by the Taoists to circulate the inner light. These methods are set out in the neo-Taoist treatise, *The Secret of the Golden Flower*, translated by R. Wilhelm with a commentary by C. G. Jung.[3] Since this text is very well known I will only dwell on certain features of it directly useful to our subject. "Essence and Life", it tells us, "cannot be seen: it is contained in the Light of Heaven. The Light of Heaven cannot be seen. It is contained in the two eyes".*

One must use the two eyes therefore to look inwards. In meditating, somewhat in the manner of a yogin (for the breath must be made rhythmical), the lids are closed and then the eyes no longer look outwards but light the inner space. And it is then that one discovers the Light.[4] Another exercise consists in concentrating the thoughts in the space between the eyes, which allows the Light to penetrate deep into the body.[5] The essential is not so much the discovery of the light as putting it into circulation within the body. Several methods are recommended, but

---

[1]H. Maspéro, *op. cit.*, p. 375.   [2]H. Maspéro, *op. cit.*, p. 376
[3]English translation, London and New York, 1931.
[4]*Op. cit.*, pp. 40, 43.   [5]*Op. cit.*, p. 40.
*The author translates "The Essence of Life . . . is contained in the Light of the Heart."

the most important seems to be what the text calls "the backward-flowing way", or "going against the stream". By means of this psycho-physiological exercise the thoughts are gathered in the Place of Heavenly Consciousness, the Heavenly Heart—and there, we are told, the Light is master.[1]

It is impossible to comment here on this method, which presents analogies both with the Tantric technique, *ulta-sadhana*[2] (litt. "going against the stream") and the Taoist way of "return to the origin".[3] Let us observe only that as a result of this exercise, the inner Light is circulated and that if it is allowed to move long enough in a circle it crystallizes, that is to say gives birth to what is called the "natural Spirit-Body".[4] The circulation of the Light produces within the body the "true seed" which is transformed into an embryo. When heated, nourished and bathed for a whole year by this method, which is certainly alchemical (for the text alludes to "the fire"), the embryo comes to maturity,[5] that is to say a new being comes to birth.

Another passage states that by making the light circulate, one obtains the crystallization, in the form of a seed, of the cosmic powers, symbolized by Heaven and Earth, and that a hundred days later in the middle of the Light, the "seed-pearl"[6] is born. Several images serve to suggest the crystallization of the Light: the Golden Flower which buds and opens, the seed that matures and becomes an embryo, or a pearl. These cosmological, embryological and alchemical metaphors converge and complete one another. The final result is the attainment of the Elixir of immortality, symbolized by the Golden Flower.

Now the opening of the Golden Flower is announced by an experience of Light. "As soon as one is quiet, the Light of the eyes begins to blaze up, so that everything before one becomes quite bright as if one were in a cloud. If one opens one's eyes

[1] *Op. cit.*, pp. 24ff.   [2] See *Yoga*, p. 318.
[3] See M. Eliade, *Forgerons et Alchimistes*, Paris, 1956, pp. 129ff.
[4] *The Secret of the Golden Flower*, p. 24.
[5] *Ibid.*, p. 26.   [6] *Ibid.*, pp. 34ff.

and seeks the body, it is not to be found any more. This is called: 'In the empty chamber it grows light'. That is a very favourable sign. Or, when one sits in meditation, the fleshly body becomes quite shining like silk or jade. It seems difficult to remain sitting; one feels as if drawn upward. This is called: 'The Spirit returns and pushes against Heaven'. In time, one can experience it in such a way that one really floats upward".[1]

These texts are more complex than may appear from our too brief summary. But it is this experience of the interior Light that principally concerns us. What value then is attached to this experience in Taoist circles? We must observe that these techniques imply neither the aid nor even the presence of a divinity. The Light dwells quite naturally within a man, in his heart. One succeeds in waking it and putting it into circulation by a process of cosmo-physiological mysticism. In other words, the secret of the life and immortality of the body is written into the very structure of the Cosmos, and consequently into the structure of the microcosm also—for every human being is a microcosm. Accent is here laid on practice, not on metaphysical knowledge or on mystical contemplation. But for Taoism the practice is itself mystical—for it has nothing to do with effort, will, or technique in the worldly sense of the term, but with the recovery of a primordial immediacy, lost as a result of the long process of civilization; with the rediscovery of natural wisdom, that is to say, wisdom depending equally on instinct and on what one might call a "mystical sympathy": that sympathy by which the sage unconsciously revives, in the deepest part of his being, the harmony with the rhythms of the cosmos.

[1]*Ibid.*, p. 56. There is also a risk of pseudo-experiences of the light when, as the commentary to *The Secret of the Golden Flower* expresses it, one believes one is meditating, but actually allows oneself to be invaded by "fantasies"; see *op. cit.*, p. 53.

IRAN

As R. Wilhelm has already observed, the leading role of the Light in *The Mystery of the Golden Flower* reminds one of Persia.[1] Iranian influences have also been found in the Tibetan myths of Primordial Man already discussed.[2] We will not approach the very complex problem of Iranian influences in Central Asia and the Far East. Let us observe, nevertheless, (1) that it is not necessary to attribute an Iranian origin to all the forms of dualism or conflict that one finds in Asia;[3] (2) nor to explain as of Iranian influence all ideas that identify the pure spirit, or being, with the Light. We have seen that, on the level of the Brahmanas and the Upanishads, India already identified being and spirit with the light. But Iranian theories elaborated to an extent unknown elsewhere the conflict between Light and Darkness, by considering as the Light not only the good God and creator, Ahura Mazdah, but also the essence of creation and of Life and, especially, the spirit and spiritual energy. In some of his Eranos lectures Henry Corbin brilliantly expounded the various aspects and implications of the theology of the Light in Zoroastrianism and Ismaelite gnosticism, and it would be purposeless to recount here the results of his researches.[4]

Let us say only that certain images used by Zoroastrianism

[1] *Op. cit.*, p. 10; reference to P. Y. Saeki, *The Nestorian Monument in China*, 2nd ed., London, 1928. This author considers that the "religion of the golden Elixir of Life" (Chin Tan Chiao) is of Nestorian origin.

[2] G. Tucci, *Tibetan Painted Scrolls*, vol. II, pp. 730ff. According to M. Hermanns, the *bon* myths of dualist structure were of Iranian origin; cf. *Mythen und Mysterien*, pp. 338ff.

[3] Some examples of "dualism" among primitives are to be found in Father Joseph Henninger's article, *L'Adversaire du Dieu bon chez les primitifs* ("Satan, Études Carmélitaines", XXVII, Paris, 1948, pp. 107-19). See also Hermann Baumann, *Das doppelte Geschlecht*, Berlin, 1955, pp. 229ff., and Ugi Bianchi, *Il dualismo religioso*, Rome, 1958, pp. 57ff.

[4] See particularly *Terre céleste et Corps de Résurrection d'après quelques traditions iraniennes*, "Eranos-Jahrbuch", 1953, vol. XXIII, pp. 151-250.

to express the consubstantiality of spirit and light recall the imagery of India, particularly of Buddhism. The *Denkart*, for instance, states that Zarathustra's radiance in his mother's womb during the last three days before his birth was so intense that it lit up the whole of his father's village.[1] Wisdom, sanctity—pure spirituality, in brief,—are symbolized here, as in India, by the most intense radiance. And just as the doctrine of the *Upanishads* identified the *atman* with the inner light, a chapter of the Great *Bundahishn* related the soul with *xvarnah*,[2] the "Light of Glory", the "pure radiance which constitutes the creations of Ohrmazd in their origin".[3] But in the case of ancient Persia, unlike that of India, we know relatively little about the *experience* of the inner Light.[4]

What seems certain is that the Iranians considered the manifestations of the Light and, especially, the appearance of a supernatural Star, as the principal annunciatory sign of the birth of the Cosmocrator and Saviour. And because the birth of the future Redeemer-King of the World will take place in a cave,[5] the Star or Column of Light will shine above the cave. It is probable that the Christians borrowed the imagery of the nativity of the Cosmocrator-Redeemer from the Parthians and applied

[1]*Denkart*, v, 2, 2; VII, 2, 56–8.

[2]The comparison has been made by Schaeder; see R. Reitzenstein and H. H. Schaeder, *Studien zum antiken Synkretismus aus Iran und Griechenland*, Leipzig, 1926, p. 230, note 1; see also H. Corbin, *Terre céleste*, p. 110.

[3]H. Corbin, *Terre céleste*, p. 109.

[4]On the eternal Light in Zoroastrianism, see the texts translated and commented on by R. C. Zaehner, *Zurvan. A Zoroastrian Dilemma*, Oxford, 1955, pp. 199ff. (the third chapter of the Great *Bundahishn*), 210ff., 389ff. and *passim*. On the theology of the Light in *Manichaeism*, see texts commented on by A. V. Williams Jackson, *Researches in Manichaeism*, New York, 1932, pp. 8ff., 177, 183, 191, 216, etc. See also Geo. Widengren, *The Great Vohu Manah and the Apostle of God*, Uppsala, 1945, pp. 27ff.; H.-Ch. Puech, *Le Manichéisme*, Paris, 1949, pp. 74ff. and notes 285ff. (pp. 159ff.).

[5]On this point, cf. Geo. Widengren, *Iranisch-semitische Kulturbegegnung in parthischer Zeit* ("Arbeitsgemeinschaft fur Forschung der Landes Nordrhein-Westfalen", Helft 70, Cologne and Opladen, 1960) pp. 62ff. This deals with a mythico-ritual drama depending, ultimately, on the Mithraic cult.

it to the Christ (see Widengren, *op. cit.*, p. 70). The oldest
Christian sources to place the Nativity in a cave are the Prot-
evangelism of James (xviii, 1ff.), Justin Martyr and Origen.[1]
Justin attacked the initiates of Mithraic mysteries who, "urged
by the devil, deemed to perform their initiations in a place they
call *speleum*".[2] This attack proves that already by the second
century Christians saw the analogy between the Mithraic *speleum*
and the cave at Bethlehem.

But primarily it is the Star and the light shining above the
cave that have played the important role in Christian religious
beliefs and iconography. Now, as Monneret de Villard and
Widengren have lately shown, this motif is most probably
Iranian. The Protevangelium (xix, 2) spoke of the blinding light
that filled the cave at Bethlehem. When it began to wane, the
Child Jesus appeared. This amounts to saying that the Light
was consubstantial with Jesus, or was one of his manifestations.

But i is the anonymous author of the *Opus imperfectum in
Matthaeum* (Patr. Gr., lvii, col. 637-8) who introduced new
elements—probably of Iranian origin—into the legend. According to him, the twelve Magi lived near the Mount of Victories.
They knew the secret revelation of Seth about the coming of
the Messiah and, every year, climbed the mountain, in which
was a cave with springs and trees. There they quietly prayed
to God for three days, waiting for the Star to appear. Finally it
appeared in the form of a small child, and the child told them
to go to Judea. Guided by the Star, the Magi travelled for two
years. On returning home they spoke of the miracle they had
witnessed; and when, after the Resurrection, the Apostle Thomas
came to their country, the Magi asked to be baptized (Monneret
de Villard, pp. 22ff.).

With some very suggestive developments this legend is found
again in the *Chronicle of Zuqnin*, a Syrian work long known

[1] Ugo Monneret de Villard, *Le leggende Orientali sui Magi evangelici*, p. 63.
[2] Justin le Martyr, *Dialogue avec Tryphon*, ch. lxxviii, etc., quoted by Monneret
de Villard, p. 63.

under the name of the *Pseudo-Dionysus of Tell Mahre*. The *Chronicle of Zuqnin* dates only from the years 774-5, but its prototype (as also that of the *Opus imperfectum*) must be older than the end of the sixth century (Monneret de Villard, p. 52). Here is a résumé of the passages relating to our subject: having set down in a book all that Adam had revealed to him about the coming of the Messiah, Seth placed the writing in the Treasure-Cave of the Secret Mysteries. He communicated the substance of these mysteries to his sons, enjoining them to climb the mountain every month and enter the cave. The twelve "Wise Kings" of the country of Shyr, "Kings and sons of Kings", faithfully performed the ritual ascent of the mountain, awaiting the fulfilment of Adam's prophecy. One day they perceived a column of ineffable light surmounted by a Star whose light was brighter than many suns. The Star entered the Treasure Cave, which became bright. A voice invited the Kings to go in. As they did so, they were blinded by the light and fell on their knees. But the light shrank and, a little later, took the form of a humble little man, who told them he had been sent by the heavenly Father. He advised them to take the treasure which had been hidden in the cave by their ancestors and to go to Galilee. Led by the Light, the Kings arrived in Bethlehem, and found there a cave like that of the Treasures. The miracle was repeated: the column of light and the Star descended and entered the cave. Hearing a voice that bade them go in, the Kings entered the cave. They bowed before the glorious Child and laid their crowns at his feet. Jesus greeted them as "Sons of the East of the Supreme Light", "worthy to see the primal and eternal Light". Meanwhile the cave became entirely bright. The Child, "Son of the Light", talked to them for a long time, calling them "those who have received the Light and are worthy to receive the perfect Light". The Kings took their way homeward. At their first stop, while they are eating their food, they have new experiences of the light. One of them sees "a great Light like no other in the world"; another "a Star whose brightness darkened the Sun", etc. When they arrive home the Kings tell what they have seen. Later on the apostle Judah Thomas comes to Shyr and begins to spread the faith. The Kings are baptized, and a Child of Light then descends from Heaven and speaks to them.[1]

From this prolix and clumsy tale let us take the motifs which bear directly on our subject: (1) the predominance of luminous manifestations (Column of Light, Star, bright Child, blinding light, etc.) all of which reflect the conception of Jesus as the ineffable Light; (2) the Nativity in a cave; (3) the name of the country, called Shyr in the *Chronicle,* is a corruption of Shyz, the birthplace of Zarathustra;[2] the "Mount of Victories" is therefore situated in the land of Shyz;[3] (4) this "Mount of Victories" seems to be a replica of the Iranian Cosmic Mountain, Hara Barzaiti, that is to say the *Axis Mundi* which connects Heaven and Earth.[4] It is therefore at the "Centre of the World" that Seth hides the prophecy of the Messiah's coming, and it is there that the Star announces the birth of the Cosmocrator-Redeemer. According to Iranian traditions, the *xvarna* shining above the holy mountain is the sign announcing the Saoshyant, the Redeemer miraculously born of the seed of Zarathustra. Finally let us note the symbolism of the periodical ascent of the Mount of Victories: it is at the "Centre of the World" that the eschatological Light is first to be perceived.

All these elements form an integral part of the great syncretist myth of the Cosmocrator-Redeemer, much modified by Persian influence. In one form or another this myth certainly influenced late Judaism and Christianity. Some of these religious ideas, however, are older than the cult of Mithras and Irano-Semitic syncretism. To cite only one example, according to

[1]Italian translation, G. Levi Della Vida, in U. Monneret de Villard, pp. 27-49; Latin translation by J.-B. Chabot, *Chronicon Pseudodionysianum vulgo dictum* (Scriptores Syri, Ser. III, t. I, Louvain, 1949), pp. 45-70.
[2]G. Widengren, *op. cit.,* p. 79.
[3]L.-I. Ringbom, *Graltempel und Paradies. Beziehungen zwischen Iran und Europa im Mittelalter,* Stockholm, 1951, pp. 243ff.
[4]On this symbolism, see *The Myth of the Eternal Return,* pp. 12-13; *Images and Symbols,* pp. 51ff.; *Centre du Monde, Temple, Maison* (in *Le Symbolisme cosmique des Monuments religieux,* Rome, 1957, pp. 57-82).

Jewish traditions the Messiah will appear on the summit of the Mountain.[1]

Now this idea derives from the image of the divine Mountain —Zion—situated in the "north" (cf. for example, Psalm 48, 2) a conception already found among the Canaanites,[2] but also well known among the Babylonians. In a more or less systematic manner, the religions of the ancient Near-East had assembled in a mythico-ritual drama the following elements: Cosmic Mountain—"Paradise"—Palace of the supreme God or birth-place of the Cosmocrator (redeemer)—Salvation of the World (cosmic regeneration) effected by the enthronement of a new Sovereign. What concerns our argument is that the Iranian version of the Nativity of the Cosmocrator-Redeemer was dominated by images of the Light, the Star and the Cave, and that these are the images that were borrowed and developed by popular Christian beliefs.

OLD TESTAMENT AND JUDAISM

It is impossible to review the religious valuations of the light and the various mystical experiences of the light in Judaism, Hellenistic syncretism, Gnosticism and Christianity. Not only is the subject vast, and unsuitable for summarizing or quick generalization, but it has been amply studied by many scholars. It will be enough to refer, for the Old Testament, to the notes collected by Sverre Aalen in his book, *Die Begriffe 'Licht' und 'Finsternis' im Alten Testament, im Spätjudentum und im Rabbinismus*, (Oslo, 1951);[3] for Philo and the mystical experience of the divine Light in Hellenistic Judaism, to Professor Erwin Goodenough's *By Light, Light. The Mystical Gospel of Hellenistic Judaism* (New

[1] Cf. Harald Riesenfeld, *Jésus transfiguré*, Lund, 1941, pp. 221ff.
[2] At Ugarit there is a mention of Mount Sapan or Ba'al Sapan where Ba'al assumes his throne and becomes king of the gods and men.
[3] See also A. M. Gierlich, *Der Lichtgedanke in den Psalmen. Eine terminologisch-exegetische Studie* ("Freiburger Theologische Studien", H.56 Freiburg im Berisgau, 1940).

Haven, U.S.A., 1935); for the symbolism of the Light at the end of classical antiquity to R. Bultmann's study, *Geschichte der Lichtsymbolik im Altertum*;[1] to the recent studies of Hanukkah, the Jewish festival of the Light, by O. S. Rankin, J. Morgenstern and Werblowsky;[2] to F. J. Dölger's researches into the symbolism of *Lumen Christi et Sol Salutis*,[3] and the list is far from exhaustive. We are now touching on particularly complex religious ground and, to be useful, all comparison between the various symbolisms and mystical experiences of the Light must be finely shaded. Account must be taken of cultural individuality and the divergencies of religious ideas as well as of the many convergences and syncretisms.

It would be out of the question to attempt the problem as a whole. We must content ourselves therefore with a few observations. It is important, for example, to observe that in the Old Testament, the Light is not identical with God and is not thought of as a divine power; it was created by Jahve and it is not the light of the Sun, for the Sun was created on the fourth day.[4] Nor can

[1]*Philologus*, XCVII, 1946, pp. 1ff.

[2]O. S. Rankin, *The Origins of the Festival of Hanukkah, The Jewish New Age Festival*, Edinburgh, 1930; Id, *The Festival of Hanukkah* (in *The Labyrinth*, edited by S. H. Hooke, London, 1935, pp. 159-209); J. Morgenstern, *The Chanukkah Festival of the Calendar of Ancient Israel* ("Hebrew Union College Annual", XX, 1947, pp. 1ff.; XXI, 1948, pp. 365ff.); R. J. Zwi Werblowsky, *Hanouca et Noël ou Judaïsme et Christianisme* ("Revue de l'Histoire des Religions", January–March 1954, pp. 30-68). See also Sverre Aalen, *op. cit.*, pp. 130ff.

[3]F. J. Dölger, *Sol Salutis*, Münster i. W., 1920; 2nd ed., *Ibid*, 1925; Id, *Lumen Christi. Untersuchungen zum abendlichen Licht-Segen in Antike und Christentum. Die Deo-gratias-Lampen von Selinunt in Sizilien und Curcul in Numidien* ("Antike und Christentum", V, 1936, pp. 1-43); see also *Die Sonne der Gerechtigkeit und der Schwarze: eine religionsgeschichtliche Studie zum Taufgelöbnis* ("Liturgiegeschichtliche Forschungen", II, Münster, 1918). See also H. Rahner, *Das christliche Mysterium von Sonne und Mond* ("Eranos-Jahrbuch, 1943", vol X, pp. 305-404), especially pp. 352ff.; G. Widengren. *Iranisch-semitische Kulturbegegnung*, pp. 56ff.

[4]See H. G. May, *The Creation of Light in Genesis*, I, 3-5 ("Journal of Biblical Literature", vol. 58, 1939, pp. 203ff.) and especially Sverre Aalen, *Die Begriffe 'Licht' und 'Finsternis' im Alten Testament*, pp. 14ff.

one interpret in a dualist sense Jahve's battle with Night or with the primordial Ocean. Darkness, like the great waters and the Dragon, symbolises the powers of Chaos—and Jahve's battle is, in fact, an act of cosmogenesis. Moreover, darkness is rarely associated with the primordial Ocean and the Dragon, or identified with them.[1] Darkness does not stand for the enemy of God—as was the case in Iran. The great originality of the Old Testament is that Jahve radically transcends the cosmic order of sanctity. In Judaism the light is not sanctified because, by virtue of its own order of being, it constitutes the analogue of Spirit and the spiritual life; it is sanctified because it was created by God. For Philo, the Light corresponds to Spirit, but has this virtue only because it emanates directly from God.[2]

BAPTISM AND TRANSFIGURATION

Similar theological positions have been taken up by the other two monotheistic religions, Christianity and Islam. But as it is not theology but the experience of the inner light that primarily concerns us, let us see how it was known and evaluated by primitive Christianity. One of the essential incidents in the Christian mystery—the Transfiguration of Christ—is a manifestation of the divine Light. The mystical light is equally important in the principal Christian sacrament, Baptism.

The symbolism of Baptism is of course extremely rich and complex, but elements of illumination and fire play a very important role in it. Justin, Gregory Nazianzen and other Fathers of the Church call baptism "illumination" (*photismos*); they base themselves, as we know, on two passages of the Epistle to the Hebrews (6, 4; 10, 32) in which those who have been initiated in the Christian mystery, that is to say baptized (for this is the interpretation given in the Syriac translation of these passages), are distinguished by the name *photisthentes*,

[1] Cf. S. Aalen, *op. cit.*, pp. 12ff., refuting Gunkel.
[2] Cf. E. R. Goodenough, *By Light, Light*, pp. 7ff. On the mystical experience of the "Divine Light" (identified by Philo with God) see *Ibid.*, pp. 146ff., 166ff.

"illumined". Already in the second century Justin (Dial., 88) mentions a legend according to which at Jesus' baptism "fire sprang up on the Jordan".[1] A whole group of beliefs, symbols and rites crystallized around the idea of baptism by fire.[2] The Holy Ghost is represented as a flame; sanctification is expressed by images of fire or flames. Here is one of the doctrinal sources for the belief that spiritual perfection—that is to say sanctity—not only makes the soul capable of seeing Christ's light-body, but that it is also accompanied by outward phenomena: the saint's body irradiates light or shines like a burning fire.

The other source of this belief is evidently the mystery of Christ's Transfiguration on the Mountain (afterwards identified with Mount Tabor[3]). Since every act of Jesus becomes an exemplary model for the Christian, the mystery of the Transfiguration also forms a transcendent model of spiritual perfection. By imitating Christ, the saint earns, by divine grace, transfiguration in this life on earth; this, at least, is how the Eastern Church understands the mystery of Tabor. Since transfiguration is the basis of the whole Christian mysticism and theology of the divine Light, it would be interesting to know in what sense it was expected or anticipated by Judaism.

Harald Riesenfeld, in his book *Jésus transfiguré* (Lund, 1947), has thrown into relief the Jewish background of this mystery. Certain of his interpretations, particularly that which touches on the cultural aspects of kingship among the Israelites, have been disputed. But this has no direct repercussion on our researches. These are the important points concerning the Jewish background of the Transfiguration: (1) the idea of light is contained in the concept of divine "Glory"; to meet Jahve

[1] Cf. H. Usener, *Das Weihnachtsfest*, 2nd ed., Bonn, 1911, pp. 62ff.

[2] See C. M. Edsman, *Le Baptême de feu*, Uppsala-Leipzig, 1940, pp. 182ff.

[3] The Gospels speak of a "high mountain" (Matth. 17, 1; Mark 9, 2). For Mount Tabor, see Judges 4, 6ff.; Ps. 89, 12; the Gospel according to the Hebrews (Hennecke, p. 54). See later references to Mount Tabor (Simeon, hesychasm, etc.) in Max Pulver's article, *Die Lichterfahrung im Johannes-Evangelium, im Corpus Hermeticum, in der Gnosis und in der Ostkirche* ("Eranos-Jahrbuch", 1944, vol. X, pp. 253-96), pp. 288ff.

is to enter the Light of Glory; (2) Adam was created as an effulgent being, but sin caused him to lose his Glory; (3) one day Glory will reappear with the Messiah, who will shine like the Sun. For the Messiah *is* Light and brings the Light; (4) in the world to come the just will have shining faces, for the Light is the characteristic sign of the future world, the world renewed; (5) when Moses descended from Mount Sinai (Exodus, 34, 29ff.) his face shone so that Aaron and all the people were afraid.[1]

It is important to bring out the Old Testament and Messianic context of Jesus' transfiguration, for it improves one's understanding of the historic roots of primitive Christianity. But, on a close examination, one observes that the Old Testament and Messianic ideology implicit in the mystery of Mount Tabor, although historically part of the religious experience of Israel, and to a certain extent of the earliest religious experience of the Near East, is not radically foreign to other religious climates. That the light is an exemplary manifestation of divinity is, as we have seen, a commonplace of Indian theologies. One can compare with the effulgent Adam the primordial Light-Man of Iranian and Indo-Tibetan myths; similarly, the shining of those who have realised spiritual perfection or received grace to contemplate the divinity face to face, is a motif frequently found in India.

Let us be clear: it is not a case of exact equivalence, of an identity of religious content or ideological formulation, but of similarities, agreements, congruences. Everything depends in the final instance on the theological or metaphysical value attached to the mystical experience of the Light; and we shall see in a moment that within a single religion, Christianity, these valuations may be divergent and contradictory. But it is no less important to establish that there is a relationship and congruence between the Figures, the symbols and even the ideologies of Asiatic religions and those of the outstanding revealed religion, Jewish monotheism, and consequently of Christianity. This fact leads us to suppose that, in addition to a

[1] H. Riesenfeld, *Jésus transfiguré*, pp. 98ff., 110ff., etc.

certain unity on the level of mystical experience itself, there is a real equivalence of the images and symbols used to express the mystical experience. It is at the point where the mystical experience is conceptualized that the differences are defined and the disagreements appear.

THE "FLAMING" MONKS

We will return to this problem in our conclusions to these comparative researches. Let us continue our analysis of the facts concerning Christianity, leaving aside the image and vocabulary of the mystic Light to be found in early Christian literature and patristic theology. As in other religions, two categories of facts primarily interest us: the subjective experience of the Light, and the objective phenomena—that is to say the objective light seen by witnesses. If one is "illumined" by baptism; if the Holy Ghost is visualized as a manifestation of fire; if the Light of the Transfiguration perceived by the Apostles on Mount Tabor represents the visible form of Christ's divinity, then the perfect Christian mystical life should logically reveal itself by luminous phenomena. This was taken by the Egyptian Fathers as an essential sign. The monk, we read in *The Book of Paradise* "shines with the light of Grace".[1] Abba Joseph claims that one cannot be a monk without becoming like a flaming fire. When one of the brothers paid a visit one day to Abba Arsenius in the desert, he saw him through the window of his cell "like a fire".[2] It was particularly when at prayer that the monk radiated light. When Pisentius was deep in prayer, his cell was filled with light.[3] Above the place where hermits prayed a magnificent pillar of light was to be seen. In the ascetic literature of the time, every perfect man was considered as a column of fire and

[1] Wallis Budge, *The Book of Paradise*, I-II, London, 1904, p. 1009; C.-M. Edsman, *Le baptême de feu*, p. 155.
[2] P. G., vol. LXV, col. 229 C (cf. Budge, *op. cit.*, p. 950, no. 440; Edsman, *op. cit.*, p. 156); P. G., vol. LXV, col. 95 C. (Budge, p. 798, no. 611; Edsman, *Ibid.*)
[3] C.-M. Edsman, *op. cit.*, p. 162.

this image reveals its true significance when we remember that theophanies or Christophanies in the form of a column of fire abound in Gnostic and ascetic writings. Once Abba Joseph stretched his hands towards Heaven and his fingers became like two flames of fire. Then, turning to one of the monks, he said: "If you wish, you may become entirely like fire!"[1]

In his *Life of Saint Sabas*, Cyril of Scythopolis reports that Justinian (in the year 530) saw "a divine grace in the form of burning light, and shaped like a crown, on the old man's head (Sabas was more than ninety) and that it radiated light like the sun".[2] When Abba Sisoès was at the point of death, and the fathers were sitting round him, "his face began to shine like the sun. And he said to them: 'Here is Abba Antony coming'. Then a little later: 'Here is the band of prophets', and his face shone brighter. Then he said: 'Here is the band of apostles' and the light of his face shone brighter still". Finally Sisoès "gave up the ghost, and it was like a flash of lightning".[3]

It would be purposeless to multiply examples. Let us add only that one Christian sect, the Messalians, went so far in their exaltation of the mystic Light that they measured a soul's degree of perfection by his capacity to perceive, in vision, Jerusalem, the city of light, or the Lord clothed in glory. For the Messalians, the final aim was the soul's ecstatic union with the light-body of Christ. This extreme doctrine did not fail to put certain official theologians on their guard against the experience of the mystic Light.

PALAMAS AND THE LIGHT OF TABOR

In the fourteenth century Barlaam, a Calabrian monk, accused the Hesychasts of Mount Athos of Messalianism, basing his attack on their own assertion that they enjoyed the vision of the

---

[1] *Ibid.*, pp. 157, 159ff.
[2] *Vita S. Sabae*, ed. E. Schwartz, p. 173; J. Lemaitre, *Dictionnaire de Spiritualité*, 1952, col. 1850.
[3] P. G., 65, 396bc.; J. Lemaitre, *op. cit.*

uncreated Light. But indirectly the Calabrian monk did a great service to Eastern mystical theology. For he gave the great theologian, Gregory Palamas, Archbishop of Thessalonica, an opportunity of defending the Hesychasts of Mount Athos at the Council of Constantinople (in 1341), and of elaborating a whole mystical theology around the light of Tabor.

Palamas had no difficulty in showing that Holy Scripture abounds in references to the divine light and the Glory of God, and that God himself is called Light. Furthermore, he marshalled an abundant mystical and ascetic literature—from the Desert Fathers to Simeon the New Theologian—to prove that deification by the Holy Ghost and the visible manifestations of Grace are marked by a vision of the uncreated Light or by emanations of light. For Palamas, wrote Vladimir Lossky, "the divine Light is a prerequisite of mystical experience. It is the visible form of divinity and of the powers by which God communicates and reveals himself to those who have purified their hearts".[1] This divine and deifying Light is Grace. The transfiguration of Jesus evidently constitutes the central mystery of Palamas' theology. His argument with Barlaam bore principally on the issue whether the Light of the Transfiguration was created or increated. The majority of the Church Fathers considered the Light seen by the Apostles as increated and divine, and Palamas set out to develop this point.[2] For him the Light is by nature a property of God, it exists outside Time and Space and is made visible in the theophanies of the Old Testament. On Mount Tabor there was no change in Jesus, but there was a transformation in the Apostles; they, by divine grace, were enabled to see Jesus as he truly was, blinding by his divine light. Adam had had this power before the fall, and it will be restored to man in

[1]Vladimir Lossky, *La Théologie de la Lumière chez saint Grégoire Palamas de Thessalonique* ("Dieu Vivant", I, 1945, pp. 93-118), p. 107. Cf. the same author's *Essai sur la théologie de l'Église d'Orient*, Paris, 1944, especially pp. 214ff. Also Jean Meyendorff, *Saint Grégoire Palamas et la mystique orthodoxe*, Paris, 1959, pp. 88ff.
[2]V. Lossky, *La Théologie de la Lumière*, pp. 110ff.

the eschatological future. In other words the perception of God in his increated Light is connected with the perfection of the beginning and the end, with the Paradise before history and the *eschaton* which will put an end to history. But those who make themselves worthy of the Kingdom of God enjoy the vision of the increated Light here and now, like the Apostles on Mount Tabor.

Moreover, developing the tradition of the monks of Egypt, Palamas affirms that the vision of the increated Light is accompanied by an objective luminosity in the saint. "He who shares the divine energy . . . becomes himself in some sort light; he is joined to the Light, and with the Light he sees in full consciousness all that is hidden from those who have not received this grace".[1]

Palamas relied principally on the mystical experience of Simeon the New Theologian. In the *Life* of Simeon written by Nicetas Stethatos, there are some particularly precise details of this experience. "One night when he was at prayer and his purified mind was joined with the primal Mind, he saw a light in the sky which suddenly threw its beams down on him, a great and pure light which illumined all things and cast a splendour as bright as day. It illumined him also, and he felt as if the whole building with the cell in which he was had vanished and passed in the wink of an eye into nothingness, that he himself had been snatched into the air and had entirely forgotten his body". On another occasion, "a light like that of dawn began to shine from above . . . it gradually grew, making the air brighter and brighter, and he felt as if he and his whole body had quitted the things of this world. As this light continued to shine with ever increasing brightness and became like a midday sun shining in splendour above him, he saw that he was himself at the centre of the light and that the sweetness invading his whole body from so near filled him with joy and tears. He saw the light unbelievably uniting with his flesh and gradually

[1] *Sermon pour la fête de la Présentation au Temple de la Sainte Vierge*, trans. by Lossky, *op. cit.*, p. 11c

pervading his limbs. He saw this light finally invading his body, his heart and his bowels, the whole light invading his whole body and turning him completely to fire and light; and as just before it had destroyed the outline of the house, so now it destroyed for him all awareness of the shape, position, bulk and appearance of his body".[1]

These conceptions have been retained till this day by the orthodox Churches. I will quote, as an example of the body throwing light, the famous case of Saint Seraphim of Sarov at the beginning of the nineteenth century. The disciple who afterwards set down the "Revelations" of the saint tells that once he saw him so bright that it was impossible to look at him. "I can't look at you, Father", he cried, "your eyes flash lightnings, your face is more dazzling than the sun, and it hurts my eyes to look at you". Seraphim then began to pray and his disciple was able to look at him. "I looked", he wrote, "and was seized with pious fear. Imagine the face of a man speaking to you from the middle of the sun, from the brightness of its dazzling midday beams. You see his lips moving, the changing expression in his eyes, you hear his voice, you feel his hands holding you by the shoulders, but you do not see those hands or the body of the man who is speaking to you, nothing but the shining light that spreads for many yards around him, revealing with its beams the snow-covered field outside and the white flakes that steadily go on falling".[2] It would be exciting to compare this experience of Saint Seraphim's disciple with the account given by Arjuna in chapter XI of the *Bhagavadgita* of the manifestation of Krishna.

We must remember also that Sri Ramakrishna, a contemporary of Saint Seraphim of Sarov, sometimes appeared luminous or as if surrounded with flames. "His tall figure . . . looked

[1]*Vie de Syméon le Nouveau Théologien*, no. 5, pp. 8-10, no. 69, pp. 94-5, texts quoted by J. Lemaitre, *op. cit.*, col. 1852, 1853.
[2]*Révélation de Saint Séraphim de Sarov*, fragment translated by Lossky, *op. cit.*, pp. 112-13. On the radiance of the saints, see the important collection of examples by O. Leroy, *La Splendeur corporelle des saints*, Paris, 1936.

much taller and as light as a body seen in a dream. Getting lighter, the dark colour of his body became converted into a firm complexion . . . The bright colours became one with the lustre of his body and he was mistaken for a person surrounded by flames of fire". (Saradananda, *Sri Ramakrishna, the Great Master*, ed. 1952, p. 829 adapted.)

MYSTICISM OF THE LIGHT

Any phenomenological study of the mystic light should take into account the light that blinded Saint Paul on the road to Damascus, various experiences of the light by Saint John of the Cross, Pascal's famous and mysterious paper on which the word "Fire" was written in capitals, and Jacob Boehme's ecstasy, which was started by the sun's reflection on a dish and followed by an intellectual illumination so perfect that he seemed to have understood all mysteries; also many other less famous experiences like that of the Venerable Serafina di Dio, a Carmelite of Capri (d. 1699) whose face in prayer or after Communion shone like a flame, and whose eyes threw sparks like a fire;[1] and even those of the unfortunate Father Surin who, after suffering for so many years for the deeds of the devils of Loudun, knew some hours of beatitude: once when he was walking in the garden "the sunlight seemed to grow incomparably brighter than usual, and yet was so soft and bearable" that he seemed "to be walking in Paradise".[2] No less significant are the luminous visions that accompany the Moslem mystics' different phases of the *dhikr;* the seven "coloured lights" seen successively by the inner eye of the ascetic at the stage of the *dhikr* of the heart,[3] and the

[1] See Montagu Summers, *The Physical Phenomena of Mysticism*, 2nd imp., London, 1950, p. 71.
[2] See Aldous Huxley, *The Devils of Loudun*, 1952, p. 305.
[3] Louis Gardet, *La mention du nom divin* (dhikr) *dans la mystique musulmane* ("Revue Thomiste", 1952, pp. 641-79; 1953, pp. 197-213), particularly, 1952, pp. 669ff. On the "seven luminous sheaths", see L. Massignon, *Recueil de textes inédits concernant la mystique en pays d'Islam*, Paris, 1929, p. 143, and

effulgent light to which one attains during the most inward *dhikr*, which is a divine light that never goes out.[1]

SPONTANEOUS EXPERIENCES OF THE LIGHT

But here we must conclude our examples of religious experiences involving the light. I should like, however, to quote also a few interesting cases of persons indifferent to or almost entirely ignorant of theology and the mystical life. We shall now in fact return to the spiritual horizon of that American merchant whose inward adventures we related at the beginning of this study. One particularly instructive case is that of Dr. R. M. Bucke (1837-1902), one of the best known Canadian psychiatrists of his time. He occupied the chair of Nervous and Mental Diseases at Western University, Ontario, and in 1890 was elected President of the American Medico-Psychological Association. At the age of thirty-five he had a strange experience, which I will relate and which radically changed his ideas of life. A little before his death he published *Cosmic Consciousness*, a book which William James considered "an important contribution to psychology". Dr. Bucke believed that certain persons are capable of attaining a higher level of consciousness, which he named "cosmic consciousness". The reality of this state seemed to him to be proved in the first instance by an experience of subjective light. His book assembles a great number of such experiences, from those of the Buddha and Saint Paul to those of his own contemporaries. His analyses and interpretations have only a slight interest, but

note 1 concerning Ala al Dawla Simnani, b. 1336, the first mystical writer and the forerunner of the modern "chief of congregation", who carefully classifies the "coloured lights seen during esctasy in repeating the various phrases of the *dhikr*".

[1]"The fires of the *dhikr* never go out, and its lights never fade . . . You always see some lights ascending and some descending; the fires around you are bright, very hot and flaming" (Ibn 'Ata' Allah, quoted by Gardet, *op. cit.*, p. 677). "This is the stage at which the effects of the *dhikr* might be compared with the great illuminations of the Byzantine tradition. Profound differences in the conceptual picture must, however, also be noted" (Gardet, *Ibid.*).

the book is valuable for its documentation: he gives many unpublished experiences, gathered principally from his contemporaries.

This is how Dr. Bucke describes in the third person what happened to him in the early spring, at the beginning of his thirty-sixth year: He and two friends had spent the evening reading Wordsworth, Shelley, Keats, Browning, and especially Whitman. They parted at midnight, and he had a long drive in a hansom (it was an English city). "He was in a state of quiet, almost passive enjoyment. All at once, without warning of any kind, he found himself wrapped round as it were by a flame-coloured cloud. For an instant he thought of fire, some sudden conflagration in the great city; the next he knew the light was within himself. Directly afterwards came upon him a sense of exaltation, of immense joyousness accompanied or followed by an intellectual illumination impossible to describe. Into his brain streamed one momentary lightning-flash of Brahmic splendour, leaving thenceforward for always an after-taste of Heaven . . . He saw and he knew that the Cosmos is not dead matter but a living Presence; that the soul of man is immortal . . . that the foundation principle of the world is what we call love and that the happiness of everyone is, in the long run, absolutely certain. He claims that he learnt more within the few seconds during which the illumination lasted than in previous months or even years of study, and that he learnt much that no study could have taught him".[1]

Dr. Bucke adds that for the rest of his life he never had a similar experience. And these are the conclusions he comes to: the realization of cosmic consciousness comes as a sense of being immersed in a flame or in a rose-coloured cloud, or, perhaps rather a sense that the mind is itself filled with such a cloud or haze. This sensation is accompanied by an emotion of joy, assurance, triumph, "salvation", and with this experience comes, simultaneously or instantly afterwards, an intellectual illumination quite impossible to describe. The instantaneousness

[1] R. M. Bucke, *The Cosmic Consciousness*, pp. 7-8.

of the illumination can be compared with nothing so well as with a dazzling flash of lightning in the middle of a dark night, bringing the landscape that had been hidden into clear view.[1]

There is much that could be said about this experience. Let us be content to make a few observations: (1) the inner light is at first perceived as coming from without; (2) not until he understands its subjective nature does Dr. Bucke feel inexplicable happiness and receive the intellectual illumination which he compares to a lightning-flash passing through his brain; (3) this illumination definitely changed his life, bringing a spiritual rebirth. Typologically, one could relate this case of illumination to the illumination of the Esquimo shaman and, to a certain extent, to the self-illumination of the *atman*. A friend and admirer of Whitman, Dr. Bucke speaks of "cosmic consciousness" and of "Brahmic splendour": these are retrospective conceptions, derived from his own ideology. The character of the experience—its transcendence of the personality and its association with love recall rather a Buddhist climate of thought. A Jungian psychologist or a Catholic theologian would say that it was a realisation of selfhood. But the fundamental point, in our opinion, is that, thanks to this experience of the inner light, Dr. Bucke had access to a spiritual world the existence of which he had not even suspected till then, and that the access to this transcendental world constituted for him an *incipit vita nova*.

A very interesting case is that of a woman to whom Dr. Bucke refers only by her initials, A.J.S. As a child, she fell and sustained a spinal injury. She had a fine voice and worked hard to become a singer, but her physical frailty was a great obstacle. After her marriage she had a nervous breakdown, and despite every care her health began dangerously to decline. The pains in her spine became so unbearable that she was completely unable to sleep and had to be sent to a sanatorium. No improvement took place and she was waiting for a suitable opportunity to commit suicide when she had this experience. One day, lying in bed,

[1] *Ibid.*, pp. 60-2.

she suddenly felt a great calmness. "I fell asleep only to wake a few hours after to find myself in a flood of light. I was alarmed. Then I seemed to hear the words 'Peace, be still!' over and over again. I cannot say it was a voice, but I heard the words plainly and distinctly . . . I lay for what seemed to me then a long time in that condition, when gradually I was again in the dark".

After that night her health quickly improved. She became well and strong both physically and mentally, but her way of life changed. Formerly she had loved the excitement of a public life; now she loved the quiet of home life and a few friends. She discovered in herself the power of healing others; with a touch or, in some cases, by looking into their eyes she could put sufferers from insomnia to sleep. At the time she first saw she light she was twenty-four, and during the rest of her life the saw it only twice more. Once her husband was beside her, and she asked him if he did not see it too, but he had noticed nothing. In her autobiographical account, sent to Dr. Bucke, she confessed that it was impossible for her to express in words what was revealed to her "during this experience and immediately following the presence of the light. . . . It is *seeing inwardly*, and the word *harmony* would perhaps express part of what is seen". "The mental experiences following the light", she adds, "are always essentially the same—namely an intense desire to reveal man to himself and to aid those who are trying to find something worth living for in what they call 'this life' ".[1]

What seems to us remarkable in this experience is not only its non-religious atmosphere but also its modern and one might say "humanitarian" character. Indeed, there was nothing terrifying about the light and the very human voice brought no transcendental message, but quite modestly counselled calm. The rapid, almost miraculous, cure also marked the beginning of a new life, but the fruits of this second birth were confined to the level of human activities: the young woman acquired the power of healing, particularly insomnia, and the spiritual result

[1]Bucke, *op. cit.*, pp. 300ff.

of her enlightenment was a desire to help people find a significance in their lives.

LIGHT AND TIME

Here now is an account of a contemporary experience recorded by W. L. Wilmhurst, author of *Contemplations*. It occurred to him in a village church during the singing of the *Te Deum*. "I caught sight," he writes, "in the aisle at my side, of what resembled bluish smoke issuing from the chinks of the stone floor. Looking more intently, I saw it was not smoke, but something finer, more tenuous—a soft, impalpable, self-luminous haze of violet colour, unlike any physical vapour. Thinking I experienced some momentary optical defect or delusion, I turned my gaze farther along the aisle, but there too the same delicate haze was present . . . I perceived the wonderful fact that it extended farther than the walls and roof of the building and was not confined by them. Through these I now could look and could see the landscape beyond . . . I saw from all parts of my being simultaneously, not from my eyes only. Yet for all this intensified perceptive power there was as yet no loss of touch with my physical surroundings, no suspension of my faculties of sense . . . I felt happiness and peace—beyond words. Upon the instant the luminous blue haze engulfing me and all around me became transformed into golden glory, into light untellable . . . The golden light of which the violet light seemed now to have been as the veil or outer fringe, welled forth from a central immense globe of brilliancy . . . But the most wonderful thing was that these shafts and waves of light, that vast expanse of photosphere, and even the great central globe itself, were crowded to solidarity with the forms of living creatures . . . a single coherent organism filling all space and place, yet composed of an infinitude of individual existences . . . I saw moreover that these things were present in teeming myriads in the church I stood in; that they were intermingled with and

were passing unobstructedly through both myself and all my
fellow-worshippers . . . The heavenly hosts drifted through
the human congregation as wind passes through a grove of
trees".[1]

I will break this astonishing story here; the states that follow
are less important for our purpose than for their bearing on the
general phenomenology of mystical experience. The singularity
of this experience is that it was not sudden, but developed in
time. No spontaneous illumination but the passing of a bluish
smoke like a mist into a violet haze and finally into a blinding
golden light. The vision altered, continually changing its nature.
At the beginning space filled with violet light extended on all
sides, and the writer saw in all directions, saw through walls
beyond the church and the village. After this experience he felt
"happiness and peace—beyond words"; and it is in this state of
spiritual calm that the light becomes golden and he perceives
the central globe, and afterwards discovers the myriads of
spiritual beings.

This vision was followed by another in which everything of
time and place and form vanished from the consciousness and
only "the ineffable eternal things" remained. "My consciousness", he wrote, "leapt to its utmost limit, and passed into the
region of the formless and uncreated". Then he was no longer
conscious of the physical world around him. But this rapture
lasted only a few seconds, for when he came back to himself
the *Te Deum* had not concluded. The rapidity of the change
from one mode of vision to another, from the perception of
physical light to that of a pure, transcendent world beyond Time
and space, is most remarkable. It is like a rapid mystical initiation
running at full speed.

A similar though much briefer experience is described by
Warner Allen in *The Timeless Moment* (1946); it took place
between two successive notes of Beethoven's Seventh Symphony
and involved no conscious hiatus in listening to the music.

[1]W. L. Wilmhurst, *Contemplations*, pp. 142ff., quoted in R. C. Johnson, *The
Imprisoned Splendour*, London and New York, 1953, pp. 306-7.

Here is Warner Allen's description: "I closed my eyes and watched a silver glow which shaped itself into a circle with a central focus brighter than the rest. The circle became a tunnel of light proceeding from some distant sun in the heart of the Self. Swiftly and smoothly I was borne through the tunnel and, as I went the light turned from silver to gold. There was an impression of drawing strength from a limitless sea of power and a sense of deepening peace. The light grew brighter, but was never dazzling or alarming. I came to a point where time and motion ceased . . . I am absorbed in the Light of the Universe, in Reality glowing like fire with the knowledge of itself, without ceasing to be one and myself, merged like a drop of quicksilver in the Whole, yet still separate as a grain of sand in the desert. The peace that passes all understanding and the pulsating energy of Creation are one in the centre . . . where all opposites are reconciled".[1]

The interest of this experience is primarily metaphysical; it reveals the paradox of a mode of existence both in Time and out of Time, a sort of *coincidentia oppositorum*. The writer is aware of being himself and at the same time absorbed in the whole, he enjoys simultaneously a personal consciousness and a consciousness that transcends personality; and at the same time an ontological centre is revealed to him, an *Urgrund* where contraries are reconciled. The preliminaries of this revelation—the tunnel of light that linked the Self to a distant Sun—would deserve individual study. But I must go on to quote one further account which is particularly instructive because its author is at the same time a careful observer and an informed scholar. Indeed, J. H. M. Whiteman, Professor of Mathematics at Cape Town University, is familiar with the metaphysics and mystical theology of both East and West. But he has also made a con-

[1]Warner Allen, *The Timeless Moment*, London, 1946, pp. 30-3, quoted in R. C. Johnson, *The Imprisoned Splendour*, pp. 309, 310. Other particularly interesting experiences of the inner light are to be found in Bucke, *Cosmic Consciousness*, pp. 267-73; Johnson, *The Imprisoned Splendour*, p. 302 (quoting Payne and Bendit, *The Psychic Sense*, London, 1943, pp. 183-4).

siderable number of personal observations on various parapsychological states.[1]

Here is his account of an experience which he had at twenty-eight. During the night, but not in a dream, he saw himself "separated" from the body and raised very quickly to a great height. "All at once, without any further change, my eyes were opened. Above and in front, yet in me, of me, and around, was the Glory of the Archetypal Light. Nothing can be more truly light, since that Light makes all other light to be light; nor is it a flat material light, but a creative light of life itself, streaming forth in Love and Understanding, and forming all other lives out of its substance". (N.B. I omit the rest of the analysis since it does not bear directly on our subject.)

"Far below, as things can be seen at these times without turning away, there appeared something like the surface of the Earth. But this was only for a moment, in a representative vision, to make clear the immense height to which the soul had been raised, and her nearness to the Sun.

"How can source be described? How its direction? Though

---

[1]He has published and commented on some of his experiences in his study, *The Process of Separation and Return in experiences fully "out of the body"* ("Proceedings, The Society for Psychical Research", May 1956, pp. 240-74). Certain of these experiences "out of the body" also involve an experience of light. Thus, for example, when at the age of twelve he had an accident while making an experiment with phosphorus, he observed "the light in the room becoming bright and taking on a dreamlike quality, and at that moment his ears became deaf" (*op. cit.*, p. 248). In a dream, while detached from his body, he felt himself carried to a great distance and saw a magnificent palace or temple at the top of which a strong light flowed through a large window. A few moments later he received a revelation of an intellectual kind—and felt himself enveloped in a still brighter light. In another dream, at the age of forty-three, he saw himself leave his body and enter a park; "the light was remarkably bright" (p. 252). In his vision he seemed to go through a tunnel, in a state close to a dream, and come out on the other side, where he found a sunny landscape, bathed in light (p. 254). In this dream he suddenly became conscious of a burst of light of a spiritual kind (p. 259). On another occasion he seemed able to distinguish the light of another world from that of the physical world (p. 266).

upwards and forwards, it was not a geometrical direction, more or less so, and in relation to something else, but an absolute direction, exactly so, by its own archetypal nature. Source it was, of Life and Truth, being the Source of all ideas of life and truth; yet manifested as in space.

"And Lo! suddenly, without any shift of direction, the light was seen in a point. And in that point was the Idea of *Twelve*; not a 'twelve' that could be counted or that appeared separable into parts; but nevertheless the Idea of Twelve that enters into our concepts of twelve; incomprehensible, except in the Godhead. And passing even within that Light . . . I came to the archetypal idea and name of the Father. But now understanding and obedience began to wane, and obscurity of mind insensibly took hold, because of the encroachment of Self. For a moment I seemed to see, at a lower level, a representation of the Idea of Seven; but whether this was objective, or prompted by imagination, could not be distinguished. Then presently consciousness settled again in the physical body".[1]

I have deliberately concluded with this experience in which one again finds the number twelve, already met with in the dream of the American merchant. The richness and precision of the story are remarkable; one can see that the author is a mathematician and has read the philosophers and theologians. What he tells us about the perception of the Light, about the direction of its source, and the *source* of the *ideas* of Life and Truth, makes us think that the vagueness and imprecision with which certain similar experiences are described are primarily due to a lack of philosophical training in those who describe them. That which we are told is "impossible to describe" or beyond our comprehension does not only tell us about the experience itself but also about the lack of philosophical knowledge of the person who experienced it. In contrast to the other modern examples I have cited, this is the experience of a believer who is at the same time a philosopher. That is why—according to Professor Whiteman —this meeting with the divine Light did not cause a break in

[1] J. H. M. Whiteman, *The Mystic Life*, London, 1961, pp. 35-6.

his life, as was the case, for example, with Dr. Bucke; it merely deepened his faith and illumined it philosophically.

FINAL OBSERVATIONS

We have just reviewed some beliefs and experiences of the Light vouched for, somewhat indiscriminately, by people of different countries, subscribing to different religions or even to non-religious ideologies.[1] Let us now try to see in what respects these experiences are alike, and in what respects they differ. First of all it is important to differentiate between the subjective light and the phenomena of light objectively perceived by other people. In the Indian, Iranian and Christian traditions the two categories of experience are lumped together; and fundamentally the justifications offered for this failure to distinguish are alike: the divinity (or in India the being) being Light or emanating from light, sages (in India) or those who attain the *unio mystica* give out light (*Bhagavad-gita, bhakti;* shamanism).

The morphology of the subjective experience of Light is extremely large. Certain of the more frequent forms can however be noted:

(1) The Light may be so dazzling that it somehow blots out the surrounding world; the man to whom it appears is blinded. This was the experience of Saint Paul, for instance, on the road to Damascus, and of many other saints—also, up to a point, of Arjuna in the *Bhagavad-gita.*

(2) There is the Light that transfigures the World without blotting it out: the experience of a very intense supernatural light, which shines into the depths of matter, but in which forms remain defined. This is like the Heavenly Light which reveals the World as it was in its primal perfection—or, according to the Judaeo-Christian tradition, as it was before Adam's fall.

[1] In his little book, *Heaven and Hell,* London and New York, 1956, Aldous Huxley has shown the part played by pure bright colours in visionary and artistic experiences.

In this category lie the majority of experiences of the light undergone by mystics, Christian and non-Christian.

(3) Rather close to this type is the illumination (*qaumanek*) of the Esquimo shaman, which enables him to see far into the distance, but also to perceive spiritual entities: an extra-retinal vision, as one might say, which permits him to see not only very far, but in all directions at once, and finally reveals to him the presence of spiritual beings, or unveils to him the ultimate structure of matter, and brings him a staggering growth of understanding. Here one must also note the differences between the various Universes mystically perceived during the experience: the Universe whose structure seems to be like that of the natural Universe, with the difference that now it is truly understood— and the Universe that reveals a structure beyond the reach of the intelligence in the waking state.

(4) A distinction must also be made between the instantaneous experience and the various types of progressive perception of the light, in which the growing intensity is accompanied by a feeling of deep peace or a certainty that the soul is immortal, or a comprehension of a supernatural kind.

(5) Finally we must distinguish between a light which reveals itself as a divine, personal Presence and a light which reveals an impersonal holiness: that of the World, Life, man, reality— ultimately, the holiness one discovers in the Cosmos contemplated as a divine creation.

It is important to stress that whatever the nature and intensity of an experience of the Light, it always evolves into a religious experience. All types of experience of the light that we have quoted have this factor in common: they bring a man out of his worldly Universe or historical situation, and project him into a Universe different in quality, an entirely different world, transcendent and holy. The structure of this holy and transcendent Universe varies according to a man's culture and religion—a point on which we have insisted enough to dispel all doubt. Nevertheless they share this element in common: the Universe revealed on a meeting with the Light contrasts with the worldly

Universe—or transcends it—by the fact that it is spiritual in essence, in other words only accessible to those for whom the Spirit exists. We have several times observed that the experience of the Light radically changes the ontological condition of the subject, by opening him to the world of the Spirit. In the course of human history there have been a thousand different ways of conceiving or evaluating the world of the Spirit. That is evident. How could it have been otherwise? For all conceptualization is irremediably linked with language, and consequently with culture and history. One can say that the meaning of the supernatural light is directly conveyed to the soul of the man who experiences it—and yet this meaning can only come fully to his consciousness clothed in a pre-existent ideology. Here lies the paradox: the meaning of the light is, on the one hand, ultimately a personal discovery and, on the other, each man discovers what he was spiritually and culturally prepared to discover. Yet there remains this fact which seems to us fundamental: whatever his previous ideological conditioning, a meeting with the Light produces a break in the subject's existence, revealing to him—or making clearer than before—the world of the Spirit, of holiness and of freedom; in brief, existence as a divine creation, or the world sanctified by the presence of God.

II

Mephistopheles and the Androgyne
or the Mystery of the Whole

About twenty years ago, happening to reread the "Prologue in Heaven" of Goethe's *Faust*, and having just reread Balzac's *Séraphita*, I seemed to see a kind of parallel between the two works which I could not define. What both fascinated and worried me in the "Prologue in Heaven" was the indulgence or even sympathy shown by God to Mephistopheles. "Von allen Geistern", said God,

> Von allen Geistern, die verneinen,
> Ist mir der Schalk am wenigsten zur Last.
> Des Menschen Tätigkeit kann allzuleicht erschlaffen,
> Er liebt sich bald der unbedingte Ruh;
> Drum geb' ich gern ihm den Gesellen zu,
> Der reizt und winkt und muss als Teufel schaffen.[1]

This sympathy, furthermore, is reciprocal. When the Heavens close and the archangels disappear, Mephistopheles, left alone, confesses that he too "likes to see the Governor now" and then: "Von Zeit zu Zeit seh' ich den Alten gern . . ."

[1]Of all the spirits of negation
The rogue is least of burdens to be borne.
Man's efforts sink below his proper level,
And since he seeks for unconditioned ease,
I send this fellow, who must goad and tease
And toil to serve creation, though a devil.
Transl. Philip Wayne (Penguin, 1949).

One knows that in Goethe's *Faust* no word is used fortuitously. It seemed to me therefore that the repetition of the adjective "gern", spoken first by God and then by Mephistopheles, must have some significance. Paradoxically, there was an unexpected "sympathy" between God and the Spirit of Negation.

Of course, taken in the context of Goethe's whole work, this "sympathy" becomes comprehensible. Mephistopheles stimulates human activity. For Goethe evil, and also error, are productive. "Wenn du nicht irrst, kommst du nicht zu Verstand",[1] says Mephistopheles to Homunculus (v. 7847). "It is contradiction that makes us productive", wrote Goethe to Eckermann on March 28, 1827. And in one of the *Maxims* (no. 85) he observed: "Nature doesn't worry about mistakes. She repairs them herself and doesn't ask herself what the upshot of it all may be".

In Goethe's conception, Mephistopheles is the spirit who denies, protests and, above all, *halts* the flux of life and prevents things from being done. Mephistopheles' activity is not directed against God, but against Life. Mephistopheles is "the father of all hindrance" ("der Vater . . . aller Hindernisse". *Faust*, v. 6209). What Mephistopheles asks of Faust to do is to *stop*. "Verweile doch!" is the essential Mephistophelian formula. Mephistopheles knows that the moment Faust stops he will have lost his soul. But a stop is not a negation of the Creator; it is a negation of Life. Mephistopheles does not directly oppose God, but his principal creation, Life. In place of movement and Life he tries to impose rest, immobility, death. For whatever ceases to change and transform itself decays and perishes. This "death in Life" can be translated as spiritual sterility; it is, taken all in all, damnation. A man who has let the roots of Life, in the deepest part of himself, perish falls into the power of the negating Spirit. The crime against Life, Goethe gives one to understand, is a crime against salvation.

[1]Unless you err, naught can be truly known. Transl. Wayne, *Faust*, part 2, Penguin, 1959.

However, as has often been observed, though Mephistopheles uses every means to oppose the flux of Life, he stimulates Life. He fights against the Good but ends by doing Good. This demon who denies Life is all the same a collaborator with God. This is why God, with his divine foresight, willingly gives him to man as a companion.

It would be easy to multiply the lines that show how, in Goethe's view, error and evil are necessary not only for human existence but also for the Cosmos, for what Goethe called the "All-one". The sources of this metaphysic of immanence are, of course, well-known: Giordano Bruno, Jacob Boehme, Swedenborg. But a study of sources did not seem to me the obvious way of reaching a better understanding of the "sympathy" between the Creator and Mephistopheles. Besides, I was not intending an exegesis of *Faust*, or a contribution towards the history of Goethe's thought. I had no skill in this sort of research. What interested me was to relate the "mystery" suggested in the "Prologue in Heaven" to certain traditional ideas associated with analogous "mysteries".

To set my thoughts in order I wrote a short study of *The Divine Polarity*. While writing this I understood why I sensed a parallel between the "Prologue in Heaven" of *Faust* and Balzac's *Séraphita*. Both works are concerned with the question of the *coincidentia oppositorum* and with totality. The mystery is hardly perceptible in the "sympathy" that binds God to Mephistopheles, but it is perfectly recognisable in the myth of the Androgyne borrowed by Balzac from Swedenborg. A little later I published another study on the mythologies of the Androgyne and, in 1942, I joined both texts in a little book entitled *The Myth of Re-integration* (*Mitul Reintegrării*, Bucarest, 1942).

I have no intention of resuming today all the themes dealt with in that work of my youth. I propose to present only a certain number of traditional rites, myths and theories associated with the union of contraries and the mystery of the totality, with what Nicholas of Cusa called the *coincidentia oppositorum*. It is well known that for Nicholas of Cusa the *coincidentia oppositorum* was the least imperfect definition of God.[1] It is well-known also that one of the sources of his inspiration was the Pseudo-Areopagite. Now, as the Areopagite said, the union of opposites in God constitutes a mystery. But I do not intend to enlarge on these theological and metaphysical speculations, though they are of the highest interest for the history of Western philosophy. It is the pre-history of philosophy, the presystematic phase of thought that should, I think, claim our principal attention at the present day.

I will not dwell either on the importance of the concept of totality in the work of C. G. Jung. It is sufficient to recall that the expressions, *coincidentia oppositorum, complexio oppositorum*, union of opposites, *mysterium coniunctionis*, etc., are frequently used by Jung to describe the totality of the Self and the mystery of the dual nature of Christ. According to Jung the process of individualization essentially consists of a sort of *coincidentia oppositorum*, for the Self comprises both the whole consciousness and the contents of the unconscious. In *Die Psychologie der Übertragung* and the *Mysterium Coniunctionis* are to be found the most complete exposition of the Jungian theory of the *coincidentia oppositorum* as the ultimate aim of the whole psychic activity.[2]

---

[1]Heraclitus wrote long ago (fr. 67) "God is day and night, winter summer, war peace, satiety hunger—*all the opposites, this is the meaning.*" See text and commentary in C. S. Kirk and J. E. Raven, *The Presocratic Philosophers*, Cambridge, 1937, pp. 191ff.

[2]See C. G. Jung, *Die Psychologie der Übertragung*, Zurich, 1946, English translation by R. F. C. Hull, *Psychology of the Transference*, in *The Practice of Psychotherapy:* The Collected Works of C. G. Jung, vol. XVI, London and New York, 1954, pp. 163-321: Id., *Mysterium Conjunctionis, Untersuchung über die Trennung und Zusammensetzung der seelischen Gegensätze in der Alchemie*, I-II, Zurich, 1955-6. To avoid all misunderstanding, let us add that we have not relied on the Jungian conception of the "psychic totality" in the pages that follow. Jung's views on the reality of evil have aroused passionate discussion. See, for instance, H. L. Philp, *Jung and the Problem of Evil*, New York, 1959; Victor White, *Soul and Psyche*, London, 1960, especially pp. 141ff.

For the historian of religions, the *coincidentia oppositorum* or the mystery of the totality can as easily be found in the symbolism, theories and beliefs concerned with the ultimate reality, the divine *Grund*, as in cosmogonies explaining the Creation as the fragmentation of a primordial unity. It is to be seen in orgiastic rituals aimed at the reversal of human behaviour and the confusion of values, in the mystical techniques for the union of contraries, in the myths of the androgyne and the rites of androgynization, etc. In general, one can say that all these myths, rites and beliefs have the aim of reminding men that the ultimate reality, the sacred, the divine, defy all possibilities of rational comprehension; that the *Grund* can only be grasped as a mystery or a paradox, that the divine conception cannot be conceived as a sum of qualities and virtues but as an absolute freedom, beyond Good and Evil; that the divine, absolute and transcendent are qualitatively different from the human, relative and immediate because they do not constitute particular modalities of being or contingent situations. In a word, these myths, rites and theories involving the *coincidentia oppositorum* teach men that the best way of apprehending God or the ultimate reality is to cease, if only for a few seconds, considering and imagining divinity in terms of immediate experience; such an experience could only perceive fragments and tensions.

All this does not imply a necessary awareness of the act one is performing in a ritual or the thought behind one's myth. In certain cultures, at certain moments of history, and for certain categories of men, the metaphysical implications of the *coincidentia oppositorum* are clearly understood and accepted. The Indian examples which we shall shortly give perfectly illustrate this act of consciousness. But the majority of our examples do not belong to this class. The myths and legends concerning the consanguinity of God and Satan, for instance, or of the Saint and the Devil-woman, are myths which, though arising from learned sources, have met with enormous success among the common people; which proves that they corresponded to an obscure desire to pierce the mystery of the existence of evil or of the imperfection of the divine Creation. These myths and legends certainly did not appear to the farmers and shepherds who heard them and spread them, as matters of philosophy or theology. But one cannot say either that they considered them merely amusing or entertaining stories. Religious folklore always contains instruction. The whole man is engaged when he listens to myths and legends; consciously or not, their message is always deciphered and absorbed in the end.

One example admirably illustrates this point and brings us immediately to the heart of the problem. This is the fundamental idea of Iranian Zervanism, according to which Ohrmazd and Ahriman were both born of Zervan, the god of boundless Time. Here we face the supreme effort of Iranian theology to transcend dualism and postulate a single principle that will explain the world. Whatever we think of the origins of Zervanism, one thing is certain: these fundamental doctrines have been thought out and elaborated by minds trained in theology and philosophy.

Now it is important to observe that similar doctrines are to be found in the religious folklore of South-East Europe. There are examples of Rumanian beliefs and proverbs according to which God and Satan are brothers.[1] Here we are confronted with two distinct but congruent themes: the gnostic myth that Christ and Satan are brothers, and the archaic myth of the relationship, indeed the half-brotherhood of God and the Devil. As for the first myth, it is to be found among the Bogomils; according to the information passed down by Euthymius Zigabenus, the Bogomils believed that Satanaël was the first-born of God, and Christ the second.[2] The belief in the brother-

[1] Proverbs collected and published by Zane: see *Traité d'Histoire des Religions,* Paris, 1949; 3rd edition, 1959, p. 356.
[2] Euthymius Zigabenus, *Panoplia,* P. G., vol. 130, col. 1290.

hood of Christ and Satan was shared by the Ebionites; which
leads us to suppose that some such conception must have circulated in Judaeo-Christian circles.[1] But in the case of the Bogomils
this belief most probably derived from an Iranian source, since
in the Zervanite tradition also Ahriman was considered to be
the first-born.[2]

But we need not dwell on the problem of the origin of these
ideas about the blood relationship of Christ and Satan and the
friendship between God and the Devil. What is important is
the fact that such myths continued to circulate among the peoples
of the Near East and Eastern Europe up to the last century.
This proves that these myths and legends fulfilled a popular need.
The blood relationship of the representatives of Good and Evil
is also illustrated by a cycle of legends concerned with the struggle
between a Saint and his sister, a Devil-woman who steals and
kills children. In the Ethiopian versions the Saint is called
Susnyos and his sister Uerzelia. The Saint begs Jesus for the
strength to murder his own sister. In the end Susnyos stabs her
with a spear and kills her.[3] Here we have the very old myth
of the hostile brothers reinterpreted and christianized. The fact
that the Saint and the Devil-woman are thought of as brother
and sister proves that this collection of fables reproduces at
different levels and in different contexts the exemplary tale of
the consanguinity of Good and Evil.

---

[1]See R. Schaerf, *Die Gestalt des Satans im Alten Testament*, in C. G. Jung,
Symbolik des Geistes, Zurich, 1948, p. 252, n.60.

[2]See R. C. Zaehner, *Zervan, A Zoroastrian Dilemma*, Oxford, 1955, pp. 419ff.
In a Yakut myth, Christ makes the World and Satan claims to be his elder
brother (see W. Schmidt, *Ursprung der Gottesidee*, vol. xii, Münster i W., 1955,
p. 34). Very probably we have here the christianization of an older idea: the
Evil Spirit as elder brother of the Good Spirit.

[3]See Eliade, *Notes on Demonology* ("Zalmoxis", i, 1938, pp. 197-203); *Id.*, *Mitul
Reintegrării*, pp. 56ff. The origin of the legend is probably Iranian; see H. A.
Winkler, *Salomo und die Kârina*, Stuttgart, 1931, p. 154; Erik Peterson, *Eis
Theos*, Göttingen, 1926, p. 122.

THE ASSOCIATION OF GOD AND THE DEVIL
AND THE COSMOGONIC DIVE

The motif of the association, indeed the friendship, between God and the Devil is particularly noticeable in a type of cosmogonic myth that is extremely widespread[1] and can be summed up as follows: In the beginning there were only the Waters, and on those Waters walked God and the Devil. God sent the Devil to the bottom of the ocean with orders to bring him a little clay with which to make the World. I omit the details of this cosmic dive and the results of this collaboration by the Devil in the work of Creation.[2] All that concerns our purpose are the Central Asian and South-Eastern European variants which stress the fact that God and the Devil are blood-brothers, or that they are co-eternal or, indeed, God's inability to complete the World without the Devil's help.

A Russian myth proclaims, for instance, that neither God nor the Devil was created, that they have existed together from the beginning of Time.[3] On the other hand, according to myths related by the people of the southern Altai, the Abakan-Katzines and the Mordvinians, the Devil was created by God.[4] But it is the manner of his creation that is revealing. For, in a sense, God creates the Devil out of his own flesh. This is how the Mordvinians describe it: God was alone on a rock. "If only I had a brother, I would make the World!" he said, and he spat on the Waters. From his spittle a mountain was born. God split it

[1]This myth presents a certain number of problems which we must pass over. The only theme that interests us here is the association of God and the Devil in the Creation of the World: a theme which is not present in the oldest versions of the myth.

[2]The essentials of the argument are to be found in O. Daenhardt, *Natursagen*, I, Leipzig-Berlin, 1907, pp. 1-89; Wilhelm Schmidt, *Ursprung der Gottesidee*, vol. XII, pp. 9-173; M. Eliade, *Preistoria unui motiv folkloric românesc* ("Buletinul Bibliotecii Române din Freiburg", vol. III, 1955-6, pp. 41-54).

[3]Daenhardt, *op. cit.*, p. 338ff.   [4]W. Schmidt, *op. cit.*, pp. 129-30.

with his sword, and out of the mountain came the Devil (Satan). As soon as he appeared the Devil proposed to God that they should be brothers and create the World together. "We will not be brothers, but companions", answered God. And together they proceeded to the creation of the World.[1]

In the variant belonging to the Transylvanian gipsies, God is unhappy alone. He acknowledges aloud that he does not know how to make the World, nor any reason why he should make it. He then throws down his wand—and it is from this that the Devil emerges.[2] In a Finnish variant God looks at himself in the water and, seeing the reflection of his face asks it how to make the World.[3] But it is the Bulgarian legends that give the Devil the most sympathetic and in fact the creative role. According to one of them, God was walking alone when he noticed his shadow and cried: "Get up, comrade!" Satan arose from God's shadow and asked him to divide the Universe between them; the Earth for him, the Heavens for God; the living for God, the dead for him. And they signed an agreement on those terms.[4] Other Bulgarian legends call attention to what one might call "God's stupidity". For after making the Earth, God perceived that there is no place for the Waters and, not knowing how to solve this cosmogonic problem, sends the angel of War to Satan, to ask for his advice.[5]

In certain variants of the cosmogonic myth (Altai-Kizi, Buryats, Voguls, and Transylvanian Gipsies) God himself recognizes that he is incapable of making the World[6]—and appeals to the Devil. This motif of God's cosmogonic powerlessness is united with another theme: God's ignorance about the origin of the Devil. But this ignorance is variously interpreted

[1]Daenhardt, *op. cit.*, pp. 61ff., 101ff.; U. Harva, *Die religiösen Vorstellungen der Mordwinen*, Helsinki, 1954, pp. 134-5.

[2]Daenhardt, *op. cit.*, pp. 34ff.   [3]W. Schmidt, *op. cit.*, p. 49.

[4]Daenhardt, *op. cit.*, p. 44; W. Schmidt, *op. cit.*, p. 123.

[5]A. Strauss, *Die Bulgaren*, Leipzig, 1898, pp. 6ff.; Daenhardt, *op. cit.*, pp. 2ff. "God's stupidity" is a mythical expression for "God's fatigue" after he had finished making the World.

[6]See W. Schmidt, *op. cit.*, pp. 136-7.

in the myths. In certain cases (Altai-Kizi, eastern Yakuts, Voguls, Bukovina) the fact that God does not know where the Devil comes from throws his incapacity and powerlessness into still higher relief. In other variants of the same myth (Mordvinians, Gipsies, Bukovina, Ukraine)[1] God fully displays his cosmogonic power but still does not know the origin of the Devil. This is another way of saying that *God has nothing to do with the origin of Evil*. He does not know where the Devil comes from; therefore he is not responsible for the existence of Evil in the world. In fact, this is a desperate attempt to remove *God's responsibility for the existence of Evil*. We have here a moralising reinterpretation of an older mythical theme. In exactly the same way, in certain Ugrian and Turco-Mongol variants the fact that the Devil was born from God's spittle is not regarded as a proof of his quasi-co-substantiality with God, but on the contrary as a flagrant proof of his inferiority.[2]

All these myths and legends deserve a far more thorough analysis than we can undertake here.[3] Enough that we have established that, on the level of religious folklore, there has survived a feeling, among Central Asiatic and European people long converted to Islam or Christianity, of the necessity of making a place for the Devil, not only in the creation of the World—which could be understood as the need to explain the origin of Evil—but also close to God, as a companion born of God's desire to escape from his solitude. It does not much affect our purpose to decide whether we are dealing with inventions of folklore which are heretical, in other words learned, in origin. What is important is that such myths and legends have circulated among the common folk, and even enjoyed a certain popularity. For one finds them still alive after seven or eight centuries of anti-heretical ecclesiastical crusades.

[1]*Ibid.*, p. 126
[2]*Ibid.*, p. 127; see also, W. Schmidt, *Ursprung*, vol. VI, pp. 38ff., on the same motif in North-American mythologies.
[3]See my article, *Preistoria unui motiv folcloric romånesc*, and my study in course of preparation, *Folklore sud-est-européen et mythologies asiatiques*.

In fact these myths and legends form a part of Christian folklore by the same right as other "depaganized" mythical material which has been absorbed by Christianity. What counts for us is that the popular mind has been pleased to imagine the loneliness of God and his comradeship with the Devil, and the Devil's role as God's servant, collaborator and even chief counsellor; to imagine, moreover, the divine origin of the devil, for essentially God's spittle is nothing less than divine; to imagine, in fact, a certain "sympathy" between God and the Devil which cannot fail to remind us of the "sympathy" between the Creator and Mephistopheles.

Let me repeat that all this belongs to folklore, to that immense reservoir of beliefs, myths and unsystematized ideas that are at the same time archaic and modern, pagan and Christian. It is even more significant to observe that more or less similar themes have served as subjects of meditation for Indian worshippers, sages and mystics. But in turning to India we make a radical change of background.

DEVAS AND ASURAS

India has been obsessed with the problem of ultimate reality, with the Unitary Being hidden behind a veil of multiplicity and variety. The Upanishads have identified this ultimate reality with Brahman-*atman*. Subsequently the philosophic systems explained multiplicity, either—like the Vedanta—as cosmic illusion, *maya*, or like the Samkhha and Yoga—by the force of matter in continuous movement, continuously changing in order to incite man to seek deliverance. But the pre-systematic stage of Indian thought is still more important for our researches. In the Vedas and Brahmanas, the doctrine of a single reality is implicit in both myths and symbolism. The Vedic mythology and religion present us with a situation which is at first sight paradoxical. On the one hand there is a distinction, opposition and conflict between the Devas and the Asuras, the gods and the "demons", the powers of Light and of Darkness. A considerable part of the *Rig Veda* is devoted to the victorious battles of the god and champion Indra against the dragon Vritra and the Asuras. But, on the other hand, numerous myths bring out the consubstantiality or brotherhood of the Devas and Asuras. One has the impression that Vedic doctrine is at pains to establish a double perspective: although, as an immediate reality, and as the world appears to our eyes, the Devas and the gods are irreconcilably different by nature and condemned to fight one another, at the beginning of time, on the other hand, that is to say before the Creation or before the world took its present form, they were consubstantial.[1]

In fact they are the sons of Prajapati, or Tvashtri: brothers engendered by the one father. The Adityas—that is to say the sons of Aditi, the "Suns"—were originally serpents. Having sloughed their old skins—that is to say acquired immortality ("they have conquered Death")—they have become gods, Devas. (*Pancavimsha Brahmanha*, XXV, 15, 4). In Vedic India, as in many other traditions, to slough the skin is to deliver the "old man" and rediscover youth, or to attain a higher mode of being. The image frequently recurs in Vedic texts. But what surprises is that this reptilian behaviour is thought to be proper for the Gods. When it rises at dawn, says the *Shatapatha Brahmana* (II, 3; 1, 3 and 6) the Sun "is delivered from Night . . . just as Ahi (the Serpent) is sloughed of its skin". In the same way, the god Soma, "just like Ahi, climbs out of his old skin".[2] The act of stripping an

---

[1]Ananda K. Coomaraswamy has studied this problem in several of his publications. See particularly *Angel and Titan: an Essay in Vedic Ontology*, "Journal of the American Oriental Society", 55, 1935, pp. 373-419; *The Darker Side of Dawn*, "Smithsonian Miscellaneous Collections", vol. 94, no. 1., Washington, 1935; *Atmayajna: Self-Sacrifice*, "Harvard Journal of Asiatic Studies", 6, 1942, pp. 358-98; Coomaraswamy perhaps commits the error of excessive metaphysical systemization. There is no reason to believe that theoretical agreement is necessarily the result of a systematic reflexion; it has already taken place at the stage of image and symbol; it is an integral part of mythical thought.

[2]*Rig Veda*, IX, 86, 44; see other references in Coomaraswamy, *Angel and Titan*, p. 405.

animal's skin and climbing out of it plays an important role in ritual; the performer is considered to have freed himself from the worldly condition, from sins or old age. But the god Soma not only behaves like the mythical Serpent, Ahi: *Shatapatha Brahmana* identifies him literally with Vritra, the primordial Dragon.[1]

This paradoxical identification of a God with the exemplary Dragon is not exceptional. Already the *Rig Veda* described Agni as the "Asura priest" (VII, 30, 3), and the Sun as the "Asura priest of the Devas". In other words *the Gods are, or once were, or are susceptible of becoming Asuras or non-gods.* Agni, the god of Fire and the hearth, the god of light *par excellence*, is consubstantial with the Serpent Ahi Budhnya, symbol of the subterranean Darkness and homologous with Vritra. In the *Rig Veda* (I, 79, 1) Agni is called a "fierce serpent". *Aitareya Brahmana* (IU, 36) affirms that Ahi Budhnya is in invisible form (*parokshena*) what Agni Garhapatya is in visible form (*pratyaksha*). In other words, the Serpent is a potentiality of Fire while Darkness is unmanifested Light. In the *Vajasaneyi Samlhita* (v, 33) Ahi Budhnya and the Sun (*Aja Ekapad*) are one.[2]

Perhaps the ophidian nature of Agni derives from the image of the birth of fire. Fire is "born" from darkness or from opaque matter—the chthonian matrix—and crawls like a snake. In the *Rig Veda* (IV, 1, 11-12) the lit fire—"when it is born on its ground" —is described as being "without foot or head, hiding its two extremities" (*guhamano anta*) like a coiled serpent.[3] In other words, it is represented as an Ouroboros, a symbol both of the union of extremes and the primordial totality. The act of separating the feet from the head symbolizes, in India, the fragmentation of the primal unity, therefore the Creation. In the cosmogony contained in the *Rig Veda* (x, 90, 14) the Creation

[1]"Soma was Vritra", *Shatapatha Brahmana*, III, 4, 3, 13; III, 9, 4, 2; IV, 4, 3, 4.
[2]On this motif, see Coomaraswamy, *Angel and Titan*, p. 395 and note 30.
[3]On the ophidian attributes of the Dawn, see Coomaraswamy, *The Darker Side of Dawn*, p. 7 and *passim*.

began with the separation of the head from the feet of the giant
Purusha. Let us add that the daradox of the double nature of
Agni—Serpent and God at the same time—appears also in the
religious ambivalence of fire. Fire, according to the *Rig Veda*
(x, 16, 9, etc.), is at once the destructive power of man, which
must at all costs be avoided, and the herald (*duta*) of the Gods,
the friend (*mitra*) and guest (*atithi*) of men.

VRITRA AND VARUNA

The ambivalence of the divinity is a theme constant to the
whole religious history of humanity. What is holy attracts
man and at the same time frightens him. The gods reveal
themselves as at once benevolent and terrible. In India, beside
his gracious and kindly form, each god has a "terrible form"
(*krodha murti*): his fierce, menacing and frightening aspect.
Varuna in particular is a god who both attracts and frightens.
Numerous Vedic texts speak of the "toils of Varuna"[1] and one
of the most frequent prayers is to be "delivered from Varuna"
(for example, *Rig Veda*, x. 97, 16, etc.). And yet the worshipper
cries "When shall I at last be with Varuna?" (*Rig Veda*, VII, 86, 2).
Varuna too is assimilated with the Serpent Ahi and the Dragon
Vritra.[2] In the *Atharva Veda* (XII, 3, 57) he is called "viper".
The names Vritra and Varuna probably share the same etymology.[3]
Furthermore there is a certain structural correspondence between
them. The "night" side of Varuna allows him to be a god of the
Waters, thus relating him to Vritra who "stops" or "binds" the
Waters.[4] There is a "demonic" aspect of Varuna, the fearful
magician who "binds" men from a distance and paralyses them,
just as Vritra seals and "binds" the waters in the hollow of the
Mountain, threatening to extinguish Life and plunge the Universe

[1] See *Images and Symbols*, p. 95.
[2] See the references arranged by Coomaraswamy, *Angel and Titan*, p. 391, note.
[3] See *Images and Symbols*, p. 98.
[4] On this theme see *Images and Symbols*, pp. 95-9.

back into Chaos. And yet these ophidian and "demonic" aspects *could not* enter into the nature of Varuna, the cosmic god and Universal Sovereign, the god of the starry Sky, the god "with a thousand eyes", etc.[1] But like all the great gods, Varuna is an ambivalent god—and Indian thought has endeavoured to interpret this ambivalence either as a divine unity-in-duality or as a *coincidentia oppositorum*.

The attempt of Indian thought to arrive at a single *Urgrund* for the World, Life and the Spirit, has attained equal success with Vritra, the exemplary ophidian monster. Vritra symbolizes darkness, inertia and immobility, and at the same time the potential, amorphous and undifferentiated; in short Chaos. The conflict between Indra and Vritra—the typical enemy of the Gods—plays a considerable role in Vedic mythology. The battle between the Dragon and the god or solar hero is, as is well-known, an extremely widespread motif of mythology, which is to be found in all the ancient systems of the Near East, in Greece and among the ancient Germans. In the form of a duel between the Serpent—the symbol of Darkness—and the Eagle, bird of the Sun, it is to be found throughout central and northern Asia and even in Indonesia.[2] The battle between the Dragon and the God champion is capable of many interpretations. We do not intend to study here the various fields of reference of this exemplary myth. It will be enough to recall that Indra's victory has, in India, a cosmological significance. By liberating the

[1]On Varuna, see *Traité d'Histoire des Religions*, pp. 70ff., 365ff. We will not dwell here on the different but complementary functions of Mitra and Varuna brilliantly examined by Georges Dumézil: see *Mitra-Varuna*, Paris, 1940; 2nd edition, 1950; *Jupiter, Mars, Quirinus*, Paris, 1941, etc. We will observe, however, that metaphysical speculation has identified Varuna with the unmanifest, the potential and eternal, and Mitra with the manifest (see *Rig Veda*, I, 164, 38). Subsequently, the two aspects of Brahman—*apara* and *para*—"lower" and "higher", visible and invisible, manifest and unmanifest—have been used by contemplatives as a means of expressing the different aspects of total reality.

[2]On this motif see my study in course of preparation: *L'Aigle et le Serpent*.

Waters immobilized by Vritra, Indra saves the Universe, that is to say, in mythical terms, *creates it anew*.

Now it is surprising to find that this dangerous adversary is, in some way, Indra's "brother", since he was begotten by Indra's father, Tvashtri. According to the myth, he had omitted to invite his son Indra to a *soma* sacrifice. But Indra managed to attend the sacrifice and took the *soma* by force. His father, in a fury, threw the rest of the divine drink on the fire, crying: "Grow up and become Indra's enemy!" Vritra was born from the remains of the *soma* poured on the fire,[1] and before long he devoured the gods Agni and Soma, so that the other gods were afraid. Tvashtri himself was so alarmed that he gave Indra his weapon, the thunderbolt, thus assuring him the final victory.

We will not recount all the phases of the combat. Certain sources[2] relate that the Sky and the Earth were made from Vritra's body—just as, in Mesopotamian mythology, Marduk created the Sky and the Earth from the dismembered body of Tiamat. *Shatapatha Brahmana* (I, 6, 3) gives one highly significant detail: the conquered Vritra implores Indra, "Do not strike me, for you are now what I was once!" He begged Indra to cut him in two, which Indra did. From the part which contained the *soma*, Indra created the Moon. From the other part, that is to say the part that was not divine, he made the bellies of men. This is the reason for the saying, "Vritra is within us!"[3]

In conclusion we find that these myths and their theological explanation reveal a less well-known because less obvious aspect of divine history. One might almost say that this is a "secret

---

[1] *Taittiriya Samhita*, II, 4, 12 and 5, 1ff.; see *Kaushitaki Brahmana*, XV, 2-3; see also A. K. Coomaraswamy, *Angel and Titan*, p. 385. We must remember that *Vishvarupa*, Vritra's brother, is called the "priest of the Devas" (*Taitt. Samh.*, II, 5, 1).

[2] *Pancavimsha Brahmana*, XVIII, 9, 6, for instance; see Coomaraswamy, *op. cit.*, p. 386, note 18.

[3] Evidently an allusion to the serpentine appearance of the intestines. But this image has served as a point of departure for speculations on the mystical effect of food and digestion, and consequently on the divine forces dormant in man.

history" of the divinity, which is only intelligible to initiates,
that is to say to those who know the tradition and understand
the doctrine. The "secret" Vedic history reveals, on one side,
the blood brotherhood of the Devas and Asuras, the fact that
these two classes of superhuman beings sprang from one and the
same principle; and, on the other, it makes clear the *coincidentia
oppositorum* in the deep nature of the divinities, who are, by
turns or simultaneously, benevolent and terrible, creative and
destructive, solar and ophidian (that is to say manifest and virtual),
etc. One recognises the effort of the Indian spirit to discover a
single principle which will explain the World, to reach a standpoint from which contraries are resolved and contradictions
abolished. The classical metaphysic merely elaborates and
systematizes this total conception of reality, outlined in the Vedas
and Brahmanas. What appears contradictory, imperfect, evil,
"demoniac", etc., in this world is explained as a negative aspect
of reality. The Devas and Asuras are thought of as contradictory
aspects or successive moments of the same divine power.

THE TWO FIELDS OF REFERENCE

Clearly, this is only true from a transcendental and timeless
viewpoint; in man's immediate experience, in his concrete,
historical existence, the Devas and Asuras are opposed, and he
must pursue virtue and combat evil. *What is true of eternity is
not necessarily true in time.* The world came into existence as a
result of the breaking of primordial unity. The world's existence,
as well as existence *in* the world, presuppose a separation of
Light from darkness, a distinction between good and evil, a
choice and a tension. But, in India, the cosmos is not considered
the exemplary and ultimate form of reality, and existence in
the world is not thought of as the *summum bonum.* Both the
cosmos and man's existence in the cosmos are particular situations
—and no particular situation can exhaust the fabulous riches of
Being. The Indian thinker's ideal is, as is well known, the *jivan*

mukti, the man "liberated while living", that is to say someone who, while living in the world, is not conditioned by the structure of the world, someone who is no longer "fixed in place" but, as the texts put it, "free to move at will" (*kamacarin*). The *jivan mukti* is simultaneously in time and in eternity; his existence is a paradox in the sense that it constitutes a *coincidentia oppositorum* beyond the understanding or the imagination.

The efforts a man makes to transcend the opposites cause him to leave his immediate and personal situation and raise himself to a supra-subjective viewpoint; in other words, to attain metaphysical knowledge. In his immediate experience, man is made up of pairs of opposites. What is more, he not only distinguishes the agreeable from the disagreeable, pleasure from pain, friendship from hostility, but comes to believe that these opposites hold also for the absolute; in other words, that ultimate reality can be defined by the same pairs of opposites that characterize the immediate reality in which man finds himself immersed by the mere fact of living in the world. Indian myths, rites and speculations shake this human tendency to consider the immediate experience of the world as a metaphysically valid knowledge reflecting, as one might say, the ultimate reality. Transcending the opposites, is, as is well known, a constant theme of Indian spirituality. By philosophical reflection and contemplation—according to the teaching of the Vedanta—or by psycho-physiological techniques and by meditations—as recommended by Yoga—a man succeeds in rising above duality, that is to say in realising the *coincidentia oppositorum* in his own body and his own spirit.

We will recall later some Indian methods of unification. Let us say for the moment that in India as in all traditional cultures the fundamental truths are proclaimed at all levels, though the expression varies at each, the terms used being suited to the level of knowledge. The principles clearly exposed and expounded in the Upanishads or the philosophic systems are also to be found in popular worship and religious folklore. It is significant, for example, that in certain texts of mediæval

Vishnu worship, the arch-demon Vritra has become a Brahman, an exemplary warrior and even a saint![1] The demon Ravana, who had captured Sita and taken her to Ceylon, is also considered to be the author of a treatise on magical child-medicine, *Kumaratantra*. A devil the author of a treatise containing anti-demonic formulas and rituals! The goddess Hariti is said to have obtained the right to eat children as a consequence of merits gained in a previous existence.[2]

And this is no exception: many demons are reputed to have won their demonic prowess by good actions performed in previous existences. In other words: *good* can serve to make *evil*. By his ascetic efforts, a devil gains the power to do evil; asceticism leads to the possession of a reserve of magical powers which allow any action to be undertaken without distinction of "moral" value. All these examples are only particular and popular illustrations of the fundamental Indian doctrine, that good and evil have no meaning or function except in a world of appearances, in profane and unenlightened existence. From the transcendental viewpoint, good and evil are, on the contrary, as illusory and relative as all other pairs of opposites: hot-cold, agreeable-disagreeable, long-short, visible-invisible, etc.

All the myths, rites and beliefs that we have just recalled have this essential feature in common: they compel a man to behave otherwise than he spontaneously would, to contradict by thought what immediate experience and elementary knowledge show him; in fact, to become what he is not—what he cannot be—in his profane, unenlightened state, in the human condition. In other words, these myths and their interpretation have an initiatory function. We know that in traditional societies initiation prepares the adolescent to assume adult responsibilities, that is to say introduces him to the religious life, to spiritual values. Thanks to his initiation, the adolescent attains more than

[1] See M. Eliade, *Notes de démonologie* ("Zalmoxis", I, 1938, pp. 197-203), pp. 201ff.
[2] See *Notes de démonologie*, p. 201.

personal knowledge, which was previously beyond his reach.[1]
Now, as we have just seen, the Indian myths of the *coincidentia
oppositorum* help anyone who meditates on them to transcend
the level of immediate experiences and uncover a secret dimension
of reality.

MYTHS AND RITES OF INTEGRATION

The few examples we have commented on are not exceptional
in the history of Indian thought. As we have just said, to
integrate, unify, make whole, in a word to abolish the contraries
and reunite the parts, is in India the royal Way of the Spirit.
This is already evident in the Brahman conception of sacrifice.
Whatever may have been the role of sacrifice in the Indo-Aryan
beginnings and the Vedic era, it is certain that from the time
of the Brahmanas sacrifice became chiefly a means of restoring
the primordial unity. Indeed, by sacrifice the scattered limbs
of Prajapati are reunited, that is to say the divine Being, im-
molated at the beginning of Time in order that the World may
be born from his body, is reconstituted. The essential function
of sacrifice is to put together again (*samdha*) that which was
broken up *in illo tempore*. At the same time as the symbolic
reconstitution of Prajapati, a process of reintegration takes place
in the officiant himself. By ritually reuniting the fragments of
Prajapati, the officiant "recollects" (*samharati*) himself, that is
to say endeavours to regain the unity of his true Self. As Ananda
Coomaraswamy writes, the unification and the act of becoming
oneself represent at the same time a death, a rebirth and a
marriage.[2]

This is why the symbolism of the Indian sacrifice is extremely
complex; one is concerned with cosmological, sexual and
initiatory symbols, all together.

[1] On the function and morphology of initiation, see the author's *Birth and
Rebirth*, London, 1961.
[2] See *Atmayajna: Self-Sacrifice*, p. 388. See *Ibid.*, p. 372, on the "recollection"
of the officiant by means of sacrifice.

Sacrifice conceived as the pre-eminent method of unification is one of the numerous examples illustrating the irrepressible aspiration of the Indian spirit to transcend the contraries and rise to a complete reality. The later history of Indian spirituality has developed almost entirely in this direction. This is one reason why Indian thought has refused to concede any value to History, and why traditional India has had no historical consciousness. For, compared with absolute reality, what we call Universal History represents only a particular moment in a vast cosmic drama. India, we insist, has refused to grant undue significance to what, according to its ontology, is no more than a passing aspect of a particular situation; to what we call today "man's situation in History".

THE ANDROGYNE IN THE NINETEENTH CENTURY

Séraphita is undoubtedly the most attractive of Balzac's fantastic novels. Not because of the Swedenborgian theories with which it is imbued but because Balzac here succeeded in presenting with unparalleled force a fundamental theme of archaic anthropology: the androgyne considered as the exemplary image of the perfect man. Let us recall the novel's subject and setting. In a castle on the edge of the village of Jarvis, near the Stromfjord, lived a strange being of moving and melancholy beauty. Like certain other Balzac characters, he seemed to hide a terrible "secret", an impenetrable "mystery". But here it is not a "secret" to be compared with Vautrin's. The character in *Séraphita* is not a man eaten up by his own destiny and in conflict with society. He is a being different in quality from the rest of mankind, and his "mystery" depends not on certain dark episodes in his past but on the nature of his own being. For the mysterious personage loves and is loved by Minna, who sees him as a man, and is also loved by Wilfred, in whose eyes he seems to be a woman, Séraphita.

This perfect androgyne was born of parents who had been disciples of Swedenborg. Although he had never left his own fjord, never opened a book, spoken to any learned person or practised any art, Seraphitus-Seraphita displayed considerable erudition; his mental faculties surpassed those of mortal men. Balzac describes with moving simplicity the nature of this androgyne, his solitary life and ecstasies in contemplation. All this is patently based on Swedenborg's doctrine, for the novel was primarily written to illustrate and comment on the Swedenborgian theories of the perfect man. But Balzac's androgyne hardly belongs to the earth. His spiritual life is entirely directed towards heaven. Seraphitus-Seraphita lives only to purify himself—and to love. Although Balzac does not expressly say so, one realises that Seraphitus-Seraphita cannot leave the earth before he has known love. This is perhaps the ast and most precious virtue: for two people of opposite sex to love *really* and jointly. Seraphic love no doubt, but not an abstract or generalized love all the same. Balzac's androgyne loves two well-individualized beings; he remains therefore in the concrete world of life. He is not an angel come down to earth; he is a perfect man, that is to say a "complete being".

Séraphita is the last great work of European literature that has the myth of the androgyne as its central theme. Other nineteenth-century writers have returned to the subject, but their works are mediocre if not frankly bad. Let us mention as a curiosity Péladan's *L'Androgyne* (1891), the eighth volume in a series of twenty novels entitled *La décadence latine*. In 1910 Péladan treated the subject again in his brochure *De l'androgyne* (in the series "Les idées et les formes") which is not entirely without interest despite its confusion of facts and its aberrations. The entire work of Sar Péladan—whom no one has the courage to read today—seems to be dominated by the androgyne motif. Anatole France wrote that "he is haunted by the idea of the hermaphrodite which inspires all his books". But Sar Péladan's whole production—like that of his contemporaries and models, Swinburne, Baudelaire, Huysmans—belongs to quite a different category from *Séraphita;* Péladan's heroes are "perfect" in sensuality. The metaphysical significance of the "perfect man" is degraded and finally lost in the second half of the nineteenth century.

French and English decadents occasionally return to the theme of the androgyne,[1] but always in the form of a morbid or even satanic hermaphroditism (in Aleister Crawley for example). As in all the great spiritual crises of Europe, here once again we meet the *degradation of the symbol*. When the mind is no longer capable of perceiving the metaphysical significance of a symbol, it is understood at levels which become increasingly coarse. The androgyne is understood by decadent writers simply as a hermaphrodite in whom both sexes exist anatomically and physiologically. They are concerned not with a wholeness resulting from the fusion of the sexes but with a superabundance of erotic possibilities. Their subject is not the appearance of a new type of humanity in which the fusion of the sexes produces a new unpolarized consciousness, but a self-styled sensual perfection, resulting from the active presence of both sexes in one.

This idea of the hermaphrodite has probably been encouraged by the study of certain ancient sculptures. But the decadent writers did not know that the hermaphrodite represented in antiquity an ideal condition which men endeavoured to achieve spiritually by means of imitative rites; but that if a child showed at birth any signs of hermaphroditism, it was killed by its own parents. In other words, the actual, anatomical hermaphrodite was considered an aberration of Nature or a sign of the gods' anger and consequently destroyed out of hand. Only the ritual androgyne provided a model, because it implied not an augmentation of anatomical organs but, symbolically, the union of the magico-religious powers belonging to both sexes.

[1] On the whole movement see Mario Praz, *The Romantic Agony*, 2nd edition, Oxford, 1951.

GERMAN ROMANTICISM

One has only to turn to the German Romantics to see the distance separating the ideal of Péladan from that of Novalis. For the German Romantics the androgyne was the type of the perfect man of the future.[1] Ritter, a well-known doctor and friend of Novalis, had sketched in his *Nachlass eines jungen Physikers* a whole philosophy of the androgyne. For Ritter the man of the future would be, like Christ, an androgyne. "Eve", he wrote, "was engendered by man without the aid of woman; Christ was engendered by woman without the aid of man; the androgyne will be born of the two. But the husband and wife will be fused together in a single flash". The body that is to be born will then be immortal. Describing the new humanity of the future, Ritter uses alchemical language, a sign that alchemy was one of the German Romantics' sources for their revival of the myth of the androgyne.

Wilhelm von Humboldt took up the same subject in his youthful *Über die männliche und weibliche Form*, in which he dwelt particularly on the divine androgyne, an archaic and extremely widespread theme which will engage us later. Friedrich Schlegel, too, envisaged the ideal of the androgyne in his essay *Über die Diotima*, in which he attacks the value attached to the exclusively masculine or feminine character, which is only achieved by education and modern custom. For, he wrote, the goal towards which the human race should strive is a progressive reintegration of the sexes which should end in androgyny.

But of all Romantic authors Franz von Baader attached the greatest importance to androgyny. According to Baader, the androgyne had existed at the beginning—and will be again at

---

[1]On this subject see Fr. Giese, *Der romantische Charakter*, vol. 1; *Die Entwicklung des androgynen Problems in der Frühromantik*, Langensalza, 1919. See also *Mitul Reintegrării*, pp. 76, *et seq.*; Ronald D. Gray, *Goethe the Alchemist*, Cambridge, 1952, ch. x (Male and Female).

the end of time. Baader's chief source of inspiration was Jacob Boehme. He borrowed from Boehme the idea of Adam's first fall; the sleep in which his celestial companion was separated from him. But, thanks to Christ, man will again become an androgyne, like the angels. Baader wrote that "the aim of marriage as a sacrament is the restoration of the celestial or angelic image of man as he should be". Sexual love should not be confused with the instinct for reproduction; its true function is "to help man and woman to integrate internally the complete human image, that is to say the divine and original image".[1] Baader considered that a theology which will present "sin as a disintegration of man, and the redemption and resurrection as his reintegration" will conquer all other theologies.[2]

To find the sources of this revalorization of the androgyne in German Romanticism we should have to examine the opinions of Jacob Boehme and other seventeenth-century theosophists, especially J. G. Gichtel and Gottfried Arnold. Thanks to the annotated anthology of Professor E. Benz, *Adam. Der Mythus des Urmenschen* (Adam. The myth of primal man), this work could speedily be done. For Boehme, Adam's sleep represents the first fall: Adam separated himself from the divine world and "imagined himself" immersed in Nature, by which act he lowered himself and became earthly. The appearance of the sexes is a direct consequence of this first fall. According to certain of Boehme's followers, on seeing the animals copulate Adam was disturbed by desire and God gave him sex to avoid worse.[3] Another fundamental idea of Boehme, Gichtel and other theosophists was that Sophia, the divine Virgin, was originally part of primal Man. When he attempted to dominate her, the Virgin separated herself from him. According to Gottfried

[1]*Gesammelte Werke*, III, p. 309, printed by Ernst Benz in his anthology *Adam. Der Mythus des Urmenschen*, Munich, 1955, pp. 221ff.
[2]*Gesammelte Werke*, III, p. 306; Benz, *op. cit.*, p. 219. See also E. Susini, *Franz von Baader et le romantisme mystique*, Paris, 1942.
[3]E. Benz, *op. cit.*, pp. 60ff., 67ff., 110. See also J. Evola, *La metafisica del Sesso*, Rome, 1958, p. 272.

Arnold, it was carnal desire that caused the primal Being to lose this "occult bride". But even in his present fallen state, when a man loves a woman he always secretly desires this celestial Virgin.[1] Boehme compared the break-up of Adam's androgynous nature to Christ's crucifixion.[2]

Jakob Boehme probably borrowed the idea of the androgyne not from the Kabbala but from alchemy; indeed he makes use of alchemical terms.[3] Actually one of the names of the Philosophers' Stone was precisely *Rebis*, the "double being" (lit. "two things") or the hermetic Androgyne. *Rebis* was born as a result of the union of Sol and Luna or, in alchemical terms, of sulphur and mercury.[4] It would be purposeless to insist, after the fundamental labours of C. J. Jung, on the importance of the androgyne in the *opus alchemicum*.[5]

THE MYTH OF THE ANDROGYNE

It is not our purpose to pursue the history of the doctrine of the androgyne from the Renaissance back into the Middle Ages

[1]E. Benz, *op. cit.*, pp. 125ff., 129, etc. J. Evola, *op. cit.*, p. 273.

[2]*Der Weg zu Christo*, quoted by Hermann Baumann, *Das doppelte Geschlecht*, Berlin, 1955, p. 175.

[3]See J. Evola, *op. cit.*, p. 271; also A. Koyré, *La philosophie de Jakob Boehme*, Paris, 1929, p. 225.

[4]See the definition of *rebis* given by Michael Meier, 1687, and quoted by John Read, *Prelude to Chemistry*, London, 1959, p. 239. See also the description of the androgyne according to an unpublished codex in Carbonelli, *Sulle fonti storiche della chimica*, Rome, 1925, p. 17.

[5]See particularly *Psychologie der Uebertragung* (transl. Hull, *Collected Works*, vol. XVI) *passim.*; *Mysterium Conjunctionis*, II, particularly pp. 224ff. See also John Read, *op. cit.*, figs. xvi and lx, etc. See *Mitul Reintegrării*, pp. 82ff. Let us add that the androgyne continues to attract contemporary theological thought. See, for example, the work *Die Gnosis des Christentums*, Salzburg, 1939, by the Catholic theologian Georg Koepgen, in which Christ, the Church and its priests are considered as androgynes (pp. 316ff. Cf. Jung, *Myst. conj.*, II, 130ff.). According to N. Berdjaev also, the perfect man of the future will be androgynous, as Christ was. (See *The Meaning of the Creative Act*, 1916, English transl., 1955, p. 187; see also Donald A. Lowrie, *Rebellious Prophet. A Life of Nicolai Berdjaev*, New York, 1960, pp. 75ff.)

and antiquity. It is enough to recall that in his *Dialoghi d'Amore*, Leone Ebreo tried to connect Plato's myth of the androgyne with the biblical tradition of the Fall, interpreted as a dichotomy of Primal Man.[1] A different doctrine, likewise centred in the primordial unity of man's being, was held by Scot Erigena, who took his inspiration from Maximus the Confessor. According to Erigena, the division of the sexes formed part of a cosmic process. The division of substances had begun in God and continued progressively as far as the nature of man, which was thus divided into male and female. That is why the reunion of substances must begin in man and be attained once more on all planes of being up to that of God. In God there is no more division, for God is All and One. According to Scot Erigena, division into sexes was the result of sin, but it will come to an end in the reunification of man, which will be followed by the eschatological reunion of the circle of earth with Paradise. Christ has anticipated this final reintegration. Scot Erigena quotes Maximus the Confessor, according to whom Christ unified the sexes in his own nature, for in the Resurrection he was "neither man nor woman, though he was born and died a man".[2]

Let us remember also that several *midrashim* represent Adam as having been androgynous. According to the *Bereshit rabba*, "Adam and Eve were made back to back, joined at the shoulders; then God divided them with an axe stroke, cutting them in two". Others hold otherwise, that "the first man (Adam) was a man on the left side, a woman on the right; but God split him in two halves".[3] Moreover there are certain Christian gnostic sects who gave the idea of the androgyne a central place in their doctrines. According to information conveyed by Saint Hippolytus,[4] Simon Magus called the primordial spirit *arseno-*

---

[1]Leone Ebreo, *Dialoghi d'Amore*, ed. Caramella, Bari, 1929, pp. 417ff.; E. Benz, *op. cit.*, pp. 31ff.
[2]*De divisionibus Naturae*, II, 4; II, 8, 12, 14; texts quoted by Evola, *op. cit.*, p. 180.
[3]Texts quoted in *Traité d'Histoire des Religions*, p. 361. See also *Mitul Reintegrării*, pp. 90ff.
[4]*Refutatio omn. haer.*, VI, 18.

thelys, "male-female". The Naasenes also imagined the celestial Man, Adamas, as an *arsenothelys*. Terrestrial Adam was no more than an image of the celestial archetype; he too, therefore, was an androgyne. By the fact that the human race descends from Adam, the *arsenothelys* exists virtually in every man, and spiritual perfection consists precisely in rediscovering within oneself this androgynous nature. The supreme Spirit, the Logos, was itself androgynous also. And the final reintegration "of the spiritual as well as the animal and material realities will take place in a man, Jesus, the son of Mary". (*Refutatio*, v, 6). According to the Naasenes, the cosmic drama contains three elements: (1) the pre-existent Logos as a divine and universal totality; (2) the Fall, which caused the break-up of Creation and the birth of suffering; (3) the coming of the Saviour, who by his unity reintegrated the countless fragments which make up our present-day Universe. According to the Naasenes, androgyny is one moment in a vast process of cosmic unification.

In the *Epistle of Eugnostus the Blessed*, of which two manu-scripts have recently been discovered at Khenoboskion, the Father produced from himself an androgynous human being which, by union with the Sophia, produced an androgynous son. "This son is the first generative Father, the Son of Man, who is also called the Adam of the Light . . . He joins with his Sophia and produces a great androgynous light, which is, by its masculine name, the Saviour, creator of all things, and by its feminine name Sophia, the all-mother who is also called Pistis. From these two beings are born six other pairs of spiritual androgynes who produce 72, then 360 other entities. . . ."[1] As can be seen, this is a process which, beginning with an androgynous Father, repeats itself at diminishing stages (each further from the "Centre" at which is the autochthonous Father).

The androgyne is also vouched for by the *Gospel of Thomas*

---

[1] J. Doresse, *Les livres secrets des gnostiques d'Égypte*, vol. I, Paris, 1958, p. 211. The essential teaching of the *Epistle of Eugnostus the Blessed* is to be found in another gnostic document from Khenoboskion, the *Sophia of Jesus* of which another version was already available in the Berlin codex. See Doresse, I, 215ff.

which, while not properly speaking a gnostic work, testifies to the mystical climate of early Christianity. Reshaped and reinterpreted, this book was, however, fairly popular among the early Gnostics, and a translation into the Sa'idic dialect figured in the Gnostic Library of Khenoboskion. In the *Gospel of Thomas* Jesus said, in an address to the disciples: "And when you make the inner as the outer, and the outer as the inner, and the upper as the lower, and when you make male and female into a single one, so that the male shall not be male and the female (shall not) be female, then shall you enter (the Kingdom)".[1]

In another logion (no. 106, ed. Puech; no. 103, Grant) Jesus says: "When you make the two become one, you will become the son of Man and if you say 'Mountain, remove yourself', it will remove itself" (Doresse, II, p. 109, no. 110). The expression "to become one" occurs three more times (log. 4, Puech, 3 Grant; 10 Grant, 11 Puech; 24 Grant, 23 Puech). Doresse refers to some parallels in the New Testament (*John*, XVII, 11, 20-23; *Romans*, XII, 4-5; I *Corinthians*, XII, 27; etc.). Outstandingly important is *Galatians* III, 28: "There is neither Jew nor Greek, there is neither bond nor free, there is neither male nor female: for ye are all one in Christ Jesus". This is the unity of primal creation, before the making of Eve, when "man" was neither male nor female (Grant, p. 144). According to the *Gospel of Philip* (codex X of Khenoboskion) the division of the sexes—the creation of Eve taken from the body of Adam—was the principle of death. "Christ came to re-establish what was thus (divided) in the beginning and to reunite the two. Those who died because they were in separation he will restore to life by reuniting them!" (Doresse, II, p. 157).

Other writings contain similar passages on the reunion of the sexes as an image of the Kingdom. When asked at what moment the Kingdom would come, the Lord himself replied: "When the two shall be one, the outside like the inside, the

---

[1]Doresse, *op. cit.*, vol. II, 1959, p. 95; A. Guillaumont, H.-Ch. Puech, etc., *L'Évangile selon Thomas*, 1959, log. 17-18; Robert M. Grant, *The Secret Sayings of Jesus*, New York, 1960, pp. 143ff.

male with the female neither male nor female". (*Second Epistle of Clement*, quoted in Doresse, II, 157.) The quotation from the *Epistle of Clement* probably derives from the *Gospel according to the Egyptians*, of which Clement of Alexandria has preserved this passage: "When Salome inquired when the things concerning which she asked would be known, the Lord said, 'When you have trampled on the garment of shame and when the two become one and the male with the female is neither male nor female'". (*Stromates*, III, 13, 92; Doresse, II, 158. Translation M. R. James, *The Apocryphal New Testament*, p. 11.)

This is not the place to study the origin of these Gnostic and near-Gnostic expressions of the divine totality and the androgyny of the "perfect man". We know that the sources of Gnosticism are extremely disparate: beside the Jewish gnosis, and speculations on the primal Adam and the Sophia, one finds the products of neo-Platonic and neo-Pythagorean doctrines and influences from the East, especially from Iran. But, as we have just seen, Saint Paul and the Gospel of John already counted androgyny as one of the characteristics of spiritual perfection. In fact, to become "male and female", or to be "neither male nor female" are formative expressions by which language manages to describe the *metanoia*, "conversion", the total reversal of values. It is as paradoxical to be "male and female" as to become a child again, to be born anew, to pass through the "narrow gate".

Clearly, similar conceptions were current in Greece. In the *Symposium* (183E—193D) Plato described primæval man as a bisexual being, spherical in form. What concerns our investigations is the fact that in Plato's metaphysical speculations, as in the theology of Philo of Alexandria, in the neo-Platonic and neo-Pythagorean theosophists as in the hermetic school who quote the authority of Hermes Trismegistus or Poimandres, and in a number of Christian gnostics, *human perfection is imagined as an unbroken unity*. This was merely a reflection of the divine perfection, of the All in One. Hermes Trismegistus reveals to Asclepius that "God has no name or rather he has all names, since he is at once One and All". Infinitely rich with the fertility of both sexes, he is continuously bringing to birth all those things which he planned to create.

"What, you say that God has both sexes, Trismegistus?"

"Yes, Asclepius, and not God alone but all beings animate and vegetable".[1]

THE DIVINE ANDROGYNY

This idea of universal bisexuality, a necessary consequence of the idea of the bisexual divinity as model and principle of all existence, is capable of throwing light on our investigations. For basically, what is implied in such a conception is the idea that perfection, and therefore Being, ultimately consists of a unity-totality. Everything that exists must therefore be a totality, carrying the *coincidentia oppositorum* to all levels and applying it to all contexts. This is proved by the androgyny of the Gods and in the rites of symbolic androgynisation, but also by those cosmogonies which explain the World as originating from a cosmogonic Egg or a primal totality in the shape of a sphere. One finds such ideas, symbols and rites not only in the Mediterranean world of the ancient Near East but in a number of other exotic and archaic cultures. Such diffusion can only be explained by the fact that the myths offered a satisfactory picture of divinity, in other words of the ultimate reality, as an indivisible totality, and at the same time invited man to approach this plenitude by means of rites or mystical techniques of reintegration.

A few examples will help us to a better understanding of this religious phenomenon. In the oldest Greek theogonies, neutral or feminine divine Beings engender unaided. According to the tradition transmitted by Hesiod (*Theogony*, 124ff.), from Chaos (neuter) was born Erebus (neuter) and Night (feminine). Earth gave birth unaided to the starry Sky. These are mythical statements of the primal totality, containing all powers, therefore all pairs of opposites: chaos and form, darkness and light, the

[1] *Corpus Hermeticum*, II, 20, 21.

virtual and the manifest, male and female, etc. As an exemplary expression of the creative power, bisexuality is ranged among the glories of divinity. Hera alone engendered Hephaistos and Typheus, and "that nuptial goddess first appears as an androgyne".[1] At Labranda, in Caria, they worshipped a bearded Zeus with "six breasts placed triangularly on his chest".[2] Heracles, the most virile of heroes, changed clothes with Omphale. In the mysteries of the Italiot Hercules Victor, the god as well as the initiates were dressed as women; as Marie Delcourt has well shown this rite was supposed to "promote the health, youth, vigour and longevity of a person and perhaps even to confer a kind of immortality".[3]

In Cyprus there was a cult of a bearded Aphrodite, called Aphroditos, and in Italy of a bald Venus. As for Dionysus, he was the most bisexual of the gods. In a fragment of Aeschylus (fragment 61) someone cries out on seeing him: "Where have you come from, man-woman? What is your country? What is that garment?"[4]

Originally Dionysus was thought of as a stout, bearded being, doubly potent because of his double nature. Later, in the Hellenistic age, art made him effeminate.[5] We will not refer to the other androgynous deities of the syncretic pantheon, the Phrygian Great Mother, for example, and her bisexual progeny Agditis and Mise. As for the divine figure whom the ancients called by the name of Hermaphrodite, it took shape rather late,

[1] Marie Delcourt, *Hermaphrodite, Mythes et rites de la bisexualité dans d'Antiquité classique*, Paris, 1958, p. 29.

[2] Marie Delcourt, *op. cit.*, p. 30.   [3] *Ibid.*, p. 36.

[4] Text quoted by Marie Delcourt, *op. cit.*, p. 40.

[5] "It takes away the garments that symbolized his double nature: the saffron veil, the girdle, the golden *mitra*. It makes him naked, not stripped of his virility but too weak to make use of it." Ovid (*Metam.*, IV, 20) and Seneca *Oedipus*, 408) give him " 'the face of a virgin', which would have surprised the archaic painters who portray him with a heavy beard" (Marie Delcourt, *Hermaphrodite*, pp. 42-3). On the hermaphrodism of Dionysus, see also Karl Lehmann-Hartleben and E. C. Olsen, *Dionysiac Sarcophagi in Baltimore*, Baltimore, 1942, pp. 34ff., and the bibliography cited in note 89.

about the third or fourth century, and its somewhat complex story[1] is less important for our investigations.

We will not recall here the androgynous gods to be found in other religions.[2] Their number is considerable, and they are as frequent in complex and developed religions—among the ancient Germans, for example, in the ancient Near-East, in Iran, China, Indonesia, etc.—as among people of archaic culture, in Africa, America, Melanesia, Australia and Polynesia.[3] The majority of vegetation and fertility gods are bisexual or bear traces of androgyny. *"Sive deus sis, sive dea"*, said the ancient Romans of the gods of agriculture; and the ritual formula *sive mas sive femina* occurs frequently in invocations. In certain cases (for example among the Estonians) the gods of the fields were considered male one year and female the next.[4] But the most curious thing is that the outstanding male and female gods are androgynous, which is explicable if one takes account of the traditional conception that one cannot be anything *par excellence* unless one is at the same time the opposite or, to be more precise, if one is not many other things at the same time.

Zervan, the Persian god of boundless Time, was androgynous,

[1] It can be found in a richly detailed chapter of Marie Delcourt, pp. 65ff.

[2] See M. Eliade, *Mitul Reintegrării*, pp. 99ff.; *Traité d'Histoire des Religions*, pp. 359ff.

[3] A rich documentation is to be found in Hermann Baumann, *Das doppelte Geschlecht*, pp. 129-249. We will not attempt here the problem of chronology, which is formidable. H. Baumann estimates that divine bisexuality is not clearly proved before the megalithic cultures (see also our remarks in the *Revue d'Histoire des Religions*, 1958, pp. 89-92). As for the bisexual interpretation given by L. F. Zotz to certain palaeolithic idols (*Bull. Soc. Préh. Franc.*, 48, 1951, pp. 333ff.), it has been rejected by H. Breuil (*Ibid.*, 49, 1952, p. 25) and K. J. Narr (*Anthropos*, 50, 1955, pp. 543ff.). This is not to say that the concept of divine androgyny was necessarily unknown to primitive peoples (see, for example, Clive Kluckhorn in *Myth and Mythmaking*, edited by Henry A. Murray, New York, 1960, p. 52). Let us observe also that, on the level of archaic cultures, "totality" may be expressed by any pair of opposites: feminine-masculine, visible-invisible, sky-earth, light-darkness.

[4] See *Traité d'Histoire des Religions*, p. 359.

as was also the supreme Chinese divinity of Darkness and Light.[1] These two examples clearly show us that androgyny was the particular expression of totality. For, as we have seen, Zervan was the father of the twins Ohrmazd and Ahriman, the gods of Good and Evil—and Darkness and Light, in China as in India, symbolize the manifest and unmanifest aspects of ultimate reality.

Numerous divinities were called "Father and Mother".[2] This was both an allusion to their completeness or actual autogenesis, and an indication of their creative powers. It is equally probable that a certain number of "divine pairs" are later elaborations of a primordial androgynous divinity or a personification of its attributes. Since androgyny is the distinguishing sign of an original totality in which all possibilities are found united, primordial Man, the mythical Ancestor of humanity, is thought of in many traditions as androgynous. We have already cited the example of Adam. Tuisto, the first man of Germanic mythology, was also bisexual; his name is connected etymologically with the old Norwegian *tvistr* ("dual"), with the Vedic *dvis*, the Latin *bis*, etc.[3] In certain traditions the mythical androgynous ancestor has been replaced by a pair of twins; in India, for example, by Yama and his sister Yami, and in Persia by Yima and Yimagh.

RITUAL ANDROGYNISATION

All these myths of divine androgyny and primal bisexual man present exemplary models for human behaviour. Consequently androgyny is symbolically re-enacted in ritual. The purpose of this ritual androgynisation are manifold and its forms extremely complex. To study it here would be out of the question. It will suffice to recall that in a great number of primitive peoples, initiation at puberty implies the previous androgynisation of the initiate. The best-known example—though hitherto insufficiently

[1] *Traité d'Histoire des Religions*, p. 360.
[2] See Alfred Bertholet, *Das Geschlecht der Gottheit*, Tübingen, 1934, p. 19.
[3] See *Mitul Reintegrării*, p. 92.

explained—is furnished by the initiatory subincision practised by certain Australian tribes, which symbolically gives the initiate a female sexual organ.[1]

If we remember that, according to the Australians, and many other primitive peoples elsewhere, non-initiates are considered asexual, and admission to sexuality is one of the consequences of initiation, the deeper significance of this rite seems to be the following: One cannot become a sexually adult male before knowing the coexistence of the sexes, androgyny; in other words, one cannot attain a particular and well-defined mode without first knowing the total mode of being.

Initiatory androgyny is not always signified, as with the Australians, by an operation. In many cases it is suggested by the boys dressing as girls, and the girls as boys. The custom is found in certain African tribes, but also in Polynesia.[2] One may ask whether ritual nakedness, common in many initiations at puberty, does not also signify a symbolic androgynisation. Also homosexual practices, reported of various initiations, are probably to be explained by a similar belief, that is to say that the initiates, during their initiatory instruction, acquire both sexes.

Exchanges of clothing were equally frequent in ancient Greece. Plutarch recounts several customs that he found strange. "In Sparta", he writes, "the woman in charge of a young bride shaves her head, clothes her in a man's dress and shoes, then puts her on the bed alone and without light. The husband steals in to join her (Plutarch, *Lycurgus*, 15). At Argos the bride puts on a false beard for the marriage night (Plutarch, *On Virtue in Women*). In Cos it is the husband who puts on female clothes to receive the wife" (Plutarch, 58, *The Greek Question*).[3]

In all these cases intersexual transvestism is a wedding custom. Now, we know that in archaic times marriages, in Greece, followed the initiations at puberty. Transvestism also took place

[1] On this subject see *Birth and Rebirth*, pp. 25ff.
[2] H. Baumann, *op. cit.*, pp. 57-8; *Birth and Rebirth*, p. 26.
[3] Marie Delcourt, *Hermaphrodite*, p. 7.

on the occasion of the Athenian Oschophories, a ceremony in which can be distinguished "survival from male initiations, a grape-harvest festival and a commemoration of the return of Theseus. If these are so perfectly welded, it is a sign, as H. Jeanmaire has shown, that the legend of Theseus itself is rooted in an old social rite of ordeals, of which it is, in part at least, a narrative interpretation".[1]

But apart from these remains of initiatory transvestism, intersexual disguises were used among the Greeks, in the feasts of Hera in Samos and other occasions also.[2] If we remember that transvestism was very widespread at Carnival, the spring festivity in Europe, and also in certain agricultural ceremonies in India, Persia and other Asiatic countries,[3] we realise the principal function of this rite: it is, to be brief, a coming out of one's self, a transcending of one's own historically controlled situation, and a recovering of an original situation, no longer human or historical since it precedes the foundation of human society; a paradoxical situation impossible to maintain in profane time, in a historical epoch, but which it is important to reconstitute periodically in order to restore, if only for a brief moment, the initial completeness, the intact source of holiness and power.

The ritual change of costume implies a symbolical reversal of behaviour, a pretext for carnival pranks, but also for the debauchery of the Saturnalia. To be brief, it is a suspension of laws and customs, for the behaviour of the sexes is now exactly the opposite of what it should normally be. This reversal of behaviour implies a total confusion of values, a specific mark of all orgiastic rituals. There is, in fact, a formal correspondence between intersexual transvestism and symbolic androgyny on the one hand and orgiastic rituals on the other. In either case,

[1]*Ibid.*, pp. 15-16.   [2]Marie Delcourt, *op. cit.*, pp. 18ff.
[3]See *Traité d'Histoire des Religions*, p. 362. Exchanges of dress on the occasion of marriage, E. Samter, *Geburt, Hochzeit und Tod*, Berlin, 1911, pp. 92ff. On this subject, see W. Mannhardt, *Der Baumkultus der Germanen und ihre Nachbarstämme*, Berlin, 1875, pp. 200ff., 480ff.; J. J. Meyer, *Trilogie altindischer Mächte und Feste der Vegetation*, Zurich-Leipzig, 1937, I, pp. 76, 86, 88ff.

one finds a ritual "totalisation", a reintegration of opposites, a regression to the primordial and homogeneous. It is in fact a symbolic restoration of "Chaos", of the undifferentiated unity that preceded the Creation, and this return to the homogeneous takes the form of a supreme regeneration, a prodigious increase of power. This is one of the reasons for the ritual orgy performed for the benefit of the crops or on the occasion of the New Year: in the former case, the orgy assures the fertility of the fields; in the latter it symbolizes the return to precosmogonic Chaos and immersion in the limitless ocean of power that existed before the Creation of the World and rendered the creation possible. The year about to be born corresponds to the World in process of being created.[1]

THE PRIMORDIAL TOTALITY

Clearly, various interpretations can be attached to these rites of totalisation by symbolic androgyny or orgy. But all are performed in order to assure the success of a *beginning:* either the beginning of sexual and cultural life denoted by initiation, or the New Year, or the spring, or the "beginning" represented by every new harvest. Taking into account that, for man in traditional societies, the cosmogony represents the exemplary "beginning", one understands the presence of cosmogonical symbols in initiatory rituals, agricultural or orgiastic. "To begin" something signifies, indeed, that one is in process of creating that thing, therefore that one is handling an enormous reserve of sacred power. This explains the structural resemblance between the myth of the primordial Androgyne, the Ancestor of humanity, and the creation myths. In both cases the myths show that in the beginning, *in illo tempore,* there was an intact totality—and that this totality was divided or broken in order that the World or humanity could be born. To the primordial androgyne, especially the spherical androgyne described by Plato, corresponds,

[1]On this theme see, *The Myth of the Eternal Return*, pp. 60ff.

on the cosmic plane, the cosmogonical Egg or the primordial anthropocosmic Giant.

A great number of creation-myths present the original state— "Chaos"—as a compact and homogeneous mass in which no form could be distinguished; or as an egg-like sphere in which Sky and Earth were united, or as a giant man, etc. In all these myths Creation takes place by the division of the egg into two parts, representing Sky and Earth—or by the breaking up of the Giant, or by the fragmentation of the unitary mass.[1]

In the beginning there was, therefore,—both on the cosmic and the anthropological scale—a plenitude containing all potentialities. But this obsession with the "beginning", displayed in so many different myths and rites, must also be interpreted in another context. For it can be observed that the tendency towards unification and totalisation, though found on many levels, is expressed in various ways and serves different purposes. The reunion of contraries and abolition of opposites take place both in ritual orgy and initiatory androgynisation, but *their fields of realisation are not the same.* A reunion of contrary principles can also be achieved by Yoga techniques, particularly by those of Tantric yoga. Here also the aim to be pursued is "unity-totality", but the experience takes place on several levels at once, and the final unification can only be described in transcendental terms. In other words, at the obscure level of ritual orgy or androgynisation or the return to the Chaos before the Creation, we are confronted with tendencies towards reunion and unification structurally comparable with the tendency of the Spirit to return to the Unity-Totality. This is not the place to dwell on this paradoxical tendency of Life to assume the behaviour of Spirit.[2] It is important, however, to state that though all these myths, rites and mystical techniques imply the absolute *coincidentia oppositorum,* though formally the cosmogonic Egg is

[1] See M. Eliade, *Structure et fonction du mythe cosmogonique* in the volume *La Naissance du Monde,* Paris, 1959, pp. 471-95.
[2] See in this context the observations on the symbolism of ascension in M. Eliade, *Myths, Dreams and Mysteries,* pp. 99ff.

related to the ritual orgy, to androgynisation or the position of a *jivan mukta*, unity-totality is not the same in the case of man taking part in an orgiastic ritual or of one abolishing the contraries by means of yoga.

These few examples that we have just given will improve our understanding of this variety of perspectives and difference of levels. We have already said that androgyny was only accepted in Greece as a ritual reality, and that children born with marks of hermaphroditism were immediately killed by their parents. In this case, therefore, there can be no confusion between *anatomico-physiological* and *ritual* reality. In Siberian shamanism, the shaman will *symbolically* assume both sexes: his dress is decorated with female symbols and in certain cases he tries to imitate female behaviour. But we know examples of shamanism in which bisexuality is ritually, therefore concretely, assumed: the shaman behaves like a woman, wears a woman's clothing, sometimes even takes a husband.[1] This ritual bisexuality—or asexuality—is believed to be at once a sign of spirituality, of commerce with gods and spirits, and a source of sacred power. For the shaman unites in himself the two contrary principles; and since his own person constitutes a holy marriage, he symbolically restores the unity of Sky and Earth, and consequently assures communication between Gods and men.[2] This bisexuality is lived ritually and ecstatically; it is assumed as an indispensable condition for transcending the condition of profane man.

The aberrant nature of some of these shamanic practices must not blind us to the fact that the final aim and theological justifications of ritual asexuality or bisexuality were the *transformation of man*. That attempts were sometimes made to achieve this transformation by methods requiring a physiological change in the shaman in no way alters our problem. The history of religions knows other examples of the confusion of levels, examples in which men have endeavoured to obtain on the level of physio-

[1] *Shamanism*, pp. 257, 258, 351ff.
[2] See, for example, shamanism among the Ngadju-Dyaks, in *Shamanism*, pp. 352ff.

logical experience a mode of spiritual being only accessible by ritual or mystical means.

The same confusion of levels is to be found in Siberian and Indonesian shamans who reverse their sexual behaviour in order to experience ritual androgyny *in concreto*. It is unimportant whether these last examples arise from a spontaneous aberration or from the degradation of an Indian mystical technique, a technique that the shaman was unable to follow or of which he had forgotten the spiritual sense. What is important is that ritual androgynisation of the shamanic kind, especially when it appears in aberrant forms, reveals a desperate effort to attain by concrete, physiological means the paradoxical totality of Man. In other words, here too we must distinguish between the *end in view* and the *means adopted* for obtaining it. The means may be naïve, or sometimes strangely puerile; in which case they succeed in uniting the opposites in the concrete, immediate sense of the term, and arrive at a method of being which is no longer human, but is not superhuman either. But the aim pursued retains its value despite the inadequate means by which men endeavour to attain it. The best proof is that an analogous aim can be discovered in certain techniques of Tantric yoga. But it is enough to recall the metaphysic implicit in these techniques to realize immediately that one is dealing with a quite different plane of experience.

TANTRIC DOCTRINES AND TECHNIQUES

It is well known that, according to Tantric yoga, the absolute reality, the *Urgrund*, contains all the dualities and contraries gathered into a state of absolute Unity (*advaya*).[1] Creation represents the explosion of the primal unity and the separation of the two contrary principles incarnate in Shiva and Shakti. All relative existence implies a state of duality, and consequently implies suffering, illusion and "slavery". The final goal of the Tantricist is to reunite the two contrary principles—Shiva and

[1] See *Yoga*, p. 206 and *passim*.

Shakti—in his own body. When Shakti, who sleeps, in the shape of a serpent (*kundalini*), at the base of his body, is awoken by certain yogic techniques, she moves through a medial channel (*susumna*) by way of the *çakras* up to the top of the skull (*sahasrara*), where Shiva dwells, and unites with him. The union of the divine pair within his own body transforms the yogin into a kind of "androgyne". But it must be stressed that "androgynisation" is only one aspect of a total process, that of the reunion of opposites. Actually, Tantric literature speaks of a great number of "opposing pairs" that have to be reunited. The Sun and Moon must be made one, so must the two mystic veins *ida* and *pingala* (which also symbolise these two heavenly bodies) and the two breaths *prana* and *apana*. Above all *prajna*, wisdom, must be joined with *upaya*, the means of attaining it, *shunya*, the void, with *karuna*, compassion. *Hevajra Tantra* speaks also of the state of "two in one", when the female element is transformed into the male principle (II, IV, 40-7; ed. Snellgrove, pp. 24ff.). This reunion of contraries corresponds also to a paradoxical coexistence of *samarasa* and *nirvana*. "There is no *nirvana* outside *samarasa*" proclaimed the Buddha according to *Hevajra Tantra*, II, IV, 32.

All this amounts to saying that we are dealing with a [*coincidentia oppositorum* achieved on all levels of Life and Consciousness. As a result of this union of opposites the experience of duality is abolished and the phenomenal world transcended] The yogin achieves an unconditioned state of liberty and transcendence, expressed by the word *samarasa* (state of bliss), the paradoxical experience of perfect unity. Certain Tantric schools teach that *samarasa* is attainable principally by *maithuna* (ritual union of the sexes) and is characterised by the "staying" or "immobilisation" of the three principal functions of a human being: breath, seminal ejaculation and thought.[1] The unification of opposites is expressed by the cessation of the bio-somatic processes and also of the psycho-mental flux. The immobilisation of those functions that are especially fluid is a

[1]See *Yoga*, pp. 258ff.

sign that a man has left the human condition and come out on a transcendent plane.

Let us observe the religio-cosmic symbolism used to express the joining of contraries. The yogin stands both for a Cosmos and a pantheon; he incarnates in his own body both Shiva and Shakti and many more divinities who are ultimately reducible to this archetypal couple. The two principal phases of Yogo-Tantric *sadhana* are (1) the raising to the cosmic level of psycho-somatic experience; (2) the abolition of this Cosmos and the symbolical return to the initial situation when primordial Unity had not yet exploded in the act of Creation. In other words, freedom and the bliss of absolute liberty are homologous with the fullness that existed before the Creation of the World. From one point of view the paradoxical state attained by the Tantricist during *samarasa* can be compared with ritual "orgy" and pre-Cosmic darkness: in both these states the forms are reunited, tensions and opposites are abolished. But it must be noted that *these resemblances are only formal, that in transcending the world the yogin does not rediscover the bliss of existence in the womb.* All these symbolisms of unification and totalisation show that the yogin is no longer conditioned by cosmic rhythms and laws, that the Universe has ceased to exist for him, that he has succeeded in putting himself in the moment outside Time in which the Universe was not yet created.

To abolish the Cosmos is a means of saying that one has transcended all relative situations, that one has entered into non-duality and liberty. In classical Yoga "the recovery, through *samadhi*, of the original non-duality introduces a new element in respect of the primordial situation (that which existed before the twofold division of the real into object-subject). That element is *knowledge* of unity and bliss. There is a 'return to the begin-ning', but with the difference that the man 'liberated in this life' recovers the original situation enriched by the dimensions of *freedom* and *higher consciousness*. To express it differently, he does not return automatically to a 'given' situation, but he reintegrates the original completeness after having established a new and paradoxical mode of being: consciousness of freedom, which exists nowhere in the Cosmos, neither on the levels of Life nor on the levels of 'mythological divinity'—(the gods, *devas*)—but which exists only in the Supreme Being, Ishvara".[1]

It is not without interest to remark that the paradoxical state of a *jivan mukta*, of one who has realized the unconditioned state —by whatever term that state is expressed: *samadhi, mukti, nirvana, samarasa,* etc.—describes this state, which is beyond the imagination, by contradictory images and symbols. On the one side, images of pure spontaneity and freedom (the *jivan mukta* is a *kamacarin,* "someone who moves at will"; that is why it is said of him that he can "fly through the air";[2] on the other side, images of absolute immobility, of the final arrest of all movement, the freezing of all mobility.[3] The coexistence of these contra-dictory images is explained by the paradoxical situation of the man "liberated in this life"; for he continues to exist in the Cosmos although no longer subject to cosmic laws; in fact he no longer belongs to the Cosmos. These images of immobility and completion express transcendence of all relative conditions; for a system of conditions, a Cosmos, must be defined in terms of becoming, by its continuous movement and by the tension between opposites. To cease moving and no longer to be torn by the tensions between opposites is equivalent to no longer existing in the Cosmos. But, on the other hand, no longer to be conditioned by the pairs of opposites is equivalent to absolute liberty, to perfect spontaneity—and one could not express this

[1] *Yoga,* pp. 99-100. Analogous remarks are suggested by Taoist techniques. It is true that Tao is the formless totality from which emerges the threefold manifestation of the Universe (Sky, Earth, and subterranean regions); but to obtain the wisdom of Tao is to realize the exemplary human situation, that of intermediary between the two extra-terrestrial cosmic regions. See Carl Hentze, *Bronzegerät, Kultbauten, Religion im ältesten China der Shanzeit,* Antwerp, 1951, pp. 192ff., and our observations in the review *Critique,* no. 83, April, 1954, pp. 323ff.

[2] See *Myths, Dreams and Mysteries,* pp. 95ff.

[3] In western alchemy, the image in most common use is the "coagulation of mercury".

liberty better than by images of movement, play, being in two places at once or flying.

Once again, in fact, we are dealing with a transcendental situation which, being inconceivable, is expressed by contradictory or paradoxical metaphors. This is why the formula of the *coincidentia oppositorum* is always applied when it is necessary to describe an unimaginable situation either in the Cosmos or in History. The eschatological symbol, *par excellence*, which denotes that Time and History have come to an end—is the lion lying down with the lamb, and the child playing with the snake. Conflicts, that is to say opposites, are abolished; Paradise is regained. This eschatological image makes it quite clear that the *coincidentia oppositorum* does not always imply "totalisation" in the concrete sense of the term; it may equally signify the paradoxical return of the World to the paradisaical state. The fact that the lamb, the lion, the child and the snake *exist* means that the *World is there*, that there is a Cosmos and not Chaos. But the fact that the lion lies down with the lamb and the child sleeps beside the snake implies at the same time that this is no longer *our* world, but that of Paradise. In fact we are presented with a World that is paradoxical, because free of the tensions and conflicts which are the attributes of every Universe. Furthermore, certain apocryphal texts (the *Acts of Peter*, the *Acts of Philip*, the *Gospel of Thomas*, etc.) use paradoxical images to describe the Kingdom or the overturning of the Cosmos occasioned by the coming of the Saviour. "To make the outside like the inside", "what is above as below", "to make the first last", "to make the right as the left" (see Doresse, *op. cit.*, vol. II, 158ff., 207ff.) are so many paradoxical expressions which signify the total reversal of values and directions occasioned by Christ. It is to be noted that these images are used side by side with those of androgyny and of a return to the state of a child. Each one of these images denotes that the "profane" Universe has been mysteriously replaced by Another World free of laws and conditions, by a World purely spiritual in nature.

MEANINGS OF THE *coincidentia oppositorum*

What is revealed to us by all these myths and symbols, all these rites and mystical techniques, these legends and beliefs that imply more or less clearly the *coincidentia oppositorum*, the reunion of opposites, the totalisation of fragments? First of all, man's deep dissatisfaction with his actual situation, with what is called the human condition. Man feels himself torn and separate. He often finds it difficult properly to explain to himself the nature of this separation, for sometimes he feels himself to be cut off from "something" *powerful*, "something" utterly *other* than himself, and at other times from an indefinable, timeless "state", of which he has no precise memory, but which he does however remember in the depths of his being: a primordial state which he enjoyed before Time, before History. This separation has taken the form of a fissure, both in himself and in the World. It was the "fall", not necessarily in the Judaeo-Christian meaning of the term, but a fall nevertheless since it implies a fatal disaster for the human race and at the same time an ontological change in the structure of the World. From a certain point of view one may say that many beliefs implying the *coincidentia oppositorum* reveal a nostalgia for a lost Paradise, a nostalgia for a paradoxical state in which the contraries exist side by side without conflict, and the multiplications form aspects of a mysterious Unity.

Ultimately, it is the wish to recover this lost unity that has caused man to think of the opposites as complementary aspects of a single reality. It is as a result of such existential experiences, caused by the need to transcend the opposites, that the first theological and philosophical speculations were elaborated. Before they became the main philosophical concepts, the One, the Unity, the Totality were desires revealed in myths and beliefs and expressed in rites and mystical techniques. On the level of presystematic thought, the mystery of totality embodies man's endeavour to reach a perspective in which the contraries are abolished, the Spirit of Evil reveals itself as a stimulant of Good, and Demons appear as the night aspect of the Gods. The fact that these archaic themes and motifs still survive in folklore and continually arise in the worlds of dream and imagination proves that the mystery of totality forms an integral part of the human drama. It recurs under various aspects and at all levels of cultural life—in mystical philosophy and theology, in the mythologies and folklore of the world, in modern men's dreams and fantasies and in artistic creation.[1]

It is not by chance that Goethe searched throughout his life for the true place of Mephistopheles, the perspective in which the Demon who denied Life could show himself paradoxically as its most valuable and tireless partner. Nor is it by chance that Balzac, the creator of the modern realistic novel, in his finest work of fantasy took up a myth that had obsessed humanity for countless thousands of years. Goethe and Balzac both believed in the unity of European literature, and considered their own works as belonging to that literature. They would have been

[1]Nevertheless, it is important to state that all expressions of the *coincidentia oppositorum* are not equivalent. We have observed on many occasions that by transcending the opposites one does not always attain the same mode of being. There is every possible difference, for instance, between spiritual androgynisation and the "confusion of the sexes" obtained by orgy; between regression to the formless and "spooky" and the recovery of "paradisaical" spontaneity and freedom. The element common to all the rites, myths and symbols which we have just recalled lies in this: that all seek to come out of a particular situation in order to abolish a given system of conditions and reach a mode of "total" being. But, according to the cultural context, this "totality" may be either a primordial indistinction (as in "orgy" or "chaos"), or the situation of a *jivan mukta*, or the liberty and blessedness of one who has reached the Kingdom in his own soul. We should need much more space than we have reserved for this essay to discover, in the case of each example we have discussed, to what sort of transcendence the abolition of contraries has led. Moreover, every attempt to transcend the opposites carries with it a certain danger. This is why the ideas of a *coincidentia oppositorum* always arouse ambivalent feelings; on the one side, man is haunted by the desire to escape from his particular situation and regain a transpersonal mode of life; on the other, he is paralysed by the fear of losing his "identity" and "forgetting" himself.

even prouder than they were if they had realized that this European literature goes back beyond Greece and the Mediterranean, beyond the ancient Near East and Asia; that the myths called to new life in *Faust* and *Séraphita* come to us from a great distance in space and time; that they come to us from prehistory.

III

Cosmic and Eschatological Renewal

ESCHATOLOGICAL NUDISM

In the years 1944-5, a strange new cult appeared in the island of Espirito Santo, one of the New Hebrides. A certain Tieka, the founder of the cult, sent the following message round the villages: men and women must take off and throw away their cache-sexe and take off their pearl necklaces and other ornaments. "Destroy all these objects", he added, "which you got from the Whites, also all mats and basket-making tools. Burn your houses and build two large dormitories in each village: one for the men and the other for the women. Couples must no longer sleep together at night. Build also a large kitchen, in which you will prepare your meals while it is still daylight; it is strictly forbidden to cook during the night. Stop working for the Whites. Slaughter all domestic animals: pigs, dogs, cats, etc." Tieka also ordered the suppression of many tribal taboos: for example, the prohibition of marriage within the totemic group, the obligation to buy a wife, the segregation of the young mother after childbirth. Funerary customs were also to be changed; a dead man must no longer be buried in his hut but exposed on a wooden platform in the jungle. But the most sensational part of Tieka's message was that "America" would soon arrive in the island; all adepts of the cult would receive enormous quantities of goods; and what is more, they would never die, they would live for ever.[1]

[1] J. Graham Miller, *Naked Cults in Central West Santos*, "The Journal of the Polynesian Society", vol. LVII, 1948, pp. 330-41, particularly, pp. 331-3.

One recognizes in these last features the specific characteristics of the "cargo-cults", millenarist and eschatological movements in Oceania, of which we will say more hereafter. Let us note immediately that the nudist cult of Espirito Santo continued to spread for several years. In 1948, Graham Miller noted that the further inland one went, the more powerful it was. A third of the population had joined it. A common language, called *Maman* had been adopted by its members, although the villages belonged to different linguistic groups. A new unity—of a religious order—has been formed outside the traditional tribal structures. The members of the sect are convinced of the excellence of the new order and the badness of the old. The Christianity spread by the missionaries is openly repudiated. The centres of the new cult are located in villages in the centre of the island which probably no White has ever visited.[1] Like all the other millenarist movements of Oceania, this cult is anti-White in character.

Nevertheless, its success is not assured. Now that the enthusiasm of the early days is over a certain resistance seems to be appearing. The promised Utopia has not been realized; on the other hand, the gigantic destruction of goods has impoverished whole regions. Furthermore, the natives object to the nudism and orgiastic promiscuity. For, according to one of Graham Miller's informants, the real reason for the nudism is the encouragement of orgy. The founder of the cult himself is alleged to have said that the sexual act, being a natural function, should be performed publicly and in daylight, after the fashion of dogs and birds. All the women and girls belong, without distinction, to all the men.[2]

Justifiably, the natives, including even some followers of the cult, had been upset by the holocaust of their possessions and the sexual promiscuity. For eschatological nudism and the destruction of goods and tools had no sense except as ritual acts portending and preparing for a new era of prosperity, liberty, blessedness and eternal life. Since the Kingdom was slow to

[1] J. Graham Miller, *op. cit.*, pp. 334ff.   [2] J. Graham Miller, *op. cit.*, pp. 340-1.

appear, there followed what always follows in the history of millenarist movements: the initial enthusiasm was succeeded by discouragement and lassitude.

In relation to our researches, the principal interest of this eschatological nudist cult lies in its paradisaical elements. What Tieka announces in his message is in fact the imminent restoration of Paradise on Earth. Men will no longer work; they will have no more need for tools, domestic animals or possessions. Once the old order is abolished the laws, rules and taboos will lose their reason. The prohibitions and customs sanctioned by tradition will give place to absolute liberty; in the first place to sexual liberty, to orgy. For, in human society, it is sexual life that is subject to the strictest taboos and constraints. To be free from laws, prohibitions and customs, is to rediscover primordial liberty and blessedness, the state which preceded the present human condition, in fact the paradisaical state. In Judaeo-Christian language, this is the situation of Adam before the Fall. So the *malamala*, or nudists of Espirito Santo, try to make their sexual conduct like that of the animals, that is to say to cast away all shame, for they consider themselves without sin. This too is why they expect both immortality and the coming of the Americans loaded with gifts. It is hard to say whether, in the mind of the cult's founder, immortality is one of the Americans' presents or if it is the spontaneous result of the coming of the eschatological Kingdom. In either case, immortality and an abundance of food are the outstanding syndromes of Paradise. Man lives for ever and in the most perfect happiness, since he eats without having to work and love is freed of its traditional prohibitions.

It is the paradisaical syndrome that makes the eschatological nudism of Espirito Santo particularly interesting and sufficiently differentiates it from other Melanesian "cargo-cults". For eschatological nudism is at the same time a prophetic and millenary movement of the "cargo-cult" type. But in this case all the paradisaical elements are present. The era of abundance and liberty, announced by all cargo-cults, is anticipated and modified by the nudists of Espirito Santo: theirs is a real return to Paradise, for the faithful will not only enjoy the goods brought in the cargos, but absolute liberty and immortality as well.

THE COMING OF THE AMERICANS AND THE RETURN OF THE DEAD

As for the Americans, they are evidently the ancestors, the dead who return loaded with gifts. The Americans were the last of the Whites to make contact with the natives of the Oceanian islands, principally during the Second World War. In the mythical thought of the natives they have taken the place of the Dutch, the Germans, the French and the English. All are Whites, that is to say in the natives' eyes spirits of the dead, phantoms, ghosts. In fact, they come from far away, from the islands whence came in mythical times the Melanesians' Ancestors—the same islands to which the native returns after death. It is because the Ancestors came in boats that the dead are placed in little boats, which will carry them back to their country of origin.[1] This is, of course, a mythical country, lying beyond the ocean. Even if the Melanesians have kept the memory of their ancestral migrations which brought them to the islands they now occupy, this memory has quickly become mythical. The country of the Ancestors, beyond the Great Waters, is a fabulous island, a kind of Paradise where the souls of the dead await their triumphal return to the living. They will return one day, but this time in magnificent ships loaded with goods, like the giant cargo steamers which the Whites welcome every day to their ports.

Such is the religious conception from which the cargo-cults

---

[1] On the ships of the dead see *Shamanism*, p. 285; V. Lanternari, *Origine storiche dei culti profetici melanesiani*, "Studi e Materiali di Storia delle Religione", XXVII, 1956, pp. 31-86, especially pp. 77ff. On the relationship between the cult of the dead and the cargo-cults see A. Lommel, *Der "Cargo-Cult" in Melanesien. Ein Beitrag zum Problem der "Europaïsierung" der Primitiven*, "Zeitschrift für Ethnologie", vol. 78, 1953, pp. 17-53.

emerged. They are all prophetic and millenarist cults,[1] and proclaim the imminence of a fabulous era of abundance and blessedness. The natives will once more be masters of their islands and will no longer work, for the dead will bring them fantastic quantities of provisions. This is why the majority of these movements require on the one hand the destruction of goods, beginning with objects bought from the Whites, and on the other the construction of vast storehouses where the provisions brought by the dead will be placed. We will discuss certain types of "cargo-cults" later. But first we must explain how the appearance of cargo-boats along the Melanesian shores could have stimulated such prophetic and millenarist minor religions. The fundamental idea is, as we have seen, the myth of the triumphal return of the dead, loaded with gifts. Now, for the natives the arrival of cargo vessels in the White man's ports is a fact reputedly miraculous. They have seen that the Whites receive provisions and quantities of manufactured objects in the making of which they have had no part. The natives have only seen the goods, they do not know the long process of

---

[1]The literature of the prophetic and millenarist cults of Melanesia is already considerable. The bibliography up to 1951 has been drawn up by Ida Leeson, *Bibliography of Cargo-Cults and other Nativistic Movements in the South Pacific*, South Pacific Commission, Paper no. 30, September, 1952. A note of the most important works to appear since 1951 can be found in Lanternari, *op. cit.*, p. 39, note 2 and *passim*. Add *Archives des Sociologies des Religions*, Paris, vol. IV, (July-December, 1957) and V (January-July, 1958) which are devoted to the problems of Messianism and Millenarism. See particularly, Jean Guiart, *Institutions religieuses traditionelles et Messianismes modernes à Fiji*, vol IV, pp. 3-30; Jean Guiart and Peter Worsley, *La répartition des mouvements millénaristes en Mélanésie*, vol. V, pp. 38-46 with map; Peter Worsley, *The Trumpet shall Sound, A Study of "Cargo" Cults in Melanesia*, London, 1957; A. Buehler, *Kulturkontakt and Kulturzerfall*, "Acta Tropica", XIV, 1957, pp. 1-35. On the problem of Messianism in primitive cultures see R. Lowie, *Le Messianisme primitif*, "Diogène", no. 19, 1957, pp. 1-15; Guiglielmo Guariglia, *Prophetismus und Heilserwartungsbewegungen als völkerkundlicher und religionsgeschichtliches Problem*, Vienna, 1959; W. Koppers, *Prophetismus und Messianismus als völkerkundliches und universalgeschichtliches Problem*, "Saeculum", X, 1959, p. 38-47.

manufacture that took place far from their islands.[1] Hence their conclusion—from their standpoint perfectly logical—that these goods have been made either by magic or by the dead.[2] Under the second hypothesis the goods rightfully belong to them, since the dead have worked for them, not for the Whites. Very often, the natives have believed that the merchant ships sent by their dead have been confiscated by the Whites—and this injustice has added to the tension already existing between Blacks and Whites. If, however, the goods were created by magic, they belonged to them just the same; for it was, after all, their gods and their magic which produced them.

PAGAN-CHRISTIAN SYNCRETISM

All these elements have combined to create an atmosphere of frustration and mutal suspicion. On the one side, at least at the beginning, the Whites were regarded as Ancestors who came to bring gifts. In fact they had white skins, like the spirits of the dead, and came in ships. On the other side, once established in the islands the Whites behaved as masters, despised the natives, compelled them to work very hard and tried to convert them to Christianity. These ambivalent feelings towards the Whites offer as good an explanation of the anti-Western movements of national liberation as envy, jealousy and mechanical imitation of Western values. In nearly all the "cargo-cults" the rejection of Christianity is more or less categorical. And yet Christian eschatology has made more than one contribution to the Melanesian Millenarist myth. Thus Upikno, a native hermit, who retired into the jungle of the Huon Peninsula, took the name of Lazarus in obedience to a command from God. One of the millenarist movements of the Rai Coast (1936) announced Christ's second coming. Mambu, a native Catholic of the Madang District, raised a syncretist pagan-Christian movement

[1] A. Lommel, *op. cit.*, p. 58, brings this fact out very well. See also V. Lanternari, p. 84; Peter Worsley, *The Trumpet shall Sound*, p. 44.
[2] See Worsley, *op. cit.*, p. 97.

directed against the Whites and the missions.[1] Another Melanesian cult, known as the "Assisi cult", foretold Christ's arrival on a cargo ship. After this event, the natives would change skins and become white and would be the masters of the Whites, who would become black. At Kaimku, Filo, a girl of seventeen, founded a new prophetic and syncretist cult. One of her uncles took the name of "God", the other of "Jesus". The adherents sang and danced day and night round the altars reciting Catholic and native prayers. Filo had predicted that God would send them goods, but also arms to expel the Europeans: the missions would be attacked first, because they spread a false religion; then would come the turn of the police.[2]

Sanop, one of the heads of a millenarist cult at Buka, accused the Europeans of having kept back part of the Christian ritual and dogma.[3] According to the followers of a cult in Dutch New Guinea, the Europeans, by tearing out the first page of the Bible, had hidden the fact that Jesus was a Papuan and, by this sharp practice had arrogated to themselves the privileged place in Christianity which rightfully belongs to the Papuans. To repair this injustice, the faithful renamed their villages Galilee, Jericho, etc., and one of their leaders, whose name was moreover Moses, retired to meditate on a mountain which was renamed Mount Carmel.[4] In 1939 an old leper woman, who prophesied the coming of the cargo-boats, renamed the Schouten Islands, Judea and Gadara; her village became Bethlehem and a small river the Jordan.[5] Furthermore, in a number of cases, millenarist movements have also rejected the traditional forms of Melanesian religion. The masks of the secret societies have been destroyed and women allowed to participate in the esoteric ceremonies. The traditional religion has sometimes been com-

[1]Peter Worsley, *op. cit.*, pp. 104ff.   [2]Peter Worsley, *op. cit.*, pp. 111ff.
[3]*Ibid.*, p. 119.   [4]*Ibid.*, p. 137.
[5]P. Worsley, *op. cit.*, p. 138. See other examples of pagano-Christian syncretism, *ibid.*, pp. 199ff., 209ff., 245ff., etc. Let us add that the majority of prophetic and messianic movements developed among primitive peoples as a result of contacts with Christianity and western culture. See studies by G. Guariglia and W. Koppers, quoted above, 5.

pletely abandoned. Not that the natives have become a-religious overnight and thrown aside both Christianity and their ancestral religion in a single gesture. On the contrary, this reversal has marked the resurgence of a truer religious life, infinitely more creative because nourished by a prophetic millenarist experience. The people were preparing for the Kingdom—and all religious forms of the past had to be abolished. They were expecting a new life, regenerated from the roots, an existence doubly precious because it proclaimed itself blessed and without end. We have noticed the same phenomenon in the nudist cult of Espirito Santo, which rejected Christianity, the ethical and economic values of the Whites, and the traditional tribal customs and prohibitions, all at once. They were preparing for the return of Paradise.

Of course, all these millenarist movements in Oceania arose as a sequel to precise historical situations, and express a desire for economic and political independence. Numerous works have explained the socio-political context of the "cargo-cults".[1] But the historico-religious interpretation of these millenarist minor religions has hardly begun. Now, all these prophetic phenomena become completely intelligible only in the perspective of the history of religions. It is impossible to discover the significance and assess the extraordinary success of the "cargo-cults" without taking into account one mythico-ritual theme which plays a fundamental part in Melanesian religions: the annual return of the dead and the cosmic renewal that it implies.[2] The Cosmos must be regenerated each year, and at the New Year ceremonies —which perform this regeneration—the dead are present. But this mythico-ritual complex is extended and completed in the

[1]To the works quoted in Note 6 add J. Poirier, *Les mouvements de libération mythique aux Novelles-Hébrides*, "Journal de la Société des Océanistes", vol. v, 1949, pp. 97-103; Tibor Bodrogi, *Colonization and Religious Movements in Melanesia*, "Acta Etnografica Academiae Hungaricae", vol. ii, Budapest, 1955, pp. 259-92; Jean Guiart, *Espirito Santo*, Paris, 1958.

[2]The great merit of Lanternari's book is that it isolates this mythico-ritual background to the Melanesian "cargo-cults"; see *op. cit.*, pp. 45ff., 55ff., and *passim*. See also G. Guariglia, *op. cit.*

myth of the Great Year, that is to say the radical regeneration of the Cosmos by the destruction of all existing forms and their return to Chaos, which is followed by a new Creation.

THE DESTRUCTION OF THE WORLD AND THE INTRODUCTION OF THE GOLDEN AGE

The theme of the periodic destruction and re-creation of the Cosmos is an extremely widespread religious motif, which will engage our attention later. For the moment, let us try to isolate the syndrome of the Great Year, as we find it in some prophetic Melanesian cults. To take an example, the prophet Tokeriu of Milne Bay (New Guinea) announced in 1893 a *true* New Year and a *true* feast of the dead which would introduce the new era of abundance. But before this a terrifying cataclysm—volcanic eruptions, earthquakes and floods—would destroy all infidels, that is, all those who had not joined the cult. After this catastrophe of cosmic proportions—in which one can recognize the exemplary image of the end of the World—the winds will suddenly change and bring good weather. The gardens will overflow with taro and yams, the trees will bow beneath their fruit, the dead will come in a ship to visit the living; and their arrival will usher in the era of abundance and blessedness. Adherents of the cult had to abstain from using objects of European origin.[1]

In 1929 and 1930, the myth of the Golden Age spread among the Baining of New Britain. An earthquake was to destroy all Europeans and unbelieving natives; the mountains would collapse into the valleys to give place to a great plain covered with gardens and orchards which would require no work; the dead, including pigs and dogs, would return to life.[2] The prophet Ronovuro of Espirito Santo announced in 1923 a deluge to be

[1]See Charles W. Abel, *Savage Life in New Guinea*, London, 1902, pp. 104-28, resumed by Lanternari, *op. cit.*, p. 45, and P. Worsley, *op. cit.*, pp. 51ff.
[2]P. Worsley, *op. cit.*, p. 90.

followed by the return of the dead in cargo-boats loaded with rice and other provisions.[1] Sometimes after many years the prophecies are considered to have been actually realized. The movement, known by the name of "Vailala Madness"—which first appeared in 1919 and declined towards 1923, to disappear completely in 1931—began to be considered by the natives, in 1934, as having literally fulfilled its prophecies. In fact in that year the natives claimed to remember quite clearly that the earth had trembled, the trees had tottered, and plants had flowered between one day and the next. They also remembered that the dead had come and gone away again during the night. Next day the marks of their European shoes and even their bicycles had been seen on the beach.[2] The prophecies are fulfilled backwards, in the past, but in the end they are fulfilled all the same.

In the Markham Valley (Morobe District) of New Guinea, a native called Marafi declared in 1933 that Satan had visited him and taken him into the bowels of the Earth to introduce him to the spirits of the dead who live there. The spirits told him that they would gladly return to Earth but that Satan prevented them. They added that if Marafi could convince the villagers that Satan was the Supreme Being, they might come back. It is to be noted that Marafi drew the logical conclusion of a revolt against the religious and political usurpation of the Whites; the true god of the new prophetic religion could only be Satan, the anti-god of the Whites. We have here of course, a figurative expression of the antagonism between Black and White, but also a condemnation of the historical and religious situation, of the fact that the Christianity of the Whites does not correspond to the spirit of the Gospels.

But, more significant still, is the announcement that the

[1] V. Lanternari, *Origine storiche dei culti profetici melanesiani*, p. 47.
[2] F. E. Williams, *The Vailala Madness in Retrospect*, in "Essays presented to C. G. Seligmann", London, 1934, pp. 369-79, pp. 373ff.; P. Worsley, *op. cit.*, pp. 90ff. See also Lanternari, p. 46.

return of the dead will be preceded by a cosmic catastrophe: an earthquake will overthrow everything, and then a rain of flaming kerosene will destroy the houses, gardens and all living things. Marafi therefore advised the building of a house big enough to shelter entire communities at the first sign of the cataclysm, that is to say when the earth began to shake. Next day they would find the dead already there loaded with gifts: tinned meat, tobacco, rice, clothing, lamps and guns. Henceforth the people would not have to work their gardens.[1]

The announcement of earthquakes and darkness preceding the arrival of the dead is a fairly widespread theme in Melanesian "cargo-cults". A familiar myth in the Dutch Indies announces that the return of the hero Mansren will usher in the Golden Age: in the place where he now lives (Indonesia or, according to some versions, Singapore or Holland) Mansren will plant a tree the top of which will touch the Sky (we recall the image of *axis mundi*); then the tree will lean towards the island of Miok Wundi, Mansren's birthplace, and a miraculous child called Konor will run up its trunk. The arrival of this *puer aeternus* will mark the beginning of the Golden Age; old men will become young, the sick will recover, and the dead will return to earth. There will be plenty of food, women, ornaments and arms. No one will be forced to work or pay taxes.[2]

In recent versions of the myth, the arrival of Mansren and the *puer aeternus* will radically alter not only the social situation, that is the mode of man's existence, but even the structure of the Cosmos. Yams, potatoes and other roots will grow on trees, while coconuts and other fruit will grow as roots. Sea creatures will become land creatures and vice versa. All these are figurative expressions of an absolute reversal of the forms and laws of the actual world; what is at present above will be below and vice versa. The whole Cosmos will be renewed; Heaven and Earth

[1]P. Worsley, *op. cit.*, p. 102.
[2]On the Mansren myth, see F. C. Kamma, *Messianic Movements in Western New Guinea*, "International Review of Missions", vol. 41, 1952, pp. 148-60·
P. Worsley, *op. cit.*, pp. 126ff.

will be destroyed and a new Heaven and a new Earth will be created in their place.[1]

The celebrated John Frum prophesied that Tana, one of the New Hebrides, would be flattened by a cataclysm; the volcanic mountains would crumble and fill the valleys, thus giving place to a fertile plain. (The crumbling of the mountains and levelling of the earth are an apocalyptic theme particularly frequent in India and the Near East.) Then the old will become young again, there will be no more sickness, no one will work in the gardens, the Whites will depart and John Frum will found schools to replace the mission-schools.[2]

In a wild region of New Guinea, discovered barely twenty years ago, the millenary myth has taken still more striking forms. There will be a Great Night, after which Jesus will come with the Ancestors and the merchandise. To be warned of their arrival, the natives erected bamboo trunks in the belief that they were putting up telegraph receivers. They also erected posts with steps cut in them to allow Jesus to descend to earth and themselves to mount to the Sky (once again we find the theme of the *axis mundi*). The graves were meticulously cleaned, and goods and arms destroyed. It had also been announced that black skins would become white and that all the White man's goods would pass to the Blacks. After the air battles between the Japanese and the Allies, the natives believed that a number of Ancestors would come in aeroplanes. The first airmen to land in these regions were received with great ceremony as the advance-guard of the Ancestors.[3]

[1]On these recent forms of the Mansren myth, see P. Worsley *op. cit.*, pp. 136-7.
[2]On John Frum's movement see Jean Guiart, *John Frum Movement in Tanna*, "Oceania", XXII, 1951, pp. 165-77; V. Lanternari, p. 44; P. Worsley *op. cit.*, pp. 152ff.
[3]R. M. Berndt, *A Cargo Movement in the East Central Highlands of New Guinea*, "Oceania", XXIII, 1952-3, pp. 40-65, 137-58, pp. 53ff., 60ff.; resumed in Worsley, *op. cit.*, pp. 199ff.

THE EXPECTATION OF THE DEAD AND RITUAL INITIATION

In all Melanesian "cargo-cults", the expectation of the catastrophe which will precede the Golden Age is marked by a series of actions expressing an absolute detachment from ordinary values and behaviour. Pigs and cows are massacred; all savings are spent in order to be done with European money, and coins are even thrown into the sea;[1] barns are built to store provisions; the cemeteries are tidied and planted with flowers, new paths are made,[2] men stop work in order to await the dead around the banquet tables.[3] In the John Frum movement a certain licence is allowed on the occasion of these collective feasts; Friday, the day on which the Golden Age will begin, is the holy day, and Saturday is spent in dancing and drinking *kava*. The young men and women live in a communal house; they bathe together by day and dance during the night.[4]

Divorced from their syncretist and Christian elements, all these Melanesian minor religions share the same central myth; the coming of the dead is taken as the sign of cosmic renewal. Now, we know that this is a fundamental religious idea of the Melanesians. The "cargo-cults" have merely resumed, amplified, revalorised and charged with prophetic and millenary power the traditional religious theme that the Cosmos renews itself periodically, or to be more exact that it is symbolically re-created every year. New Year's day is a replica of the cosmogony: a new World has just been born, a fresh, pure, rich world with all its potentialities intact and unworn by time; in other words the World as it was on the first day of Creation. This idea, which is,

[1] The John Frum movement, Worsley, *op. cit.*, p. 154; prophetic cult of Rambutjon Island, *Ibid.*; p. 188, etc.
[2] See P. Worsley, *op. cit.*, p. 118.
[3] See, among others, Worsley, *op. cit.*, pp. 84ff.
[4] See Jean Guiart, *John Frum Movement*, pp. 167ff.; P. Worsley, *op. cit.*, pp. 155ff.

by the way, very widespread, reveals the religious man's desire
to deliver himself from the weight of his past, to escape the work
of Time, and to begin his life again *ab ovo*.[1]

In Melanesia the great agricultural feast of the New Year
contains the following elements: the coming of the dead, the
prohibition of work, offerings on platforms for the enjoyment
of the dead or a banquet offered to spirits, in fact a collective
feast of an orgiastic kind.[2] In this lay-out for the great agricultural
New Year's feast it is easy to recognize the most characteristic
elements of the "cargo cults": expectation of the dead, enormous
holocaust of domestic animals, offerings to the spirits, orgiastic
rejoicings, and the refusal to work. Europeans were particularly
struck by the vast destruction of goods and the absolute stopping
of activity. To confine ourselves to one example, this is how
an Acting Resident Magistrate described his visit to one of the
regions of Papua infected by what was called Vailala Madness.
"They all sat motionless and not a word was uttered for the
several minutes that I stayed there looking at them. It was
enough to make anyone furious, to see them behaving in this
idiotic manner: a whole group of strong, well-built natives,
wearing new clean clothes and sitting in silence like stones or
tree-trunks in the full afternoon, instead of working or attending
to some job like reasonable beings. You would have said that
they were ripe for a lunatic asylum".[3]

It was difficult for a Westerner to understand this ritual
immobility: it was not just laziness but pure madness. And yet,
the natives were engaged in celebrating a rite: they were waiting
for the dead and were therefore forbidden to work. But now it
was not merely the return of the dead on New Year's day, and

[1]On all this, see *The Myth of the Eternal Return*.

[2]See V. Lanternari, *Origine storiche dei culti profetici melanesiani*, p. 46; *Id.*,
L'annua festa "Milamala" dei Trobriandesi: interpretazione psicologica e funzionale,
"Rivista di Antropologia", xlii, 1955, pp. 3-24 of the offprint. These pages
had already been written when the same author published his book, *La Grande
Festa. Storia del Cappodanno nella civiltà primitive*, Milan, 1959.

[3]*Papua, Annual Report*, 1919-20, appendix v, text reproduced by P. Worsley,
p. 84.

the annual renewal of the World; they were watching for what might be called the inauguration of a new cosmic era, the beginning of a Great Year. The dead would come back for good, never to leave the living again. The abolition of death, old age and sickness would destroy all differences between the living and the dead. This radical renewal of the world was practically the inauguration of Paradise. And therefore, as we have just seen, it was to be preceded by terrible cataclysms; earthquakes, floods, darkness, fiery rain, etc. This time there would be a total destruction of the old world, to allow of a new cosmogony, the inauguration of a new way of life: a paradisaical existence.

If so many "cargo-cults" assimilated millenarist Christian ideas, it is because the natives rediscovered in Christianity their old, traditional eschatological myth. The resurrection of the dead, proclaimed by Christianity, was a familiar idea to them. If the natives were disappointed by the missionaries, if the majority of "cargo-cults" ended by becoming anti-Christian, it was not because of Christianity itself, but because the missionaries and converts did not seem to behave like true Christians. The natives were frequently and tragically disappointed by their encounters with official Christianity. For what most attracted them to Christianity was precisely the proclamation of a radical renewal of the World, of the imminent coming of Christ and the resurrection of the dead; it was the prophetic and eschatological aspects of the Christian religion that woke the deepest echo in them. But these were just the aspects of Christianity that the missionaries and converts seemed to pass over and despise. The millenarist movements became wildly anti-Christian when their chiefs realized that the missionaries, who had indirectly inspired them, did not believe in the reality of the ships of the dead with their cargos of gifts; in fact did not believe in the imminence of the Kingdom, the resurrection of the dead and the inauguration of Paradise.

One of the most significant episodes in the conflict between the millenarist ideology of the "cargo-cults" and official Christianity is the misadventure of the famous Yali, a figure of the first importance in the prophetic movements of the Madang religion. I will end this account of the Melanesian millenary cults by telling his story. Yali had been drawn by the popular fervour into a millenarist movement which contained many features drawn from Christian eschatology. But in 1947 he was summoned to Port Moresby, the capital of Papua in New Guinea, to a meeting with certain high officials who were alarmed by his activities. While he was at Port Moresby, he learnt that the European Christians did not believe in the reality of the marvellous cargo-boat. A native showed him a book on evolution, and informed him that European Christians *really* believed in this theory. The information deeply disturbed Yali; he discovered that the Europeans believed they were descended from animals, in other words, shared the old totemist belief of his own tribe. Yali felt he had been deceived, became rabidly anti-Christian and returned to the religion of his ancestors.[1] He preferred to acknowledge his descent from one of his familiar totemic animals rather than from an obscure monkey who was said to have lived, far away from his island, in a fabulous geological era.

THE NEW YEAR AND THE RESTORATION OF THE WORLD AMONG THE CALIFORNIANS

The tribes of which we will now speak do not cultivate root crops or raise pigs like the Melanesians. They do not live in a tropical region but in a territory that lies between the North-West coast of California and the Klamath, Salmon and Trinity rivers. We are principally concerned with different branches of the Karuk, Hupa and Yurok tribes who practise not only agriculture but salmon fishing. The Hupa also gather acorns, which they grind to make a flour from which they make a sort of broth.

These tribes call their principal religious ceremony "the

[1] P. Lawrence, *The Madang District Cargo Cult*, "South Pacific", VIII, 1955, pp. 6-13; P. Worsley, *op. cit.*, pp. 216ff.

restoration of the World", the *repair* or the *fixing* of the World. They call them by the English name New Years, because, at least originally, this ceremony took place at the native New Year.[1] It is an annual ceremony, the purpose of which is to re-establish or stabilize the Earth for the coming year or two. The natives call this "putting props under the World". The fact that the ceremony is so arranged as to begin with the new moon also indicates the symbolism of renewal.[2] But all these ideas of renewal, restoration, repair, stabilization, etc., represent in the religious consciousness of the Californians the ritual repetition of the Creation of the World. In effect, the priest is supposed carefully to repeat the gestures and words of the "Immortals", that is to say, spirits who inhabited the World before humanity and left it or were turned into stones when the Californian tribes occupied their territories. Now, as we shall soon see, the "Immortals" really created the World in which the Californians were to establish themselves and, furthermore, they originated the customs and civil and religious institutions of that people.

The ceremonial is in two parts: the one esoteric, performed by the priest alone and in great secrecy, and the other public, the latter consisting of dancing and archery contests restricted to the young people. These public ceremonies contain a rich religious symbolism, but we can neglect them. The core of the esoteric rite consists of a story or dialogue relating the words of the Immortal Spirits. The recitation is accompanied by mimes symbolizing the actions of the Immortals in mythical times. All the rituals together amount to a presentation of the building of the Cosmos. The ceremonial house in which the dances take place is partially reconstructed or repaired, and this work symbolizes the restabilizing of the World. Among certain Yurok tribes, the restabilization of the World is effected by

[1]For all that follows, see A. L. Kroeber and E. W. Gifford, *World Renewal, a Cult System of Native North-West California*, "Anthropological Records", XIII, no. 1, University of California, Berkeley, 1949.
[2]Gifford in Kroeber and Gifford, p. 106.

the ritual reconstruction of the bath-hut.[1] There is no need to remind the reader that the cult-house constitutes an *imago mundi*. Among Amerindian tribes as far apart as the Kwakiutl and the Winebago, the cult-house represents the Universe and is called "Our World".[2]

A second ritual consists of the lighting of a new fire, the flames and smoke of which are tabu to the populace. As is well known, in many parts of the world the fire is put out on New Year's Eve to be ritually relighted on New Year's Day. The cosmogonic symbolism is obvious: the fireless nights represent the primordial night; the new fire signifies the appearance of a new World.[3] A third ritual consists of a long peregrination by the priest, who visits all the sacred sites, that is to say the places where the Immortals have performed certain actions. As we shall see, the itineraries followed not only faithfully imitate those of the Immortals but also imply the repetition of their actions in mythical times, actions which caused the World to take the form which it preserves to this day. Vigils performed by the priest in the bath-hut, prayers and benedictions also form part of the ceremonial. But one of its essential constituents is the ritual meal of salmon or acorn broth. This is a sacrifice of the firstfruits, for it gives the signal for the beginning of the salmon-fishing or the raising of the veto on the new nut harvest. After symbolically re-creating the Universe, the priest ceremoniously divides the firstfruit of the New Year.

[1]Kroeber, *op. cit.*, p. 5. In order not to overburden this essay, we will not dwell on the parallel beliefs found among other Amerindian tribes. For the symbolism of the repair of ritual huts among the Cheyenne, see Werner Mueller, *Die Religionen der Waldlandindianer Nordamerikas*, Berlin, 1956, pp. 306ff.

[2]See Werner Mueller, *Die blaue Hütte*, Wiesbaden, 1954, pp. 6off.; *Ibid.*, *Weltbild und Kult der Kwakiutl-Indianer*, Wiesbaden, 1955, pp. 17ff.

[3]A summary proof is to be found in my *The Myth of the Eternal Return*, p. 54 and pp. 67-9.

THE KARUK RITUAL

Variants can certainly be observed between the ceremonials performed by different tribes, but the outline of the scenario remains the same. To simplify our exposition we will follow the broad lines of the Karuk ritual.[1] The priest represents or rather incarnates the Immortals. This is stressed by his titles and by the tabus to which he is subject. He is called an "immortal person" or "spirit-person". During the ceremony—especially when he lights the fires and when he is eating—no one may look at him. Two or three months after the ceremony, the priest is still subject to certain tabus; for example, he must eat and speak sitting down, he must not drink, etc.

The essential rites are spread over ten or twelve days. The priest spends a certain number of hours in the bath-hut, fasting and praying. But it is the rites that he performs and the words that he speaks during his peregrination that are significant. A Karuk priest (of the Inam tribe) told Gifford, with plentiful details, all that he does and says in the course of his pilgrimage to the sacred sites.[2] He dives into a river and, swimming under water, he "thinks" a prayer. He comes out and thinks as he starts walking; "So the Immortals walked in mythical times". And he continues to pray for the well-being of the community. He comes to a place where there is a stone and slowly turns it round so as to make the World firmer; he goes to a sacred site and lights the fire. He starts sweeping and says, "The Immortal is sweeping for me. All those who are sick will now recover". He sweeps the edges of the World, to the east and the west. Then he climbs a mountain. He looks for a branch from which he makes a stick, saying as he does so: "The World is broken, but when I begin to drag this stick along the ground, all the

[1]Gifford in A. L. Kroeber and E. W. Gifford, *World Renewal*, pp. 6ff., 10ff., 19ff. and 48ff.
[2]Gifford, *op. cit.*, pp. 14-17. We shall closely follow this exciting document and partially translate the traditional words pronounced by the priest.

cracks will be filled and the Earth will be solid again". Here too he lights a fire and sweeps, as before, all the edges of the World.

He then goes down to the river. There he finds a stone which he firmly fixes, saying, "The Earth has been rocking. Now it shall be made firm again. The people will live (long) and will be stronger." Then he sits on the stone. "When I sit on the stone", he explained to Gifford, "the World will not rise up again or rock". This stone has been there since the time of the Immortals, that is to say since the beginning of the World. It was brought by Isivsanen, the divine Being whose name signifies "World, Universe".

On the sixth day the priest incarnates the most powerful of the Immortals (*ixkareya*), Astexewa wekareya. When he says anything, for example: "He who performed this work will live long and will not be ill", he adds, "Astexewa wekareya says this". When he chooses the place for the archery contest, he says: "It is Astexewa wekareya, myself, that chooses this place". He climbs the mountain again and lights a fire. He cuts down the weeds and prays: "The World is full of sickness. Astexewa wekareya cuts down the sicknesses in the World". He starts sweeping the place and says: "Now Astexewa wekareya is sweeping away all the sicknesses, everywhere in the World. My child will not be ill". (The expression "my child" covers all the children in the world.) He cuts a stick and places it on the ground, saying: "Astexewa wekareya places this stick. May everyone have better luck, and may there be no more sickness in the World. Game and fish shall be easier to catch and plentiful". When the fire goes out, he departs and repeats the same ceremony in another place, five or six kilometres further on.

In the evening the Fawn Dance takes place in camp. When the priest is about to light the fire someone shouts and everyone hides his face with a blanket or a branch. Some time later the priest throws water on the fire and jumps from a rock some feet high into the river. This is a signal that the spectators may uncover their faces. Next day the priest goes to the two fires lit on the mountain and carefully takes away the ashes.

The Karuk priest's ten days' journey was instituted by the Immortals. Each spot visited corresponds to a place where an Immortal disappeared after performing certain rites. The Immortals have decreed that the priest shall return each year, during the ceremony of the Renewal of the World and repeat exactly everything they did.

The Hupa agree with the Yurok and the Karuk, that a race of Immortals (*kixunai*) preceded man on earth, founded human institutions and established the ceremonies. The myths and formulas recited relate to the acts of the Immortals. Sacred stones, representing the Immortals who had not time to leave the earth before the coming of the humans, now form part of the platform facing the cult-hut.[1]

NEW YEAR AND COSMOGONY

The collection of rituals which we have just noticed forms a cosmogonic scenario. In mythical times the Immortals created the World in which the Californians were to live; they traced its boundaries, fixed its Centre and its resting places, assured an abundance of salmon and nuts and exorcised the sicknesses. But the present world is no longer the a-temporal and unchangeable Cosmos in which the Immortals lived. It is a living world, inhabited and worn down by beings of flesh and blood, subject to the laws of change, old age and death. Therefore it needs periodical repair, renewal and re-establishment. But the World can only be renewed by imitating what the Immortals did *in illo tempore*, by repeating the creation. That is why the priest follows the exemplary journey of the Immortals and repeats their deeds and words. In fact, the priest ends by incarnating the Immortals. In other words, on New Year's Day the Immortals are considered to be present on Earth again. This explains why the ritual of the annual renewal of the World is

[1]Gifford, following Goddard, *op. cit.*, pp. 58ff.

the most important religious ceremony of these Californian tribes. The World is not only restabilized and regenerated, but it is also sanctified by the symbolic presence of the Immortals. The priest who incarnates them becomes—for a certain period of time—an "immortal person", and as such must neither be looked at nor touched. He performs the rites away from men, in absolute solitude. For when the Immortals performed them for the first time, men did not yet exist on earth.

Symbolically then the World begins afresh at each New Year; the Immortals make it stable, healthy, rich and holy, as it was at the beginning of Time. This is why the priest proclaims that there will be no more illnesses or cataclysms, and that man will have abundant food. The raising of the veto on salmon fishing or on the new nut harvest allows men to consume the products of a Cosmos newly born. They eat exactly as the first human beings ate for the first time on Earth. For us moderns who have long ago lost the sense and experience of food as a sacrament, it is difficult to understand the religious value of the ritual meal of firstfruits. But let us try to imagine what the experience of touching, tasting, chewing and swallowing the *fruits of a new Cosmos*, still sanctified by the presence of the Immortals, can be for members of a traditional society. To open ourselves to such an experience we must think of a modern man's emotion on his first discovery of love, or his first journey in a distant and beautiful country, or on first seeing a work of art which will decide his artistic career. *For the first time*: that is everything; it is the key to the many rites and ceremonies aiming at the renovation of the World, the repetition of the cosmogony. One divines the profound desire to live each experience as it was lived for the first time, when it represented a sort of epiphany, the meeting with something powerful, significant, stimulating, a meeting that gives sense to the whole of existence.

The modern world has long lost the religious sense of physical work and the organic functions. Where they still survive their religious significances are threatened by the irresistible diffusion of techniques and ideologies of European origin. They can only be understood by taking into account traditional man's need periodically to rediscover the shock of initial experience; in other words to live the different phases of his existence as he lived them for the first time. Then all was new and significant and made a unit in a transcendental reality.

This need periodically to renew the Cosmos—the world in which one lives, the only world that *really* exists, *our* world,—is found in all traditional societies. Of course the expression varies from one society to another, according to the peculiar structure of each culture, and is conditioned by the particular historical inheritance. For example, to limit ourselves to the two types of society that we have just analyzed, the Melanesians and North-West Californians, the differences in religious ideology and behaviour are too noticeable to pass unobserved. With the Melanesians, it is the dead and the mythical Ancestors who return during the great agricultural feast of the New Year. With the Californians there is a symbolic return of the Immortals. In Melanesia, as among agricultural societies generally, the periodical return of the dead occasions collective rejoicings of an orgiastic kind. And as we have seen, the dramatic tension of waiting for the dead, a syndrome for the radical renewal of the World, is capable of giving rise to prophetic and millenarist movements. The religious universe of the North-Western Californians is quite different. Here we are dealing with a closed and perfect world, constructed as one might say geometrically by the Immortals and re-created annually in the person of the priest, with his solitary pilgrimages, meditations and prayers. And comparative analysis will reveal other more or less radical differences.

Despite these differences, one recognizes in the two types of society a body of ritual and religious ideology homologous in structure. In both the Cosmos must be re-created and Time periodically regenerated, and the cosmogonical scenario by means of which the renewal is effected is connected with the new harvest and the sacramentalization of food.

PERIODICAL REGENERATION OF THE WORLD

The need for a periodical regeneration of the Cosmos seems to
have been felt by all archaic and traditional societies, for it is
found everywhere.[1] The periodicity may be annual, either in
relation to the initiation ceremonies—as in Australia[2]—or to
chance events: the threat to a harvest in Fiji, or the consecration
of a king, as in Vedic India. Some, at least, of these periodical
ceremonies must originally have been New Year festivities or
have been modelled on them. For the cosmic regeneration *par
excellence*, the exemplary pattern of all renewal is the New Year's
feast. The Year represents the perfect cycle, the exemplary
image of an unbroken spatio-temporal unity.

The ritual scenario of the New Year receives its richest
development in the agricultural and urban societies of the Near
East, where the calendar has been laboriously elaborated. Here
one finds the dramatic and orgiastic elements that characterize
the annual feasts of agricultural societies. The repetition of the
cosmogony involves a ritual battle between two groups of men,
as among the Mesopotamians, the Hittites and the Egyptians:
this, as is well known, is the re-enactment of the fight between
Marduk and the sea monster Tiamat, or between Tesup and the
serpent Illuyankas, or between Re and the serpent Apophis—
a fight which took place *in illo tempore* and which, by the final
victory of the god, put an end to Chaos.

In other words, on the occasion of the New Year's feasts,
the transition from Chaos to Cosmos is re-enacted; the cosmogony
is repeated in the present. In Mesopotamia, the New Year ceremony (*akitu*) also included the *zakmuk*, the "feast of lots", so
called because lots were drawn for each month in the year; because
the twelve future months were then *created*. A whole series of
rites was added to these: the descent of Marduk into Hell, the

[1]See *The Myth of the Eternal Return, passim.*
[2]See *Birth and Rebirth: The Religious Meanings of Initiations in Human Culture,*
pp. 18ff.

humiliation of the King, the expulsion of evils by means of a scapegoat, and finally the sacred marriage of the god with Sarpanitu—an action reproduced by the king and a hierodule in the goddess's chamber as a signal for a period of universal orgy. Here we find a symbolic return to Chaos (supremacy of Tiamat, "confusion of forms", orgy) followed by a new creation (victory of Marduk, fixing of fates, hierogamy, new birth).[1]

The ritual repetition of the cosmogony which follows the symbolic destruction of the old world regenerates Time in its entirety. The aim is to begin a new life in the midst of a new Creation. The need for the total regeneration of time (to be realized by the annual repetition of the cosmogony) has also been preserved in Iranian traditions. A Pahlavi text says that "In the month of Fravardin, on the day Xurdhath, the lord Ormazd will produce the resurrection and the 'second body', and the world will be saved from impotence with the demons, the *drugs*, etc. And there will be abundance everywhere; there will be no more lack of food; the world will be pure, and man freed from the opposition [of the evil spirit] and immortal for ever". Qazwini says that "on the day of the New Year God raised the dead", and he "gave them back their souls and commanded the Sky to rain on them that day; and this is why the people have adopted the custom of pouring water on that day". The close connection between ideas of "creation by water" (aquatic cosmogony; deluge that periodically regenerates historic life; rain) and birth and resurrection is confirmed by this phrase from the Talmud: "God has three keys: of rain, of birth, of the raising of the dead".[2]

According to the tradition transmitted by Dimasqi, on the day of Nauruz, the New Year, the king proclaimed: "Here is a new day of a new month of a new year; what time has wasted must be renewed". It is on this day too that the fate of man is fixed for a whole year. Purifications by water and libations were performed to ensure abundant rains for the coming year.

[1]See *The Myth of the Eternal Return*, pp. 51ff.
[2]See references in *The Myth of the Eternal Return*, pp. 62ff.

Moreover, at the time of the Great Nawroz everyone sowed seven kinds of seed in a jar, and from their growth drew conclusions about the coming year's crops. This custom is similar to the "fixing of fates" at the Babylonian New Year that has come down to our own times in the New Year's ceremonies of the Mandaeans and the Yezidis. It is also because the New Year repeats the cosmogonic act that the twelve days between Christmas and Epiphany are still regarded today as a prefiguration of the twelve months of the year. European peasants determine the temperature and rainfall of each of the coming months by the "meteorological signs" of these twelve days. Among the Indians of the Vedic era the twelve days of midwinter were an image and replica of the whole year (*Rig Veda*, IV, 33), and the same belief is to be found in ancient China.[1]

It can be seen that in agricultural and urban societies, the scenario of the New Year contains a series of dramatic elements, of which the most important are: the repetition of the cosmogony by the symbolical return of Chaos, orgiastic confusion and ritual battles ending in the final victory of God; the driving out of sin and the return of the dead; new fire; the regeneration of Time by the "creation" of the twelve future months and the "determining" of the crops, etc. There is no need to remark that this scenario is nowhere to be found in a complete form; each culture has developed certain elements, while neglecting or not knowing others. But the fundamental theme, that is to say the regeneration of the Cosmos by the repetition of the cosmogony, is to be found everywhere. Let us add that it is in the cultural context of the ancient Near East, particularly in the tension between the religious and political ideologies belonging to agricultural, urban and pastoral peoples, that the prophetic, messianic and millenarist movements of the ancient world afterwards crystallized. The eschatology, the expectation of a Saviour—historic or cosmic—and the belief in the resurrection of the dead have their deep roots in the religious experience of the universal *renovatio* or renewal of Time.

See *The Myth of the Eternal Return*, pp. 65ff.

THE ROMAN LUDI; THE ASHVAMEDHA

As we have already said, in certain societies regeneration, although periodic, is not connected with the New Year's festivals. We have alluded to the cosmic renewal effected on the occasion of certain Australian initiatory rites. Another example of periodicity, independent of the New Year scenario, is that of the Roman ritual games. According to A. Piganiol, the principal purpose of the games was to maintain a sacred energy with which the life of Nature, a human group or an important personage was connected. Ritual games constituted an exemplary means of rejuvenating both the World and the gods, the dead and the living.[1] Among the principal occasions on which the *ludi* were performed were the anniversaries of the agricultural gods (in this case the feasts were seasonal cere-monies[2]), the anniversaries of illustrious living men (and then the ceremonies were performed *pro salute*), the anniversaries of victories (in order to renew the divine strength that had provided the victory), or the inauguration of a new period (in this case, "the purpose of the games was to assure the renewal of the world until the next celebration")[3].

But it is in Vedic India that the mechanism which allows the ritual scenario of the New Year to be moveable can best be understood. The *ashvamedha*, the famous Indian horse-ṣacrifice of Vedic times, was performed either to guarantee the fertility of the Cosmos, or for the purging of sins, or to assure sovereignty over the Universe. But it is probable that the *ashvamedha* was originally a spring festival, or, more exactly, a ritual celebrated on the occasion of the New Year.[4] Its structure contains cosmo-gonic elements.[5] The Rig Vedic and Brahman texts stress the

[1] A. Piganiol, *Recherches sur les jeux romains*, Strasbourg-Paris, 1923, p. 149.
[2] A. Piganiol, *op. cit.*, pp. 145ff.   [3] *Ibid.*, p. 148.
[4] See C. D. d'Onofrio, Le *"nozze sacre" della regina col cavallo*, "Studi e Materiali delle Religioni", XXIV-XXV, 1953-4, pp. 133-62, p. 143.
[5] See *Traité d'Histoire des Religions*, p. 92.

relationships between the horse and the Waters. It is well-known that in India the Waters are the cosmogonic substance *par excellence:* the successive Universes are born from the Waters. The Waters symbolize the seed, the potentialities; in fact all the creative possibilities. And, as we have just seen, the principal aim of the *ashvamedha* was the fecundity of the Universe. The symbolic union between the horse, now sacrificed, and the queen, *mahisi*, represents an archaic fertility rite. The obscene dialogue accompanying it reveals the great age and popular character of the ceremony.[1] But this is clearly a ritual designed to regenerate the whole Cosmos and restore all social classes and trades to their exemplary state of perfection. During the sacrifice a priest, the *adhvaryu*, recites: "May the Brahman be born in sanctity, full of the light of sanctity! May the prince be born in royal majesty, hero, archer, warrior, with the strong bow and invincible chariots! May the cow be born rich with milk, the oxen strong, the horse swift, the women fruitful, the soldiers victorious and the young men eloquent! May he who makes this sacrifice have a hero for son! May Parjyana give us at all times the rain we want! May the corn ripen plentifully for us! May our work and our rest be blessed!"[2]

THE CONSECRATION OF THE INDIAN KING

The wish to regenerate the Cosmos by the symbolic repetition of the cosmogony can also be discovered in the consecration of the Indian king, the *rajasuya*. The central ceremonies took place about the New Year. The anointing was preceded by a year of consecratory ceremonies (*diksa*), and generally followed by another year of closing ceremonies. The *rajasuya* is probably an abbreviated version of a series of annual ceremonies intended to restore the Universe.[1] The king had a central role, for in the

---

[1] On the obscene elements see P.-E. Dumont, *L'Ashvamedha*, Paris, 1927, pp. vi, xii, 276ff.

[2] *Vajasaneyi Samhita*, XXII, 22, transl. H. Oldenberg—V. Henry in *La religion du Véda*, Paris, 1903, p. 316.

character of the sacrificer *shrauta*, he in some manner embodied the Cosmos.[1]

Hocart had already revealed the structural identity between the consecration of an Indian king and the cosmogony.[2] The various stages of the ritual enacted, successively, the return of the future sovereign to the embryonic state, his gestation of a year, and his mystical rebirth as Cosmocrator, identified both with Prajapati and the Cosmos. The future sovereign's embryonic period corresponded to the process of the ripening of the Universe and was, in all probability, originally related to the ripening of the crops.[3] The ritual return to the pre-natal stage brings about the annihilation of the individual. The operation is extremely dangerous. For this reason these special ceremonies are intended to ward off the powers of evil (Nirrti, Rudra, etc.) and to liberate the king in time from the membranes of the embryo.[4] The second phase of the ritual achieves the formation of the sovereign's new body: a symbolic body obtained by the king's mystical marriage either with the Brahmin caste or with the people, which allows him to be born from their womb, as a consequence of the union of the male and female waters, or of gold—signifying fire—with water.[5]

The third phase of the *rajasuya* consists of a series of rites, as a result of which the king acquires sovereignty over the three worlds, that is to say, at the same time incarnates the Cosmos and establishes himself as Cosmocrator. The central ceremony comprises several acts. The king raises his arms, and this gesture has a cosmogonic significance: it symbolizes the setting up of the *axis mundi*. When he receives consecration, the king stands on

[1] See J. C. Heesterman, *The Ancient Indian Royal Consecration*, The Hague, 1957, p. 7.

[2] A. M. Hocart, *Kingship*, Oxford, 1927, pp. 189ff.; see *Traité d'Histoire des Religions*, p. 345. On the mystical transformation of the sacrificer into the Universe, see the texts cited by Heesterman, pp. 10, 29, etc.

[3] J. C. Heesterman, *op. cit.*, p. 67.   [4] *Ibid.*, pp. 61, 17ff.

[5] See the texts and comments in Heesterman: union of male and female waters, pp. 86ff.; marriage with the people, pp. 52ff.; marriage with the Brahmin caste, pp. 56, 78; conception by the purification of water by gold, p. 87.

the throne with his arms raised, thus incarnating the cosmic axis fixed in the navel of the Earth—that is the throne, the Centre of the World—and touching the Sky.[1] The asperging is connected with the Waters that descend from the Sky along the *axis mundi*—that is to say the King—to fertilize the Earth. Then the king takes a step towards each of the four cardinal points and symbolically mounts to the zenith. As a result of these rites the king acquires sovereignty over the four directions of space and the seasons; in other words, he becomes master of the whole spatio-temporal Universe.[2]

In historical times the *rajasuya* was only performed twice; the first time to consecrate the king, and the second to assure his sovereignty over the Universe. But in protohistoric times the *rajasuya* was probably annual and was performed to regenerate the Cosmos. It is related in structure to that class of Indian seasonal festivities called *utsava*.[3] It is also probable that in ancient times the people took a more important part in it.

It is plain by what mechanism the cosmogonic scenario of the New Year can be introduced into the consecration of a king; the two ritual systems pursue the same end: cosmic renovation. It is true that the return to the origin and, consequently, the symbolic repetition of the cosmogony are implicit also in other rituals. For, as I have had occasion to show in the Eranos lecture of 1956, the cosmogonic myth is the exemplary model of all creation.[4] But the *renovatio* accomplished on the occasion of a king's consecration has had considerable conse-

[1] The essential texts are commented on by Heesterman, pp. 102ff. On the symbolism of the throne as the "world's navel" (Centre of the World) see J. Auboyer, *Le trône et son symbolisme dans l'Inde ancienne*, Paris, 1949, pp. 79ff. See also J. Gonda, *Aspects of Early Vishnuism*, Utrecht, 1954, pp. 84ff. On the symbolism of the Centre, see *Images and Symbols*, London, 1961, pp. 27-56.
[2] J. C. Heesterman, pp. 101ff.
[3] On this type of seasonal festivity, see J. Gonda, *Skt. "utsava"-festival*, "India Antiqua", Leyden, 1947, pp. 146-55.

See M. Eliade, *La vertu créatrice du mythe*, "Eranos-Jahrbuch", xxv, 1956, p. 59-85.

quences in the later history of mankind. On the one side, the renewal ceremonies become moveable, detaching themselves from the rigid framework of the calendar; on the other, the king becomes in some manner responsible for the stability, fruitfulness and prosperity of the entire Cosmos. This amounts to saying that universal renewal is no longer connected with the cosmic rhythms, but with historical persons and events.

REGENERATION AND ESCHATOLOGY

This conception is found to be the source of future eschatologies, historical and political, In fact, at a later date men came to expect the cosmic renovation or "salvation" of the World from the appearance of a certain kind of King, Hero, Saviour or even political leader. Although in a strongly secularised form, the modern world still preserves the eschatological hope of a universal *renovatio*, to be effected by the victory of a social class, or even a political party or personage. The Marxist myth of a golden age, to be introduced by the final triumph of the proletariat, constitutes the most detailed and dazzling of all modern political eschatologies. According to Marx, the classless society of the future will put an end to all the conflicts and tensions which have characterized the history of humanity from its beginnings. There will be no more history in the true sense of the word, but a sort of earthly paradise, for man will finally be free and will eat when he is hungry, performing the minimum of work since the machines invented by scientists will look after the rest.

It is touching and significant to find at the end of our journey almost the same paradisaical syndrome that we discovered in the millenarist movements of Melanesia: plenty of food, absolute liberty, abolition of the need to work. All that is missing is the motif of the return of the dead and of immortality. But the fundamental theme is there, though emptied of its religious and eschatological significances. Of course, the cultural context is

quite different. In nineteenth-century Europe, we find societies
that are not only extremely complex but radically secularized.
Marx was at pains to charge the proletariat with a soteriological
mission, but, as was to be expected, he did not employ religious
language; he spoke of the *historical* function of the proletariat.
The argument of dialectical materialism perfectly agrees with
the general orientation of the scientific spirit in the nineteenth
century. Marx does not even trouble to "desacramentalize"
physiological processes and economic values. In themselves they
provide enough evidence, which everyone accepts. And this is
enough clearly to distinguish traditional from modern societies.
For the men of traditional societies consider the physiological
operations—nourishment and sexuality in the first place—as
mysteries also, while modern man reduces them to organic
processes.

This raises the problem of the "true" significance of all the
myths and rites which we have just been examining. As may
have been noticed, preoccupation with crops, game or fish—
in fact with everyday nourishment—can be seen in almost all
the various scenarios for the periodical renewal of the World.
One might therefore be tempted to wonder whether, after all,
we are not faced with a great spiritual mystification which should
be reduced to its true proportions, that is to say to its primary
economic and social, perhaps even physiological causes. There
is, as everyone knows, the convenient but naïve method by
which a spiritual phenomenon is reduced to its "origin", that
is to say to its material basis.[1] This is the famous demystification
which is also used by Marxist writers. But this argument of
the European scientific spirit is, in itself, the consequence of an
existential decision by modern man and, therefore, forms an
integral part of the recent history of the Western world. It is
not, as was believed in the nineteenth century, the universally
valid reasoning of the spirit, the only argument acceptable to
homo sapiens. The explanation of the world by a series of reduc-
tions has an aim in view: to rid the world of extra-mundane

[1]See *Myths, Dreams and Mysteries*, pp. 120ff.

values. It is a systematic banalization of the World undertaken for the purpose of conquering and mastering it. But the conquest of the World is not—in any case was not till half a century ago—the purpose of all human societies. It is an idiosyncracy of Western man. Other societies pursue different aims: to understand the mystery of the World in order to live as the World "lives", that is to say by perpetually renewing itself. It is the meaning of human existence that matters, and this meaning is of a spiritual order.

If there is a mystification, it is not among the primitives who see the exemplary model of their existence in the cosmic rhythms, but among modern materialists who believe that the cosmic rhythms can ultimately be reduced to the periodicity of the crops. For the men of traditional societies are tragically aware of the fact that in order to live a man must eat; no mystification on his part concerning the necessity of making sure of his food each day. The misunderstanding arises once it is forgotten that nourishment is not a physiological activity but a *human* one, since it is charged with symbolism. Nourishment, as a purely physiological act or economic activity, is an abstraction. To feed oneself is a cultural action, not an organic process. Even at the stage of earliest infancy the baby behaves towards his food as towards a symbolic world.

As for the men of traditional societies, the value they place on their food is part and parcel of their total behaviour towards the Cosmos. By means of his food, man participates in a higher reality; he eats something that is rich, strong and confers prestige; which was created by the Supernatural Beings or even—in certain cases—is the substance of those Beings; which is, in any case, the product of a mystery (for all periodical regeneration of an animal or vegetable species, like all crops, depends on a "mystery", a mythico-ritual scenario revealed to men by the Gods *in illo tempore*). Furthermore, food does not serve only as nourishment, it also provides reserves of magico-religious force, or confers prestige and, in this sense, is a sign of an individual's social status or fate—his "luck"—in the cosmic round.

A whole series of religious relationships between man and the Cosmos can be deduced from the acts by which he seeks, obtains or produces his food. For the religious man, to *exist* necessarily means to have a place in the *real* Cosmos—that is to say a Cosmos that is alive, strong, fruitful and capable of periodical renewal. But as we have seen to renew the World is equivalent to *reconsecrating* it, to making it again as it was *in principio*, and sometimes this reconsecration has the value of a return to the paradisaical stage of the World. This means that traditional man felt the need of existing in a rich and significant Cosmos; rich not only in food (for it was not always so) but also in significance. In the final instance, this Cosmos reveals itself in a cipher; it "speaks", it transmits its message by its formation, its states of being, its rhythms.[1] Man "hears"—or "reads"—these messages and consequently behaves towards the Cosmos as towards a coherent system of significances. Now this cipher of the Cosmos, when correctly interpreted, concerns para-cosmic realities.

This is the reason why the periodical renewal of the World has been the most frequent mythico-ritual scenario in the religious history of humanity. Indeed, it has been indefatigably reinterpreted and revaluated, continually integrated in many and various cultural contexts. Not only monarchic ideologies but different types of messianic and millenarist beliefs and, in modern times, movements of national liberation among colonial peoples, have depended more or less directly on this old religious belief: that the Cosmos may be renewed *ab integro*, and that this renovation involves not only the "salvation" of the World, but also the return of the paradisaical stage of existence, characterized by an abundance of food obtained without toil. Man once felt himself mystically at one with the Cosmos and knew that the Cosmos renews itself periodically; but he knew also that the renewal may be effected by the ritual repetition of the cosmogony, performed either annually (scenario of the New Year), or on the occasion of cosmic crises (drought, epidemics, etc.);

[1]On the "cipher" of the World, see ch. v.

or of historical events (installation of a new king, etc.). In the final instance, the religious man comes to *feel himself responsible for the renewal of the World*. And it is in this responsibility of a religious order that one must look for the origins of all forms of politics, both "classical" and "millenarist".

IV

Ropes and Puppets

THE "ROPE-TRICK"

Ashvagosha relates in his poem *Buddhacarita* (XIX, 12-13) that when the Buddha visited his birthplace, Kapilavastu, for the first time after his illumination, he demonstrated some "miraculous powers" (*siddhi*). In order to convince his people of his spiritual strength and prepare them for conversion, he raised himself in the air and cut his body into pieces, which he dropped to the ground and then joined together again beneath the astonished eyes of the spectators.[1] This miracle forms so intimate a part of the tradition of Indian magic that it has become the typical prodigy of fakirism. The celebrated "rope-trick" of the fakirs and conjurers creates the illusion that a rope rises very high in the sky, and the master makes his pupil climb it until he disappears from view. The fakir then throws his knife into the air and the young man's limbs fall, one after another, to the ground.

The *Suruci-Jataka* (no. 498) relates that in order to make King Suruci's son laugh, a conjurer magically created a mango-tree[2] and threw a ball of thread very high in the air, so that one end caught on one of the branches. Climbing up the thread, the conjurer disappeared at the top of the tree. His limbs fell to the ground, but a second conjurer put them together again, sprinkled them with water—and the man came to life.[3]

[1] See *Shamanism*, pp. 428ff.; *Yoga*, pp. 321ff.
[2] The Sanspareil mango is identical with the "central mango" of King Vessavana, which another Jataka (no. 281) represents as an *axis mundi*; see *Jataka*, Pali text II, pp. 397ff.; transl. Fausboll, II, p. 271.
[3] Pali text, IV, p. 324; transl. IV, p. 204.

The rope-trick must have been very well-known in eighth- and ninth-century India, for Gaudapada and Shankara use it as an example to illustrate the illusions created by *maya*.[1] In the fourteenth century, Ibn Batutah claims to have witnessed the trick at the court of the Indian king. The emperor Jahangir describes a similar spectacle in his *Memoirs*. Since the time of Alexander at least, India was considered the true home of magic, and travellers were credited with having seen one or more typically fakiric miracles. A mystic of the importance of Al Hallaj found room for a number of anecdotes from which it is clear that he went to India in order to learn white magic, "so that he might draw men to God". L. Massignon summarizes and translates a tale preserved in the *Kitab al Oyoun*, according to which when Al Hallaj reached India he "sought information about a woman, went to look for her, and talked to her. She put him off till next day. Then she went out with him to the seashore with a twisted thread tied in knots like a ladder. Then the woman said some words and climbed the thread; it supported her feet, and she mounted so high that she disappeared from our view. And Al Hallaj turned to me and said: 'It is for this woman that I came to India' ".[2]

It is impossible to examine here the voluminous records of the rope-trick in India ancient and modern. Yule and H. Cordier collected a certain number of cases in the Anglo-Indian press of the nineteenth century.[3] R. Schmidt, A. Jacoby and A. Lehmann have enriched the files and added a number of cases from outside India.[4] It is to be found in China, in the Dutch East Indies, in Ireland and in ancient Mexico. Here is a description by Ibn

[1] H. von Glasenapp, *La philosophie indienne*, transl. A. M. Esnoul, Paris, 1951, pp. 152 and 369, note 36.
[2] L. Massignon, *Al Hallaj, martyr mystique de l'Islam*, Paris, 1922, I, pp. 80-3.
[3] Sir Henry Yule and H. Cordier, *The Book of Ser Marco Polo*, London, 1921, I, pp. 316ff.
[4] R. Schmidt, *Fakire und Fakirtum im alten und modernen Indien*, Berlin, 1908, pp. 167ff.; A Jacoby, *Zum Zerstückelung und Wiederbelebungswunder der indischen Fakire*, "Archiv f. Religionswissenschaft", XVII, 1914, pp. 455-75, especially pp. 460ff.; A. Lehmann, *Einige Bemerkungen zu indische Gaukler-Kunststücken*,

Batutah of a séance in which he took part in China. The conjurer "took a wooden ball with several holes in it, through which long ropes were passed. He threw it into the air, and it mounted so high that we completely lost sight of it . . . When only a short end of the rope remained in the conjurer's hands, he ordered one of his pupils to catch hold of it and climb, which he did until he was out of sight. The conjurer called him three times and received no answer; then, as if in a great rage, he snatched up a knife, seized hold of the rope and disappeared also. After a while he threw down one of the boy's hands, tnen a foot, then the other hand, then the other foot, the body and the head. He came down, puffing and blowing, with bloodstains on his clothes . . . The Emir gave him some order, the man picked up the boy's limbs, laid them together—and the boy got up and stood before us! All this greatly astonished me. My heart beat fast, just as it had done when I saw something similar at the court of the Indian king . . ."[1]

In the seventeenth century the Dutch traveller Ed. Melton claimed to have witnessed a similar spectacle at Batavia, but here the performers were a band of Chinese conjurers.[2] Nearly identical stories are narrated by several Dutch travellers in the seventeenth and eighteenth centuries.[3]

Strange to say, the rope-trick is also recorded in Irish folklore. The most widespread story is to be found in the collection translated by S. H. O'Grady.[4] The conjurer throws a silk thread in the air and it catches on a cloud. Up this thread he sends a

---

"Jahrbuch d. Museums f. Völkerkunde zu Leipzig", XI, 1952, pp. 48-63, especially 51-9.

[1] C. Defrémery and Dr. B. R. Sanguinetti, *Voyages d'Ibn Batoutah*, Arabic text with French translation, Paris, Société Asiatique, 1822, vol. IV, pp. 291-2. We have already quoted this passage in *Shamanism*, p. 429, note 3 and *Yoga*, p. 322.

[2] Yule and Cordier, *op. cit.*, p. 316; A. Jacoby, *op. cit.*, pp. 460-2, quoting E. D. Hauber, *Biblioteca, acta et scripta magica*, 1740, pp. 114ff.

[3] Jacoby, *Ibid.*, pp. 462-3.

[4] *Silva Gadelica*, London, 1892, vol. II, pp. 321-2; Jacoby, *op. cit.*, p. 470 quotes a variant taken from *Erin, Eine Sammlung irischer Erzählungen*, VI, pp. 130ff.

rabbit followed by a dog (let us recall that the conjurer described by Jahangir in his *Memoirs* had sent a dog, a pig, a panther, a lion and a tiger, one after another, up his chain.[1]) Then he sends a young man and a girl: all disappear in the cloud. A little later on, finding that because of the lad's carelessness the dog has eaten the rabbit, the conjurer also climbs the rope. He cuts off the young man's head, but at the king's request puts it back and brings the boy back to life.

Legends containing, together or separately, the two characteristic themes of the rope-trick have been found in various parts of Europe.[2] These themes are: (1) that magicians cut up either their own limbs or someone else's, and afterwards put them together again; and (2) that conjurers, male or female, climb ropes and disappear into the air. The second motif will be dealt with later. All these European legends belong to a world of magicians; those of the first type are probably of learned origin. This is how the magician Johann Philadelphia appeared at Göttingen in 1777. He was cut in pieces and put in a barrel. But the barrel was opened too soon, and all that was found in it was an embryo that had not had time to evolve. Therefore the magician never came back to life. In the Middle Ages a similar story was told of Virgil, and Paracelsus collected tales of the same kind in the Siebengebirge.[3] In his *Disquisitiones magicae* (1599), Debrios relates that the magician Zedechia the Jew, who lived in the time of Louis the Simple, used to throw

[1] *Memoirs of the Emperor Jahangir*, p. 102, quoted by Yule and Cordier, p. 318; "They produced a chain of 50 cubits in length; and in my presence threw one of its ends towards the sky, where it remained as if fastened to something in the air. A dog was then brought forward, and being placed at the lower end of the chain, immediately ran up, and reaching the other end, immediately disappeared in the air. In the same manner a hog, a panther, a lion, a tiger, were successively sent up the chain, and all equally disappeared at the upper end of the chain. At last they took down the chain and put it into a bag, no one ever discovering in what way the different animals were made to vanish into the air in the mysterious manner above described."

[2] See the examples collected by Jacoby, pp. 466-7, 472-3.

[3] Jacoby, p. 464. On the legends collected by Paracelsus, see W. Mannhardt, *Germanische Mythen*, pp. 64ff.

men in the air, cut up their limbs and put them together again.[1]
Let us note in passing that Sahagun reports happenings of the
same kind among the Huastecs of Mexico. They concern a class
of magicians called *motetequi*, literally "those who cut themselves". The *motetequi* used to cut himself in pieces, which he
covered up; he then went under the cover and emerged almost
immediately, showing not even the slightest wound.[2] Jahangir
had witnessed the same procedure among the conjurers of
Bengal: the man cut into pieces was covered with a cloth; a
conjurer got under the cloth and, the next moment, the man
jumped to his feet.[3]

HYPOTHESES

There have been attempts to explain the rope-trick either as
collective suggestion, or the extraordinary sleight-of-hand of the
conjurers.[4] But A. Jacoby had drawn attention to the fabulous,
saga-like character of the majority of parallel European stories.[5]
But whichever explanation is advanced, suggestion or sleight-of-
hand, the problem of the rope-trick does not seem to us yet to
have been solved. Why was this sort of conjuring invented?
Why was precisely this scenario chosen—the climbing of a rope,
and dismemberment of the pupil followed by his resurrection—
to be imposed by suggestion or auto-suggestion on the audience's
imagination? In other words, the rope-trick in its present form,
of imaginative scenario, fabulous tale, or conjuring trick, has
a *history*, and this history can only be elucidated by taking into
account the religious rites, symbols and beliefs of archaic peoples.

Two elements must be distinguished: (1) the dismemberment

[1]Jacoby, pp. 464-5.
[2]Eduard Seler, *Zauberei in alten Mexico*, "Globus", vol. 78, 1900, pp. 89-91,
printed in *Gesammelte Abhandlungen zur Amerikanischen Sprach-una Altertum-
skunde*, II, Berlin, 1904, pp. 78-86, especially p. 85.
[3]*Memoirs of the Emperor Jahangir*, p. 99, quoted by Yule and Cordier, p. 318.
[4]A. Lehmann, in the article quoted, rejects the hypothesis of suggestion and
explains the rope-trick as sleight-of-hand.
[5]*Op. cit.*, pp. 464-74 and *passim*.

of the pupil, (2) the ascent into the sky by means of a rope. These are two characteristics of shamanic rites and ideology. Let us start by analyzing the first theme. We know that during initiatory dreams, apprentice shamans witness their own dismemberment by the "spirits" or "demons" who play the part of initiatory masters: their heads are cut off, their bodies are chopped to pieces, their bones are cleaned, etc., and in the end the demons "gather together" the bones and cover them with new flesh.[1] Here we find ecstatic experiences of an initiatory type: a symbolic death is followed by a renewal of the organs and the resurrection of the initiate. It is worth remembering that visions and experiences of the same kind are current among the Australians, Esquimos, and some American and African tribes,[2] which means that we have here an extremely archaic initiatory technique. Now it is remarkable that a Tantric Himalayan rite, the *tchod*, also contains the symbolic dismemberment of the neophyte: he witnesses his decapitation and tearing to pieces by the *dakinis* or other demons.[3] One can therefore consider the dismemberment of the pupil and his resurrection by the fakir as a shamanic initiation scenario almost entirely desacramentalized.

As for the second shamanic element that we have recognized in the rope-trick: the ascent to Heaven by means of a rope, this presents a more complex problem. There is, on the one hand, the archaic and extremely widespread myth of the tree, the rope, the mountain, and the ladder or bridge which at the beginning of Time connected the Sky with the Earth and assured communication between the world of the Gods and mankind. Owing to a crime of the mythical Ancestor, this communication was broken off; the tree, rope or liana has been cut down.[4] This myth is not limited to the countries dominated by Shamanism in the strict sense, but plays a considerable part in the mythologies and the ecstatic rituals of the Shamans.

[1] See *Shamanism*, pp. 428ff., also H. Findeisen, *Schamanentum*, Stuttgart, 1957, pp. 50ff.
[2] See *Shamanism*, pp. 53ff.   [3] See *Shamanism*, p. 437; *Yoga*, pp. 318ff.
[4] See *Shamanism*, pp. 482ff.; *Myths, Dreams, and Mysteries*, pp. 59ff.

TIBETAN MYTHS OF THE COSMIC ROPE

The myth of the staircase or rope that connected Heaven to Earth is very well-known in India and Tibet. The Buddha came down from the *Trayastrimsh* Heaven by a staircase to "clear a path for humankind": from the top of the staircase all the Brahmalokas could be seen above, and the depths of Hell below, for the staircase was a true *axis mundi* standing at the Centre of the Universe.[1] This miraculous staircase is represented in the reliefs of Bharhut and Sanci, and in Tibetan Buddhist painting it serves human beings as a way to Heaven.[2]

According to pre-Buddhist (Bon) Tibetan traditions, there originally existed a rope that bound Earth to Heaven. The Gods came down this rope from Heaven to meet human beings. After the "fall" of man and the coming of death, the link between Heaven and Earth was broken.[3] The first king of Tibet was said to have come down from Heaven by a rope. The first Tibetan kings did not die; they mounted again into Heaven.[4] But since the rope has been cut, only souls can ascend to Heaven; the bodies remain on Earth.[5] In many magical practices, especially Bon, men try even today to climb to Heaven by a magic rope,[6] and believe that at death the pious are drawn to Heaven by an invisible cord.[7]

All these beliefs express different aspects of a doctrine that

[1]A. K. Coomaraswamy, *Svayamatrnna: Janua Coeli* ("Zalmoxis", II, 1939, pp. 3-53), pp. 27, note 8, 42, note 64.
[2]G. Tucci, *Tibetan Painted Scrolls*, Rome, 1949, vol. II, p. 348, and *Tanka*, no. 12, pp. 14-22.
[3]Mathias Hermanns, *Mythen und Mysterien, Magie und Religion der Tibeter*, Cologne, 1956, pp. 42-3. See Also H. Hoffmann, *Quellen zur Geschichte der tibetischen Bon Religion*, Wiesbaden, 1951, p. 153.
[4]See *Shamanism*, pp. 430ff.; Tucci, *Tibetan Painted Scrolls*, II, pp. 733-4; Hoffmann, *Quellen*, pp. 141, 150, 153, 245; M. Hermanns, *op. cit.*, pp. 37ff.
[5]Hoffmann, *op. cit.*, p. 246.
[6]Hoffmann, *op. cit.*, p. 154; Hermanns, *op. cit.*, p. 42.
[7]S. H. Ribbach, *Drogpa Namgyal*, München-Planegg, 1940, p. 239, note 7; Hermanns, *op. cit.*, p. 42.

can be summed up as follows: (1) in mythical times, communication with Heaven was easy, for a rope (or tree, mountain, etc.) connected the Earth and the Sky; (2) the Gods came down to Earth, and Kings—who were also of celestial origin—climbed back into Heaven by a rope when they had accomplished their mission on Earth; (3) as a result of a catastrophic event which can be compared to the "fall" of the Judaeo-Christian tradition, the rope was cut and all communication between Heaven and Earth consequently became impossible; (4) this catastrophe changed both the structure of the Cosmos (definite separation of Earth and Heaven) and the human condition, for man became mortal; in other words, thenceforth he knew the separation of body and soul; (5) in fact, since the primordial catastrophe only the soul, at the moment of death, can mount into Heaven; (6) there are nevertheless privileged beings (pious men or magicians) who, even in our day, succeed in climbing to Heaven by means of a rope.

The doctrine that we have just resumed seems quite ancient. It is found not only among the Tibetans and in Central Asia, but also in other regions of the world. The ideology of the mystical experience of Shamans has been developed from similar mythologies of "Paradise" and the "fall".[1] The problem is too complex for us to attempt here. Moreover it does not bear directly on our subject. For purposes of this argument, it is enough for us to remember that since the "fall" the rope has become the property of privileged people: kings, magicians, priests. The rope is capable of bearing a man—or only his soul —up to Heaven. The rope is considered the best means of reaching Heaven in order to meet the Gods. But it is no longer a possession common to humanity: it is only available to a limited number of the "elect".

[1] See *Shamanism, passim.*

A NEGRITO SHAMAN'S CORD

Here now are some analogous examples, chosen from primitive peoples. During the healing seance, the shaman of the Pahang Negritos (the *halak*) holds in his fingers threads made of palm-leaves, or, according to other authorities, very fine cords. These threads or cords stretch to the Bonsu, the Sky God who lives above the seven stages of Heaven. So long as the séance lasts the *halak* is directly linked to the Sky God by these threads or cords, which the god drops down and which he raises up again after the ceremony.[1]

This amounts to saying that the healing is effected by the shaman while he is in communication with the Sky God and, ultimately, thanks to that communication. In fact, during the séance the *halak* also uses magic stones which are supposed to have been taken from the throne of the Supreme Being or the celestial vault.[2] In short, the essential element in the cure is the religious experience of the shaman, who feels himself directly connected with the Sky and the Celestial Beings. He derives his power from the fact *that he holds between his fingers an object fallen from above*: a thread, string, or stone detached from the vault of Heaven.

We will not discuss the antiquity of this belief. As is well known certain elements of Malaysian shamanism show recent influences. The conception of a Heaven on seven planes, for example, is an idea of Indian origin.[3] Nevertheless, the essentials of the ritual of the Negrito *halak* are archaic. For the magic stones that fell from Heaven play an important role in the initiations of Australian and South American medicine-men.[4]

[1] Ivor Evans, *Papers on the Ethnology and Archaeology of the Malay Peninsula*, Cambridge, 1927, p. 20.
[2] See *Shamanism*, pp. 337ff.; R. Pettazzoni, *L'Onniscienza di Dio*, Turin, 1955, p. 469, note. On the magic stones and "solidified light" see above pp. 24ff.
[3] See *Shamanism*, pp. 274ff., 406ff.; H. C. Quaritch Wales, *Prehistory and Religion in South-East Asia*, London, 1957, pp. 12ff.
[4] See *Shamanism*, pp. 52ff., 135ff.

And, as we shall see later, Australian medicine-men also tell of a magic rope which allows them to rise in the air and even to mount to Heaven.

The possession of the rope presupposes a fairly intense religious experience in the *halak*. This experience comes as a result of a "divine election". The phenomenon is too well known to require emphasis. There is always a "call" on the part of the supernatural Beings, accompanied by a series of psychopathological symptoms.[1] What is important to our theme is the fact that, in certain shamanic cults, divine election is indicated by a dream in which the "chosen" man sees a thread descend from Heaven. A Lepcha of Maria Basti tells the following story: "If in a dream a man sees a thread fall down towards him from Heaven, he must read this sign as an order from Heaven to become a shaman (Bongthing or Mun). Those who are chosen in this way must obey and devote themselves to the shamanic function. It is possible that a man may see the thread descend on another. In this case he must tell his dream to the man in question, who must obey the summons. If, however, someone cuts the thread when it is falling on a chosen person, the latter will die suddenly".[2]

This document clearly shows that: (1) the mystical vocation is a result of divine choice; (2) this choice is communicated to the shaman in the form of a thread that descends from Heaven and falls on his head; (3) the descent of the thread is a stroke of fate: it is as if destiny were suddenly revealed; (4) In fact, the chosen person feels as if he has lost his personal liberty; he feels like a prisoner "bound" by another's will, like one "in chains". The thread falling from above proclaims that the shaman's vocation has been decided by the Gods. And, as the whole history of shamanism shows, resistance to this divine decision means death.

---

[1] See *Shamanism*, pp. 50ff. and *passim*.
[2] M. Hermanns, *The Indo-Tibetans*, Bombay, 1954, pp. 51ff.

INDIA: COSMIC ROPES AND TISSUES OF BREATH

In Indian cosmological and physiological speculations, there is abundant use of images of the cord and the thread. Briefly one might say that their role is to implement *all living unity*, both cosmic and human. These primordial images serve at once to reveal the structure of the Universe and to describe the specific situation of man. Images of the rope and the thread succeed in suggesting what philosophy will afterwards make more explicit: that all things existing are, by their nature, produced, "projected" or "woven" by a superior principle, and that all existence in Time implies an "articulation" or "web". It is important, however, to distinguish between several parallel themes:

(1) The cosmic cords (that is to say, the winds) hold the Universe together, just as breath holds together and articulates the body of a man. The identity between breath (*pranas*) and the Winds is already stated in the *Atharva-Veda* (XI, 4, 15). The organs are held together by the breath, that is to say, in the final instance by the *atman:* "I know the stretched thread on which these living beings are woven; I know the thread of the thread and also the great *brahman*" (*Atharva-Veda*, X, 8, 38). This thread (*sutra*) is the *atman*, and in the *Brihadaranyaka Upanishad*, II, 7, 1, the doctrine of *sutratman* is clearly formulated: "Do you know, Kapya, the thread by which this world and the other world and all beings are bound together? . . . He who knows the thread, the ruler within, he knows *brahman*, he knows the worlds, he knows the gods, he knows *atman*, he knows all things".

(2) When, at the end of the world, the ropes of the winds are cut (*vrashcanam vatar-ajjunam*), the Universe will fall apart (*Maitri Upanishad*, I, 4). And since "it is by the air, as by a thread, that this world and the other world and all beings are strung together . . . they say of a dead man that his limbs have become

unstrung—(vyasramsisatasyan gani), for it is the Air (the breath) that binds them like a thread (Brih. Up., III, 7, 2).[1]

Let us add that similar ideas are to be found in China. Chuang tze (III, 4) affirms that "the ancients describe death as the loosening of the cord on which God had hung Life".

(3) The Sun binds the worlds to itself by means of a thread. As the Shatapatha Brahmana repeats many times, "the Sun binds (samavayata) these worlds together by a thread. Now, this thread is the same as the wind" (vayuh, VIII, 7, 3, 10; see also VII, 3, 2, 13). "The Sun is the connecting link, since these worlds are attached to the Sun by the four points of the compass"[2] (Sat. Br., VI, 7,

---

[1]This correspondence of microcosm to macrocosm, expressed by images of the thread (or rope) and unstringing, is fully elaborated in the time of the Brahmanas. The human being is "made" (samskrta) by means of rituals (Kausitaki Br., III, 8). The priests collect and consolidate (samstha) the atman, in order to make it into a perfect whole (Ait. Br., II, 40, 1-7). The exemplary model of this "unification" and "articulation" is, of course, the ritual myth of Prajapati. After the creating of the worlds, the gods and living beings, Prajapati became "unstrung" (Satapatha Br., VI, 1, 2, 12). Prajapati's "restoration" is described by the word samskr, to put together, and this putting together of Prajapati is symbolically identified with the construction of a fire altar. "With his joints unstrung he was incapable of standing up, and the gods put them together again by means of sacrifices" (samadadhuh; Sat. Br., I, 6, 3, 35-6). What the gods did in illo tempore the priest periodically repeats: "he reunites (samskaroti) Prajapati, totally and entirely" (sarvam krtsnam: Sat. Br., VI, 2, 2, 11). The integration effected by the construction of a fire altar will serve as a model for the work of the integration of the breath and the other faculties in order to "articulate" the atman.

[2]In connection with this symbolism Ananda Coomaraswamy recalls an episode in the Sarabhanga Jataka (v, 130) "where the Bodhissatta Jotipala (the 'Keeper of Light'), standing at the centre of a field, at the four corners of which posts have been set up, attaches a thread to the neck of his arrow and with one shot penetrates all four posts, the arrow passing a second time through the first post and then returning to his hand; thus, indeed, he 'sews' all things to himself by means of a single thread." (The Iconography of Dürer's "Knots" and Leonardo's "Concatenation", in "The Art Quarterly", Spring, 1944, pp. 109-28, p. 121.) Coomaraswamy has returned several times to the symbolism of the thread: see Svayamatrnna: Janua Coeli in "Zalmoxis", II, 1939—published 1941—pp. 3-51, particularly pp. 5ff.; "Spiritual Paternity" and the "Puppet-Complex" in "Psychiatry", VIII, Aug. 1945, pp. 25-35, particularly p. 29.

I, 17). The Sun is "well-meshed", because it sews together the days and the nights" (*ibid.*, IX, 4, 1, 8). This allusion to the joining of the days and the nights is closely connected with the Vedic image of the two sisters—Night and Dawn—who "like two weavers working in happy agreement weave the taut thread together" (*Rig Veda*, II, 3, 6) weaving the web of time.[1]

(4) Since it binds the World to itself by a thread, the Sun is the Cosmic Weaver, and is very often compared to a spider. "The weaver of the cloth is certainly he who shines down there, for he moves across the worlds as if across a cloth" (*Sat. Br.*, XIV, 2, 2, 22). A sacrificial *gatha* cited in the *Kausitaki Brahmana*, XIX, 3, speaks of the Sun (=the Year) as a spider. Several Upanishads use the image of the spider and its web, suiting it in each case to the religious orientation proper to itself. Sometimes it is the *atman* that is compared to a spider, sometimes the "imperishable" (*akshara*), sometimes God. "As a spider comes out with its thread . . . so from the *atman* issue all breaths, all worlds, all gods, all beings (*Brhad. Up.*, II, 1, 20; see *Maitri Up.*, VI, 32). "Just as a spider draws out and draws back (*srjate grhnate*, lit. 'pours out and dries up') . . . so all is born in this world from the imperishable (*aksarat*)" (*Mundaka Up.*, I, 1, 7). In a theistic Upanishad like the *Shvetasvatara*, it is the "only God who, like the spider, envelops himself with threads drawn from primordial Matter" (*pradhana*, VI, 10).

(5) Finally, a number of post-Vedic texts identify the Cosmic Weaver with *atman* or Brahman, or even with a personal God like Krishna in the *Bhagavad-gita*. When, in a famous passage of the *Brhadaranyaka Upanishad* (III, 6, 1), Gargi asks the question: "Yajnavalkya, if the Waters are a web on which all is woven, on what web are the Waters themselves woven?" Yajnavalkya

---

[1] An extremely complicated symbolism is developed around the "weaving of Time". See *Rig Veda*, V, 5, 6; IV, 13, 4; *Ath. Veda*, X, 7, 42ff., X, 8 37-9, etc. We will examine only certain aspects of this in the present book. Let us recall that the sacrifice is "fully stretched" (*Sat. Br.*, III, 8, 2, 2). To "stretch" a sacrifice is equivalent to "stretching" the "web" of time, that is to say, ultimately, to making the World last for one more year.

replies "On the air". The air in its turn, explains Yajnavalkya, is woven on the Worlds of the Sky, and these are woven on the worlds of the Gandharvas, and they on the Worlds of the Sun, and so on to the Worlds of Brahma. But when Gargi asks: "And the worlds of Brahma, on what web are they woven?" Yajnavalkya refuses to reply. "Do not ask too much, O Gargi, or your head will fall off. You are asking too much about a deity beyond whom there is no more to ask!" But in the following verses (III, 7, 1ff.) Yajnavalkya states that it is the "inner ruler" (*antaryaninam*) who is the true Ground of the Universe. And this inner ruler is the *sutratman*, the *atman* imagined as a thread.

In the *Bhagavad-gita* it is God who "weaves" the World. Krishna proclaims himself the Supreme Person "by whom this Universe is woven" (*yena sarvam idam tatam*, VIII, 22). "All this is woven by me" (*maya tatam idam sarvam*, IX, 4). And, after the blinding theophany of Lesson XI, Arjuna cries: "All is the Primordial God, the Ancient Spirit . . . by you all has been woven" (*tvaya tatam vishvam*, XI, 38).[1]

THE WEAVER AND THE WEB

As can be seen, one finds in the case of the Primordial Weaver, the same situation as in that of the Cosmic Spider; he is homologous either to the Sun, or to a transpersonal principal (*atman*-Brahman), or to a personal God. But, whatever the nature or form of his manifestation, the Creator is, in all these

---

[1] "All this Universe is strung upon Me, as rows of gems upon a thread" (*sutre manigana iva*) says Krishna also (VII, 7). The image occurs frequently: "As the thread of a necklace (*manisutram*) passes through a gem, so all this—that is to say the Gandharvas, the Apsaras, animals and men—is threaded on this (that is to say on the Sun, *Vayu, prana,* Brahman)"; *Jaiminya Upanishad Brahmana*, III, 4, 13; III, 5, 1 (quoted by Coomaraswamy, *Svayamatrnna*, p. 5). A. Coomaraswamy recalls a passage in the *Tripura Rahasya* in which there is mention of a town and its inhabitants, and the Spirit (*pracara*, lit. "migrant" or "newcomer") states that without him the inhabitants "would be scattered and lost like pearls without the thread of the necklace" (*Spiritual Paternity*, p. 31).

contexts, a "weaver"; which means that he holds attached to him by invisible threads or cords, the Worlds and the beings that he produces (to be more exact, that he "ejects" from himself).

To come to being and exist in Time, to endure, is to be projected by the Creator and to remain bound to him as by a thread. Even when—already in the time of the Brahmanas, but especially in the *Upanishads*—the accent falls on the necessity of "unifying" and articulating the breath in order to forge the Immortal Person, the *atman*, there is always a "creation"; the means of access to the state of transpersonal being must be created; the instrument by which a man obtains immortality must be forged. It is remarkable that even in the *Upanishads* (where the problem was quite different: how to express the ineffable experience of the discovery and conquest of Self?) the image of the thread is used in relation to the *atman*. It seems therefore that the principal streams of archaic Indian spirituality were fed by the powerful idea that whatever is living, real, existent (either in Time or in Timelessness) is essentially a well-adjusted and articulated unity. Before discovering that Being is One, Indian speculation discovered that dispersion and disconnectedness are equivalent to non-being; that, truly to exist, one must be unified and integrated. And the most satisfactory images by which to express all this were the thread, the spider, the weft and weaving. The spider's web brilliantly showed the possibility of "unifying" space from a Centre, by binding together the four cardinal points.

IMAGES, MYTHS, SPECULATIONS

These images and speculations are the product of deep experience. Every time man becomes aware of his true, existential situation, that is to say of his specific manner of existence in the Cosmos, and accepts this way of existence, he expresses these decisive experiences by images and myths which will afterwards enjoy a privileged position in the spiritual tradition of humanity.

Careful analysis will lead to the rediscovery of these existential situations which have given rise to the Indian symbolism of the thread and the web.

Cosmogonical creation, as well as the cosmos itself, are symbolized by the act of weaving. In the Brahmanas the Universe exists because all its parts are in order, because the spatio-temporal fabric is stretched as a result of sacrifice. But this idea of the weaving of the Universe and the re-articulation of Prajapati by the mysterious magic of the sacrifice is not very ancient. Prajapati, who exhausts himself and becomes unstrung while creating the World, the gods and all living beings, represents an idea exclusive to the Brahmanas. But even for the Brahmanas, it is Prajapati who created the Universe, and the sacrifice merely prolongs his existence. The exaltation of the all-powerful sacrifice must not make us lose sight of the fact that the Brahmanas also considered the Cosmos to have an author.

The Sun, the Gods or Brahman "weave" the World. *The web then depends on a weaver.* The Universe is made by someone else and, what is more, it is attached by cords to its maker. Creation is not absolutely separated from the Creator; it is attached to him as by an umbilical cord. This is important; for, in that case, Worlds and beings are not and cannot be "free". They cannot move of their own will. The thread that binds them to their Maker keeps them alive, but also dependent. "To live" is equivalent either to being "woven" by the mysterious Power that weaves the Universe, Time and Life, or to being attached by an invisible thread to a Cosmocrator (Sun, Brahman or personal God). In both cases "to live" is equivalent to being conditioned, to being dependent on someone else. This "someone else" may be God or an impersonal Principle, mysterious and difficult to identify, but his presence is felt in all temporal existence; in fact, each living being feels that he is the result of his own actions and of something else, of the fact that he is "woven", that is to say indestructibly attached to his own past. He feels that he constitutes a "web", and the "web", at a certain point in Indian speculation, comes to be considered unbreakable, in the sense that the "weaving" is no longer stopped by the death of the individual but is continued from one existence to another, constituting, in fact, the reason for innumerable transmigrations.

Probably one of the roots of the idea of karma should be sought in speculations about the cosmic web and the fabric formed by a continuous succession of sacrifices. We will not attempt here the problem of the origins of that idea. Let us say only that it does not take shape among religious men, who feel themselves attached as if by threads to a personal God; it impresses itself upon thought only when the discovery is made that man is the result of his own ritual acts, that is to say when he feels bound by himself to himself. The insistence with which he meditates on the fact that every man has a place in a series of temporal events, that he forms part of a web, that he cannot escape from his own past, proves that he is faced with an idea that can no longer be dealt with by the ritual solutions of primitive and archaic societies, which periodically regenerate Time (regeneration implying the abolition of the past).[1]

The images of the thread, the rope, the bond and the web are ambivalent; they express both a privileged position (to be attached to God, to be related to the cosmic *Urgrund*) and a pitiable and tragic situation (to be conditioned, enchained, predestined, etc.). In both cases, *man is not free*. But in the first he lives in permanent *communication with his Creator*, with the cosmic *Urgrund;* in the second, he feels himself the *prisoner of a fate*, bound by "magic" or by his own past (by the sum of his actions).

A similar ambivalence can be discovered in other expressions of the Indian symbolism of the bond, which we have discussed in a previous work.[2] Varuna and Vritra and also the gods of death are "masters of bonds"; they tie up and paralyze living beings, they bind the dead, and Vritra "imprisons" the Waters. In this Indian symbolism of bondage, magical elements are

[1] On this problem see *The Myth of the Eternal Return*.
[2] See *Images and Symbols*, pp. 92–124.

dominant: a man in bonds is paralyzed, given over to death. In fact, one finds the same images and expressions of bondage in sorcery, demonology and the mythology of death. Nevertheless, Varuna and Indra also untie and "release" human beings (Indra also "released" the Waters "imprisoned" by Vritra in the hollow of the mountain). This amounts to saying that the gods have "the power to bind and loose". (Matthew XVI, 19; etc.)

Another example: Yoga is the most perfect means of freeing oneself from slavery which is the human lot. By yoga a man gains absolute liberty. Now the word *yoga* itself to some extent denotes an action of "binding"; the root *yuj*, "join", also forms the Latin *jungere, jugum*, and the French *joug*, "yoke". This will be understood if one remembers that yoga is primarily a technique for achieving the perfect mastery of the body, the "subjugation" of the organs and the psycho-mental faculties. It is a matter of joining, articulating and unifying the activity of the organs and the psycho-mental flux. The *yukta* is the "unified" man; but he is also the man in a state of union with God.

ROPES AND PUPPETS

All these images—of Winds as cosmic ropes, of the air weaving the organs and keeping them together, of the *atman* as a thread, of the Spider, the Sun and the Weaving-gods—are closely related to other archaic conceptions, such as that of the thread of Life, of destiny as a web, of goddesses or fairies at the loom, etc. The subject is too vast to be attempted here. Let us say something, however, about the role of the cord and thread in magic. Not only are magicians supposed to enchant their victims by means of cords and knots, but one also finds the belief that they can fly in the air or disappear into the sky with the help of a string. A number of mediaeval and post-mediaeval European legends tell of sorcerers or witches escaping from prison, or even from the stake, by means of a thread or cord that someone has thrown to them.[1] This last theme of folklore strangely recalls the Indian rope-trick.

As we have just seen, the cord is not only the exemplary means of communication between Sky and Earth; it is also a key image, employed in speculations concerning Cosmic Life, human existence and destiny, metaphysical knowledge (*sutratman*) and, by extension, occult sciences and magic powers. On the level of archaic culture, the occult sciences and magic powers always take for granted the faculty of flying in the air and ascending to the sky.[2] The tree-climbing of the shaman is, essentially, a rite of ascension into Heaven. And it is significant that in traditional Indian imagery, the climbing of a tree symbolizes both the possession of magic powers and metaphysical gnosis. We have seen that the conjurer of *Suruci-Jataka* climbs a tree with the help of a magic rope, then disappears in the clouds. This is a theme of folklore which is also to be found in learned texts. The *Pancavimsha Brahmana* (XIV, 1, 12-13), for example, speaking of those who climb to the top of the great Tree, states that those who have wings—that is to say *those who know*—succeed in flying, whereas the ignorant, having no wings, fall to the ground. Here again we find the sequence: climbing the tree, esoteric knowledge, ascent to Heaven; that is to say, in the context of Indian ideology, the transcendence of this world and deliverance. Now, as will be seen in a moment, we find the same sequence among the magicians of primitive societies.

It would be useful to compare Greek and Germanic symbolisms of binding and weaving with these Indian images and speculations. We have touched on this problem in a previous work. Onians' *Origins of European Thought* also contains a great number of facts and perspicuous analyses on this subject of the symbols and rituals—related but distinct—of binding, weaving and spinning in Greece and among the ancient peoples

[1] See some examples in A. Jacoby, *op. cit.*, pp. 467ff.
[2] See *Myths, Dreams and Mysteries*, pp. 99ff., "Symbolisms of Ascension".

of Europe.[1] The problem is immense, and we make no pretence of resolving all its complexities. For the present, let us merely recall that the image of a rope binding the Cosmos and man to the supreme God (or to the Sun) is also to be found in Greece. Plato uses this image when he wishes to suggest the human condition and the means of perfecting it. "May we not regard every living being", he writes, "as a puppet of the Gods, either their plaything only, or created with a purpose—which of the two we cannot certainly know! But this we know, that these affections in us are like *cords and strings* which pull us different and opposite ways, and to opposite actions; and herein lies the difference between virtue and vice. According to the argument there is one among these cords that every man ought to grasp and never let go, but to pull with it against all the rest; and this is the *sacred and golden cord* of reason". (*The Laws*, 644, transl. Jowett. Author's italics.)

Aurea catena Homeri

The image is certainly taken from the famous "golden cord" with which Zeus could draw all things to him. One recalls the opening of the eighth book of the *Iliad:* after assembling the gods on Olympus, Zeus forbids them to bring help to the Trojans or Danaans, and threatens to throw those who disobey him into Tartarus. "For", continues Zeus, "you know by how much I am the most powerful of all the gods. Only put me to the test and you will be satisfied. Suspend a golden rope from heaven and lay hold of the end of it, all of you gods and goddesses. You will never drag Zeus, the supreme master, from the sky to the ground, however hard you try. But if I cared to pull hard from my end, I should haul you up, earth, sea and all. Then I should make the rope fast to a pinnacle of Olympus, and leave you all to dangle for your pains in mid-air. By so much does my strength exceed the strength of gods and men!" (VIII, 17-27,

[1] R. B. Onians, *The Origins of European Thought*, Cambridge, 1951, 2nd edition, 1954, especially pp. 349ff.

transl. E. V. Rieu, slightly altered). As has been observed, the image is taken from a boys' game. In fact "the Greeks knew as well as we do the game by which two teams tug a rope in opposite directions to prove their respective strengths. Zeus is inviting the gods to a trial of this kind. Only here the pull is not horizontal but vertical, Zeus standing alone at the top of the sky while the other gods below cling to the earth. He boasts that, under these conditions, he will pull the gods and the earth up to Olympus, and hang them all as a trophy on one of the peaks of the sacred mountain."[1]

It is not impossible that this anecdote reflects a hidden memory of an Indo-European mythical theme. But it is principally the symbolic interpretations of the golden cord that interest us in our research. Ever since archaic times, indeed, men have seen in Zeus' golden rope "sometimes the bonds that hold the universe in an indestructible unity, sometimes those that connect mankind with the higher powers" (P. Lévêque, *op. cit.*, p. 11). So, in the Orphic poem that scholars have called the *Rhapsodic Theogony*, Zeus asks the Night: "Mother, highest of divinities, divine Night, tell me how should I establish my proud empire over the immortals? How, by my efforts, shall the all be one and the parts distinct? Surround everything with the divine ether, then place in the centre the sky and the boundless earth and the sea and all the constellations with which the sky is crowned. But when you have placed a solid bond round all things, tying a golden chain to the ether . . ." (Lévêque, *op. cit.*, p. 14).

This is certainly an archaic idea, for Zeus comes to Night, a cosmological divinity, for counsel. "Spiritually we are close to Night as she appears in Book XIV of the *Iliad*, where she is powerful enough to save Hypnos from the anger of the master of the gods . . . close also to the primordial Night of Hesiod's *Theogony* (v. 116ff.). There is no reason to doubt that this part of the *Rhapsodic Theogony* goes back as far, probably, as the sixth

[1]The editors of the Collection des Universités de France, *Iliade*, vol. II, p. 26, quoted by Pierre Lévêque, *Aurea Catena Homeri*, Paris, 1959, p. 8.

century BC, if not in its form at least in the elements with which it makes play. It would be in Orphic circles, therefore, towards the end of the archaic era, that the Homeric image of the golden chain would have been used as an explanation of the cosmos" (P. Lévêque, *op. cit.*, p. 15).

Plato, in his *Theaetetus*, identifies the golden chain with the sun. Socrates tells the young Theaetetus: "And the palmary argument of all, which I strongly urge, is the golden chain of Homer, by which he means the sun, thereby indicating that so long as the sun and the heavens go round in their orbits, all things human and divine are and are preserved, but if they were chained up and their motions ceased, then all things would be destroyed, and, as the saying is, turned upside down". (*Theaetetus*, 153, c. d., transl. Jowett.)

In the *Republic* (x, 616 b. c.) although neither the sun nor the golden chain are mentioned, Plato uses a similar image. In explaining the structure of the Universe, he speaks of "a light that stretches from above across the sky and the earth, a light straight as a pillar and very like a rainbow, but brighter and purer. They came to this light after a day's journey; and there, in the midst of the light, they saw, stretched from this point of the heavens, the ends of its bonds; *for this light is a bond that binds the heavens as the under-girths that bind ships:* in this way it *held together all the revolving spheres*". (See also Lévêque, *op. cit.*, p. 20; author's italics.) Thus, Plato twice uses the image of a luminous cord that binds the Universe and holds its diverse parts in a single unity. Let us add that other Greek authors have seen in the golden chain the planets, or the four elements, or Aristotle's "unmoved motor", or *heimarmene*.

The other interpretation of the golden chain, notably when it is thought of as a spiritual link between Earth and Sky, between man and the higher powers, extends and completes the cosmological symbolism. Macrobius, in his *Commentary on Scipio's Dream*, considers that "since everything follows in continuous succession and deteriorates stage by stage from the first to the last degree, a wise and reflective observer must conclude that from the supreme deity to the lowest life everything is united and bound by mutual and for ever indissoluble links; this is the marvellous golden chain that Homer shows us, hanging in God's hand from the vault of heaven and descending to earth" (1, 14, 15; see also Lévêque, *op. cit.*, p. 46). The same idea occurs in Olympiodorus' *Commentary on the Gorgias* and that of Proclus on the *Timaeus* (Lévêque, *ibid.*, pp. 47-8). In addition, it is not uninteresting to note that for the Pseudo-Dionysius the Areopagite, the image of the golden chain has served as a symbol for prayer. This is what he writes in *The Divine Names*: "Let us strive therefore by our prayers to raise ourselves to the height of these divine and beneficent rays. It is as if we were to seize an infinitely bright chain hanging from the summit of the sky and descending to us, constantly striving to pull it down to us with each hand in turn. We should have the impression that we are bringing it down, but in reality our effort would be unable to move it, for it would be present as an entirety from top to bottom, and it is we who would be raising ourselves, to the highest splendours of a bright and shining perfection. Similarly, if we were in a boat, and ropes were thrown to save us which were tied at the other end to a rock, we should not be pulling the rock towards us, but rather hauling ourselves and the boat with us, towards the rock" (*The Divine Names*, 3, 1).

Let us observe that just as Indian philosophical speculation has made continual use of the archaic images of the rope, the thread and the web, so theosophists and Greek thinkers have for long been interpreting the venerable myth of Homer's golden chain in this manner. As in India, although in another perspective, the image of the golden cord has served as a point of departure both for cosmological theories and the description of the human condition. Let us add that the *aurea catena Homeri* has continued to provide food for philosophical reflection as late as the eighteenth century. An anonymous little book of Rosicrucian inspiration, *Aurea catena Homeri, oder Eine Beschreibung von dem Ursprung der Natur und natürlichen Dingen* played an important role in the formation of the young Goethe's thought.

THE "ASTRAL CORD"

The image of the cord is sometimes used to suggest the connection between the spirit (nous) and the soul (psyche). In his essay *On the Daimon of Socrates* (22) Plutarch states that the part "submerged in the body is called *psyche*, but the uncorrupted part is called *nous*"; and he continues, "the *nous* swings above the head, touching the top of the skull; it is like a cord, which must be held, and with which one must guide the lower part of the spirit for as long as it proves obedient and is not overcome by the appetites of the flesh". Very probably the conception of *nous* in the form of a cord was developed by the Neo-Platonists from Plato's description of men as puppets of the Gods and of the cord of reason. But even so this image may also represent certain parapsychological experiences. Indeed, according to those of Dr. H. Carrington and Sylvan J. Muldoon,[1] recently discussed by Raynor C. Johnson, it would appear that certain human beings are capable of feeling and, at the same time, visualizing a sort of cord or thread binding the physical body to the subtle body (which is called in pseudo-occult jargon the "astral body"). As Raynor Johnson puts it: "He [S. J. Muldoon] says that there is an astral cable or cord linking together the heads of the physical and astral body—of great elasticity . . . This exerts a considerable pull or control up to a variable range of about eight to fifteen feet. Once outside this range there is a feeling of freedom, but the cord is always present, even though quite thin, and it retains the same thickness indefinitely . . . Once the astral body has moved beyond cord-activity range . . . the cable then diminishes to a fine, thread-like structure and, as might be expected, the flow of energy from the astral to the physical body is greatly reduced . . . Death of the physical body is presumably caused by the severance of the astral cord".[2]

[1] Sylvan J. Muldoon, *The Projection of the Astral Body*, with a Preface by Dr. H. Carrington, London, 1929; *Id.*, *The Case for Astral Body* (1936).
[2] Raynor C. Johnson, *The Imprisoned Splendour*, London, 1953, pp. 230ff.

We do not need to discuss the authenticity of such experiences. Let us merely note that certain of our Western contemporaries claim to feel and see this subtle cord. The world of the imagination and the intermediate world of extra-sensory experiences are no less real than the physical world. One could, of course, object that the authors whom we have just quoted consciously or unconsciously "imagined" their experiences as a result of reading Plutarch or other, similar works.

MAGIC ROPES

But this would not invalidate the authenticity of such parapsychological experiences. For Australian medicine-men also speak of a cord miraculously tied to their bodies. It has been known since Howitt's studies that medicine-men possess a magic cord with the help of which they claim to climb to Heaven.[1] The recent researches of Ronald Berndt and Professor A. P. Elkin have discovered sensational details concerning this magic cord. Here is Elkin's description: "During the initiation of medicine-men in South-East Australia, they produce a rope from the medicine-man by means of incantations. This cord enables him to accomplish marvellous exploits, for instance to emit fire from his stomach like an electric wire. And, more interesting still is the use made of the rope to rise towards the Sky, or to the tree-tops, or into space. At the initiation parade, at the height of the ceremonial enthusiasm, the magician lies on his back under a tree, raises his rope, and climbs up to a nest placed at the treetop; he then passes to other trees, and at sunset climbs down the trunk again. Only the men see this exploit, which is preceded and followed by the whirling of the bull-roarer and other expressions of emotional excitement. In the descriptions of these exploits noted by M. Berndt and myself will be found the names of the medicine-men and details like the following: Joe Dagan, a Wongaibon magician, lying on his back at the foot of a tree

[1] A. W. Howitt, *The Native Tribes of South-East Australia*, London, 1904, pp. 400ff.; see also *Shamanism*, pp. 135ff.

made his rope rise and climbed up it, his head thrown backwards and his body loose, his legs apart and his arms at his sides. When he reached his goal, forty foot up, he waved his hands to those who were below. He came down in the same manner and, as he was lying quietly on his back, the rope re-entered his body".[1]

Professor Elkin believes that the explanation of this magical event must be sought in the powers of the collective unconscious. But, even if we are concerned with the collective unconscious, it would be interesting to know why the medicine-men chose the traditional image of ascent by means of a rope that could be produced from the body and returned at will. As we have already recalled, we have other examples also of Australian medicine-men claiming to ascend to the Sky by means of a rope. What is still more interesting is that the shaman of the Ona, one of the tribes of Tierra del Fuego, also possesses a "magic rope", nearly three metres long, which he produces from his mouth, and causes to disappear in the twinkling of an eye by swallowing it.[2] Such magical exploits must be compared to the fakirs' "rope trick".

It is remarkable that in Australia too the magic rope is the property of the medicine-man, that is to say of the man who holds the secret knowledge. We find at the Australian level of culture the same sequence that has been reported from India and in mediaeval European folklore: knowledge, magic, magic rope, tree-climbing, voice from heaven. We know, furthermore, that the initiations of Australian medicine-men are shamanic in structure, for they involve the ritual decapitation and cutting to pieces of the aspirant.[3] In brief, the two elements comprising the rope-trick ascent to the sky by means of a rope and the dismemberment of the boy are found together in the traditions of Australian magic. Does this mean that the rope-trick had an Australian origin? No, but it is loosely related to extremely

[1] A. P. Elkin, *Aboriginal Men of High Degree*, Sydney, 1946, pp. 64-5.
[2] See E. Lucas Bridges, *The Uttermost Part of the Earth*, New York, 1948, pp. 284ff.
[3] A. P. Elkin, *op. cit.*, pp. 31, 43, 112ff.; *Shamanism*, pp. 52ff.

ancient mystical techniques and speculations, and the rope-trick
is not, properly speaking, an Indian invention. India has merely
elaborated and popularized this miracle, just as Indian speculation
has built a cosmo-physiological mystique around the symbolism
of cosmic ropes and the *sutratman*.

We are now back at the point of departure of our study:
the significance and function of the rope-trick. But it is above
all the cultural function of the rope-trick—or, to be more exact,
of the archaic scenarios which made it possible—that seems to us
important. We have just seen that these scenarios and the ideology
which they imply belong to the milieu of the magicians. The
object of the exhibition is to reveal to the spectators an unknown
and mysterious world: the sacred world of magic and religion
to which only the initiated have access. The images and dramatic
themes employed, notably the ascent to Heaven by means of
a rope, the disappearance and initiatory dismemberment of the
aspirant, not only illustrate the occult powers of the magicians,
but reveal also a deeper level of reality, inaccessible to the
profane; they illustrate in fact the initiatory death and resurrection, the possibility of transcending "this world" and disappearing
on to a "transcendental" plane. The images released by the
rope-trick are capable of producing both an attachment to an
invisible, secret and "transcendental" reality and doubts as to
the reality of the familiar and "immediate" world. From this
point of view, the rope-trick—like all other displays of magic—
has a positive cultural value, for it stimulates the imagination and
reflection, one acting on the other, by the questions and problems
that it raises and, ultimately, by putting the problem of the
"true" reality of the World. It is not fortuitous that Shankara
uses the example of the rope-trick to illustrate the mystery of
cosmic illusion; from the beginnings of Indian philosophical
speculation, *maya* was the supreme magic, and the gods, to the
degree that they were "creators", were *mayin* or magicians.

Finally, we must take into account the "dramatic" function
of the rope-trick (and similar exploits). The magician is, by
definition, a stage-producer. Thanks to his mysterious science

the spectators witness a "dramatic action" in which they do not take an active part in the sense of "working" (as happens in other collective dramatic ceremonies). During the magicians' trick the spectators are passive; *they contemplate*. This is an occasion for imagining how things may be done without "working", simply by "magic", by the mysterious power of thought and will. It is also an occasion for imagining the creative power of the Gods, who do not create by working with their hands, but by the force of their words or thought. To be brief, a whole moral is pointed: that spiritual science is all-powerful, that man is free and that it is possible for him to transcend his familiar Universe. All these thoughts are raised by the contemplation of the "spectacle", by the fact that man discovers the function of a "contemplative".

SITUATIONS

These few observations on the rope-trick only concern one aspect of the symbolic complex that has engaged us. Each of the other aspects would deserve equally long comparative study. But the examples that we have just discussed have clearly brought to light this fact: whether it records a paranormal experience restricted to a few privileged individuals or is the product of human fantasy, the image of an invisible rope or thread attaching man to higher regions has served to express *exemplary human situations*: for instance the possibility of being in communication with the Sky and the Gods, and consequently of being chosen by the Gods and called to a religious vocation. In Indian speculative philosophy the image of the invisible cord is used both to describe the relations between God and his creatures and to suggest the essence of the *atman*. But in India, as well as Greece and ancient Europe, it served to symbolize the human condition in general, destiny (the "thread of life": the Goddesses who spin destiny), the web of temporal existence (*karma*), and consequently "servitude". A whole category of related images express "entanglement" by magic or death. As for the symbolism of weaving, although it depends on that of the thread, it goes further and extends it.

As we have several times observed, these images express ideas which belong together but are different. In different contexts the thread or cord is capable of suggesting different shades of meaning. It is of course the chief function of exemplary images that they invite, help and even force a man to think, to define his ideas, continually to discover new meanings, and to deepen and develop them. It is highly significant that the image of the cord or thread plays a principal role in the imaginary universe of primitive medicine-men and in the extra-sensory perceptions of modern men, as well as in the mystical experience of archaic societies, in Indo-European myths and rituals, in Indian cosmology and philosophy, in Greek philosophy, etc. This shows that the images of thread and cord continually occur in the imaginations and speculations of man, which is a proof that they correspond to extremely deep experiences and, ultimately, reveal a human situation that seems untranslatable by other symbols or concepts.

V

Observations on Religious Symbolism

THE VOGUE FOR SYMBOLISM

As we have frequently insisted, we have for some time been witnessing a vogue for symbolism.[1] Several factors have combined to give the study of symbolism the privileged position which it enjoys today. On the one hand there have been the discoveries of depth psychology, in the first place the fact that the activity of the unconscious can be detected by the interpretation of figures, images, scenarios, which cannot be taken at their nominal value, but are like the "ciphers" of situations and persons that the conscious mind will not or cannot acknowledge.

There was also, at the beginning of the century, the growth of modern art and, after the First World War, the poetical experiments of surrealism, which familiarized the educated public with non-figurative, dream worlds, only capable of presenting a meaning in so far as one managed to decipher their structures, which were "symbolic". A third factor also aroused interest in the study of symbolism: the ethnologists' researches into primitive societies and, especially, the hypotheses of Lucien Lévy-Bruhl concerning the structure and functions of "the primitive mentality". Lévy-Bruhl considered that the "primitive mentality" was pre-logical, since it appeared to be dominated by what he called "participation mystique". At the end of his life Lévy-Bruhl abandoned the hypothesis of a primi-

[1]See *Images and Symbols*, pp. 27ff.
[2]A clear exposition of the theories of Freud and Jung about the symbol is to be found in Jolande Jacobi's *Komplex, Archetypus, Symbol in der Psychologie C. G. Jung*, Zurich, 1957, pp. 86ff.

tive mentality pre-logical and radically different from the modern mentality, and actually argued against it.[1] In fact, his hypothesis had not attracted the widespread adherence of ethnologists and sociologists. Nevertheless, the hypothesis of a "primitive mentality" had been useful in so far as it aroused discussions among philosophers, sociologists and psychologists. In particular it had drawn the attention of the finest intellects to the behaviour of "primitive man", his psycho-mental life and cultural creations. The present-day interest of philosophers, particularly in Europe, in myths and symbols is in great part due to Lévy-Bruhl's books and to the controversies which they aroused.

In fact, this vogue we are discussing owes more than can possibly be said to certain philosophers, epistemologists and linguists who set out to show the symbolic character not only of language, but of all other activities of the human mind, from rite and myth to art and science.[2] Since man possesses a symbol-forming power, all that he produces is symbolic.[3]

In recalling the principal factors that have contributed to the growth of interest in symbolism we have at the same time noticed the realms in which the study of symbolism has been undertaken. These are the realms of depth psychology, of the plastic arts and poetry, of ethnology, semantics, epistemology and philosophy. The historian of religions can only rejoice at these researches, undertaken from different points of view, into a subject so important for his own field of work. Since the human sciences

[1]See Lucien Lévy-Bruhl, *Les Carnets*, edited Maurice Leenhardt, Paris, 1946.
[2]See Max Schlesinger, *Geschichte des Symbols*, Berlin, 1912; A. N. Whitehead, *Symbolism, its Meaning and Effect*, New York, 1927; W. M. Urban, *Language and Reality. The Philosophy of Language and the Principles of Symbolism*, London and New York, 1939; *Religious Symbolism*, edited by F. Ernest Johnson, New York, 1955; *Symbols and Values: An Initial Study* (xiiith Symposium of the Conference on Science, Philosophy and Religion), New York, 1954; *Symbols and Society* (xivth Symposium of the Conference on Science, Philosophy and Religion), New York, 1955. See also *Symbolon. Jahrbuch für Symbolforschung*, vol. 1, Basle, 1960.
[3]It is enough to recall the works of Ernst Cassirer, *Philosophie der symbolischen Formen*, 3 vol., Berlin, 1923-9; *Id., An Essay on Man*, Yale, 1944, and Susanne K. Langer, *Philosophy of Reason, Rite and Art*, Harvard, 1942.

are closely interlinked, any important discovery made in one sector has its repercussions on the neighbouring disciplines. Anything that psychology or semantics may teach us about the functions of the symbol is bound to affect the science of religions. Is it not fundamentally all one subject? Its purpose also is to understand man and his place in the world. Indeed the relationship between these disciplines and the science of religions would be a fruitful subject for study.

Even so, it is no less true that the field of religious science must not be confused with those of the other disciplines. The attitude proper to a historian of religions is far from identical with that of a psychologist, linguist or sociologist. The religious historian's researches differ from those of the linguist, psychologist and sociologist in that he is preoccupied only with *religious* symbols, of those belonging to a religious experience or religious conception of the world.

The attitude of the historian of religions also differs from a theologian's. All theology implies systematic reflexion on the content of religious experience, with a view to penetrating and elucidating the relationship between God the Creator and the creature man. The religious historian's ways of approach are, on the other hand, empirical. He is dealing with historico-religious facts which he tries to understand and make intelligible to others. His attention is engaged at once by the significance of a religious fact and by its *history*; he takes pains not to sacrifice either. Of course, the religious historian is also tempted to systematize the results of his researches and reflect on the structure of religious phenomena. But then he is completing his task as historian by a task of phenomenology or religious philosophy. In the broad sense of the term, the science of religions embraces both religious phenomenology and the philosophy of religion. But the historian of religions in the strictest sense can never renounce his concern with the historically concrete. He attempts to decipher, in the temporal sphere of historical actuality the fate of experiences arising from an inflexible human desire to transcend the temporal and historic.

All authentic religious experience implies a desperate effort to penetrate to the root of things, the ultimate reality. But every expression or conceptual formulation of a given religious experience lies in a historical context. Expressions and formulations consequently become "historical documents" comparable to any other cultural "facts": artistic creation, social or economic phenomena, etc. The supreme merit of any historian of religions is precisely his endeavour to discover in a "fact" duly conditioned by the historical moment and the cultural style of the age the existential situation which caused it.

Another element must also be taken into account: theology is essentially preoccupied with historical and revealed religions —the Jewish, Christian and Muslim monotheisms—and only secondarily with the ancient religions of the Near East and the early Mediterranean. A theological study of religious symbolism will necessarily take account of documents chosen from the great monotheistic religions rather than of "primitive" material.[1] Now the ambition of the historian of religion is to acquaint himself with the greatest possible number of religions, especially with archaic and primitive ones, in which there is a chance of meeting certain religious institutions at a still elementary stage.

In short, though it is advisable to take into account researches undertaken by specialists in other disciplines on the symbol in general and religious symbolism in particular, the historian of religions is ultimately obliged to approach the subject with his own means of investigation and in his own proper perspective. There exists no better perspective in which to view historico-religious facts than that of the general science of religions. It is only out of timidity that religious historians have sometimes accepted an integration proposed by the sociologists or anthropologists. In so far as general considerations can be formulated on the religious behaviour of man, no one can make a better

[1]Clearly, a theology of the History of Religions will have to take into account all these archaic and primitive religious experiences. But such a theology presupposes the existence of a History of Religions and depends on its findings.

formulation than the religious historian. In order to do so, he must of course master and integrate the results of all investigations in all the important sectors of his discipline.

THE INHIBITIONS OF THE SPECIALIST

Unfortunately this general mastery has become increasingly rare.[1] Few historians make the effort to follow researches in domains distant from their own field of specialization. Though a historian of the Greek religion may sometimes interest himself in recent studies on Iranian or Indian religions, he is less inclined to follow the results of his specialist colleagues in, let us say, the Altaic, Bantu or Indonesian religions. Should he wish to make a comparison or propose a more general explanation of the Greek of Mediterranean facts, he will turn to a *Manual*, or skim Frazer, or resort to some fashionable theory on the religion of the "primitives". In other words, he will dodge the very work expected of him as a historian of religions: that of keeping himself informed of the researches of his specialist colleagues in other fields, of assimilating and comparing their results, and of finally integrating them in order to improve his understanding of his Greek documents.

This timidity is seemingly explicable by two prejudices. The first might be formulated like this: the history of religions is a limitless field[2] that no single person can master; therefore it is better to know one sector well than to wander as a dilettante through several. The second prejudice, rather implicit than avowed, is that for a "general theory" of religions it is wiser to go to the sociologist, anthropologist, philosopher or theologian. Much could be said about comparison and integration. For the moment it is important to correct an erroneous opinion held about the work of integration. The historian of religions does

---

[1] See *Images and Symbols*, pp. 27ff.
[2] This is true of all historical disciplines. More than fifty years ago Anatole France observed that it would take several lives to read all the documents on the French Revolution alone.

not have to take the place of the various specialists or master their respective philologies. Not only is such a substitution virtually impossible, it would be of no use. The historian of religions whose field of research is, let us say, Vedic India or classical Greece, does not have to know Chinese, Indonesian or Bantu in order to use in his researches Taoist religious documents or the myths of the aborigines of Ceram or the rites of the Tongans. What he must do is to keep abreast of the progress made by specialists in all these fields. A man is a historian of religions not by virtue of mastering a certain number of philologies, but because he is capable of ordering religious facts in a general perspective. The historian of religions does not act as a philologist but as an expounder and interpreter. Mastery of his own speciality has taught to him to find his way through a maze of facts, and where to turn for the most important sources, the most reliable translations, the studies that will guide him best in his researches. As a historian of religions, he labours to understand the material put at his disposal by philologists and historians. A few weeks' work are enough for a linguist to discover the structure of an unfamiliar language. The historian of religions should be capable of arriving at similar results when working on religious facts foreign to his own field of study. For he need not make the philological effort required by specialist research, any more than a historian of the French novel needs to repeat work already done on Balzac's or Flaubert's manuscripts, or to make a new stylistic analysis of Stendhal, or reinvestigate the sources of Victor Hugo or Gérard de Nerval. His duty is to keep abreast of all this work, to use its results and to integrate them.

The methods of a historian of religions can also be compared to those of a biologist. When the biologist studies, let us say, the behaviour of a certain kind of insect, he does not take the place of the entomologist. He extends, compares and integrates the entomologist's researches. Of course the biologist too is a "specialist" in one of the branches of zoology, that is to say he has a long experience of one or another of the animal species.

But his method differs from the zoologist's: he is concerned with the *structures of animal life*, not only with the morphology and "history" of a particular species.

The second prejudice of certain historians of religions, that you must turn to another "specialist" for a world-wide and systematic interpretation of religious facts, is probably to be explained by the philosophical timidity of a great number of scholars. Two factors in particular have helped to impose and cultivate this timidity: on the one hand the very structure of the disciplines that serve as a kind of introduction to or preparation for the science of religions (it is well known that the majority of historians of religions are recruited from the philologists, archaeologists, historians, orientalists and ethnologists); on the other hand, an inhibition created by the lamentable failure of the great improvisations of the end of the nineteenth and the beginning of the twentieth century (mythology considered as a "disease of language", astral and nature mythologies, pan-Babylonianism, animism and pre-animism, etc). Be this as it may, the historian of religions considers it safer to leave the risk of syntheses and general theories to the other disciplines—sociology, psychology, anthropology.[1] But this amounts to saying that the historian of religions hesitates to complete his preparatory work as philologist and historian by an act of comprehension, which of course requires an effort of thought.

QUESTIONS OF METHOD

We have no intention of developing these few observations concerning the field and methods of the science of religions. Our purpose is more modest; we wish to show that it is possible to envisage the study of religious symbolism in the conspectus of the science of religions, and what the results of this study might be. But in discussing this precise case we shall be brought

[1]In fact all the "general theories" which have dominated the history of religion from its beginnings have been the work of linguists, anthropologists, sociologists and philosophers. See *Images and Symbols*, pp. 30ff.

up against some methodological difficulties inherent in all researches into the history of religions. In other words, we shall have to discuss certain aspects of our method, not in the abstract but as they occur during the actual course of the research.

The first difficulty which confronts a historian of religions is the enormous mass of documents; in our case the vast number of religious symbols. One question occurs at the start: even if we can succeed in mastering this mass (which is not always certain) have we the right to use them indiscriminately, that is to say by grouping them, comparing them, in fact examining them according to the convenience of the author undertaking the researches? These *religious* documents are at the same time *historical* documents; they form an integral part of various cultural contexts. In fact, each document has a particular significance, relative to the culture and the historical moment from which it has been detached.

The difficulty is a real one, and we will try later to show how it can be overcome. Let us say for the present that the historian of religions is bound to meet a similar difficulty in everything he undertakes. For, on the one hand, he wants to know all the *historical examples* of a certain religious behaviour and, on the other, he is obliged to isolate the *structure* of this behaviour, as it can be learnt from a number of examples. To take an example: there are countless variants of the symbolism of the Cosmic Tree. A certain number of these variants can be considered as deriving from centres of diffusion. The possibility may even be admitted that *all* the variants of the Cosmic Tree derive from a single centre of diffusion. In this case, it may be hoped that one day the history of the symbolism of the Cosmic Tree may be plotted; the centre of origin having been ascertained, the channels of diffusion and the different values which this symbolism took on in course of its wanderings may all be traced.

If practicable, a historical monograph of this kind would be of great service to the history of religions. But the problem of the symbolism of the Cosmic Tree would not be solved all the same. Quite another work would remain to be done: to establish the meaning of this symbol, what it *reveals*, what it shows in its quality as a religious symbol. Each type or variety reveals with a particular intensity or brilliance *certain* aspects of the symbolism of the Cosmic Tree, while leaving other aspects in shadow. In certain cases the Cosmic Tree is revealed as primarily an *imago mundi*, and in others it appears as an *axis mundi*, as a trunk that supports the Sky, connects the three cosmic zones (Heaven, Earth and Hell) and affords a means of communication between Earth and Sky. Finally, other variants principally stress its part in the periodical regeneration of the Universe, or the role of the Cosmic Tree as Centre of the World, or its creative powers, etc. I have studied the symbolism of the Cosmic Tree in several of my previous works,[1] and it would serve no purpose to resume the problem in its entirety. It suffices to say that it is impossible to understand the significance of the Cosmic Tree without considering one or several of its variants. The nature of the symbolism can only be completely deciphered when a considerable number of examples have been examined. One cannot understand the significance even of a given type of Cosmic Tree until one has studied the most important types and variants. It is only after elucidating the significance of the Cosmic Tree in Mesopotamia and in India that one can understand the symbolism of Yggdrasil or of the Cosmic Trees of Central Asia and Siberia. In the science of religions, as elsewhere, comparison is used both to relate and to distinguish.

But this is not all: it is only when an inventory of all the variants has been made that their differences in meaning stand out in full relief. It is the degree of its difference from the Altaic symbol of the Cosmic Tree that throws up the great importance of the Indonesian symbol for the history of religions. The question then arises: is there in one case or the other an innovation or obfuscation of meaning, or a loss of the original significance? Knowing the significance of the Cosmic Tree in Mesopotamia or India or Siberia, one wonders what historico-

[1]See *Traité d'Histoire des Religions*, pp. 232ff.; *Shamanism*, pp. 269ff.; *Images and Symbols*, pp. 39ff., pp. 161ff.

religious circumstances, or what internal reasons have caused the same symbol to possess a different significance in Indonesia. Diffusion does not solve the problem. For even if it could be proved that the symbol spread from a single centre one would still not have answered the question: *why have such-and-such cultures preserved certain primary significances, while others have forgotten, rejected, modified or enriched them?* Now, the understanding of this process of enrichment only becomes possible when the nature of the symbol has been isolated. It is because the Cosmic Tree symbolizes the mystery of a World in perpetual regeneration that it can symbolize—simultaneously or successively—the pillar of the Universe and the cradle of humankind, the cosmic *renovatio* and the lunar rhythms, the Centre of the World and the path by which man goes from Earth to Heaven, etc. Each of these new connotations is made possible because the symbolism of the Cosmic Tree was revealed from the beginning as a "cipher" of the World understood as a living, sacred and inexhaustible reality. The historian of religions will have to elucidate the reasons why a certain culture has kept, developed or forgotten an aspect of the symbolism of the Cosmic Tree—and, in doing so, he will come to penetrate more deeply into the soul of that culture and learn to differentiate it from the rest.

In certain respects one could compare the situation of the historian of religions with that of the depth psychologist. Both have to preserve contact with the given facts; the methods of both are empirical; their aim is to understand "situations": individual situations in the case of the psychologist, historical situations in the case of the historian of religions. But the psychologist knows that he will only succeed in understanding an individual situation, and be able to help his patient to recover to the extent that he succeeds in uncovering the structure underlying a particular combination of symptoms, to the extent that he recognizes in the peculiarities of an individual story the broad lines of the history of the psyche. Therefore the psychologist improves his means of research and rectifies his theoretical conclusions by taking into account during his work of analysis all discoveries that have been made. As we have just seen, the historian of religions is acting in just the same way when studying, for instance, the symbolism of the World Tree. Whether he feels bound to confine himself, let us say, to Central Asia or Indonesia, or on the other hand attempts to cover this symbolism in its entirety, he can only fulfil his task by taking into consideration all the important variants of the Cosmic Tree.

Man being *homo symbolicus*, and all his activities implying symbolism, every religious fact has necessarily a symbolic character. No assumption could be more certain than that every religious act and every cult object has a meta-empirical purpose. The tree that becomes a cult object is not worshipped as a *tree*, but as a *hierophany*, a manifestation of the sacred.[1] And every religious act, from the moment that it becomes *religious*, is charged with a significance which is, in the final instance, "symbolic", since it refers to supernatural values or forms.

One would therefore be justified in saying that any research undertaken on a religious subject implies the study of religious symbolism. But in the current language of the science of religions, the convention is to confine the term symbol to religious facts of which the symbolism is manifest and explicit. One speaks for example of the wheel as a solar symbol, of the cosmogonic egg as a symbol of the undifferentiated totality, of the serpent as a chthonian, sexual or funerary symbol, etc.[2]

It is current practice also to approach a given religious institution—initiation, for example—or religious behaviour—

---

[1] On the subject of hierophanies, see *Traité d'Histoire des Religions*, pp. 15ff., and *passim*.

[2] It is also conventional to reserve the term "symbolism" for a structurally coherent ensemble; we speak for example of water symbolism, the structure of which can only be understood by studying a great number of religious facts apparently heterogeneous: baptismal rites and lustration, aquatic cosmogonies, myths about floods and disasters at sea, myths whose principal feature is fecundity by contact with water, etc. . . . (*Traité*, pp. 168ff., *Images and Symbols*, pp. 125ff., and 151ff.). Clearly, the current use of the terms "symbol" and "symbolism" lacks precision, but one must adapt oneself to this state of things. In many cases the context sufficiently reveals the meaning.

the *orientatio*, let us say—solely from the symbolic angle. The aim of this kind of investigation is to put on one side the socio-religious contexts of the institution or behaviour in question in order to concentrate on the symbolism they imply. Initiation is a complex phenomenon, comprising many kinds of rites, divergent mythologies, different social contexts and disparate aims.[1] It is well known that in the final analysis all this is "symbolic". But the study of the symbolism of initiation has a further purpose: to decipher the symbolism underlying such-and-such an initiatory rite or myth (*regressus ad uterum*, ritual death and resurrection, etc.), to study each of these symbols morphologically and historically, to lay bare the existential situation which determined their formation.

The same applies to such religious behaviour as the *orientatio*. There exist innumerable rites of orientation and myths justifying them, all certainly deriving from the experience of the sacred ground. To attack this problem in its entirety presupposes the study of ritual orientation, geomancy, the rites of founding a village or constructing a temple or house, the symbolism of tents, huts and houses, etc. But as at the basis of all this lies an experience of the sacred ground and a cosmological idea, one can limit the study of the *orientatio* to the symbolism of the sacred ground. This does not mean that one fails to know or neglects the historical and social contexts of all the forms of *orientatio* that one has been at pains to examine.

One could easily multiply examples of such researches on a particular symbolism: the "magic flight" and ascension, Night and the symbolism of darkness, lunar, solar, telluric, vegetable and animal symbolisms, the symbolism of the quest for immortality, the symbol of the Hero, etc. In each of these cases the approach is essentially the same: one tries to reconstitute the symbolic significance of religious facts apparently heterogeneous but structurally related, which may take the form of ritual rites or behaviour, or of myths, legends, supernatural figures and images. Such a procedure does not imply the reduction of all

[1] See *Birth and Rebirth: The Religious Meanings of Initiation in Human Culture.*

these significances to a common denominator. One cannot sufficiently insist on this point: that the examination of symbolic structures is a work not of *reduction* but of *integration*. One compares and contrasts two expressions of a symbol not in order to reduce them to a single, pre-existent expression, but in order to discover the process by which a structure is capable of enriching its meanings. In studying the symbolism of flight and ascension, we have given some examples of this process of enrichment; the reader anxious to verify the results of such a methodological process is referred to *Myths, Dreams and Mysteries*.

WHAT THE SYMBOLS "REVEAL"

The task of the historian of religions remains incomplete if he fails to discover the function of symbolism in general. We know what the theologian, the philosopher and the psychologist have to say about this problem.[1] Let us now examine the conclusions which the historian of religions reaches when he reflects on his own documents.

The first observation that he is forced to make is that the World "speaks" in symbols, "reveals" itself through them. It is not a question of a utilitarian and objective language. A symbol is not a replica of objective reality. It *reveals* something deeper and more fundamental. Let us try to elucidate the different aspects, the different depths of this revelation.

(1) Symbols are capable of revealing a *modality of the real or a condition of the World which is not evident on the plane of immediate experience*. To illustrate the sense in which the symbol expresses a modality of the real inaccessible to human experience, let us take an example: the symbolism of the Waters, which is capable

[1] We would recall Paul Tillich's statement: "This is the great function of symbols: to point beyond themselves, in the power of that to which they point, to open up levels of reality which otherwise are closed, and to open up levels of the human mind of which we otherwise are not aware" (Paul Tillich, *Theology and Symbolism* in "Religious Symbolism", edited F. Ernest Johnson, New York, 1955, pp. 107-16, p. 109).

of revealing the pre-formal, the potential, the chaotic. This is
not, of course, a matter of rational cognition, but of apprehension
by the active consciousness prior to reflection. It is of such
apprehensions that the World is made. Later, by elaborating the
significances thus understood, the first reflections on the creation
of the World will be set in motion; this is the point of departure
of all the cosmologies and ontologies from the Vedas to the
Pre-Socratics.

As for the capacity of symbols to reveal an inner pattern of
the World, we will refer to what we said earlier about the
principal significances of the Cosmic Tree. The Tree reveals
the World as a living totality, periodically regenerating itself
and, thanks to this regeneration, continually fertile, rich and
inexhaustible. Here, too, it is not a question of considered
knowledge, but of an immediate comprehension of the "cipher"
of the World. The World "speaks" through the medium of the
Cosmic Tree, and its "word" is directly understood. The World
is apprehended as Life and, for primitive thought, Life is a
disguise worn by Being.

A corollary of the preceding observations: religious symbols
which touch on the patterns of life reveal a deeper Life, more
mysterious than that grasped by everyday experience. They
reveal the miraculous, inexplicable side of Life, and at the same
time the sacramental dimension of human existence. "Deciphered" in the light of religious symbols, human life itself,
reveals a hidden side: it comes from "elsewhere", from very far
away; it is "divine" in the sense that it is the work of Gods or
supernatural Beings.

(2) This brings us to a second general observation: for
primitives, *symbols are always religious*, since they point either
to something *real* or to a *World-pattern*. Now, at the archaic
levels of culture, the *real*—that is to say the powerful, the significant, the living—is equivalent to the *sacred*. Moreover, the
World is a creation of the Gods or of supernatural Beings: to
discover a World pattern amounts to revealing a secret or a
"ciphered" meaning of the divine work. It is for this reason

that archaic religious symbols imply an ontology; a pre-systematic ontology, of course, the expression of a judgement both of the World and of human existence: judgement which is not formulated in concepts and which cannot always be translated into concepts.

(3) An essential characteristic of religious symbolism is its *multivalence*, its capacity *to express simultaneously several meanings the unity between which is not evident on the plane of immediate experience.* The symbolism of the Moon, for example, reveals a connatural unity between the lunar rhythms, temporal becoming, the Waters, the growth of plants, women, death and resurrection, the human destiny, the weaver's craft, etc.[1] In the final analysis, the symbolism of the Moon reveals a correspondence of a "mystical" order between the various levels of cosmic reality and certain modalities of human existence. Let us observe that this correspondence is not indicated by immediate and spontaneous experience, nor by critical reflection. It is the result of a certain mode of "viewing" the World.

Even if we admit that certain of the Moon's functions have been discovered by careful observation of the lunar phases (their relation with rainfall, for instance, and menstruation), it is difficult to imagine that the symbolism could have been built up in its entirety by an act of reason. It requires quite another order of cognition to reveal, for example, the "lunar destiny" of human existence, the fact that man is "measured" by temporal rhythms which are one with the phases of the Moon, that he is consigned to death but that, like the Moon which reappears in the sky after three days of darkness, he also can begin his existence again, and that, in any case, he nourishes the hope of a life beyond the tomb, more certain or better as a consequence of initiation.

(4) This capacity of religious symbolism to reveal a multitude of structurally united meanings has an important consequence: the symbol is capable of *revealing a perspective in which diverse realities can be fitted together or even integrated into a "system".* In

[1] See *Traité*, pp. 154ff.

other words, a religious symbol allows man to discover a certain unity of the World and at the same time to become aware of his own destiny as an integral part of the World. In the case of lunar symbolism, it is clear in what sense the different meanings of the symbols form a "system". On different registers (cosmological, anthropological, and "spiritual") the lunar rhythm reveals homologous patterns: always it is a matter of modalities of existence subject to the law of Time and cyclic becoming, that is to say of existences destined for a "Life" which carries, in its very structure, death and rebirth. Thanks to the Moon symbolism, the World no longer appears an arbitrary assembly of heterogeneous and divergent realities. The various cosmic levels are mutually related, they are, in a sense, "bound together" by the same lunar rhythm, just as human life is "woven" by the Moon and predestined by the Spinning Goddesses.

Another example will illustrate even better this capacity of symbols to open up a perspective in which things can be understood as united in a system. The symbolism of Night and Darkness—which can be discerned in cosmogonic myths, in initiatory rites, in iconographies featuring nocturnal or underground creatures—reveals the structural unity between the pre-cosmogonic and pre-natal Darkness, on the one hand, and death, rebirth and initiation on the other.[1] This renders possible not only the intuition of a certain mode of being, but also the comprehension of the "place" of that mode of being in the constitution of the World and the human condition. The symbolism of cosmic Night enables man to see what existed before him and before the World, to understand how things came into existence, and where things "were" before they were there, before him. Once again, this is no speculation but a direct understanding of the mystery that things had a beginning, and that everything which precedes and concerns this beginning

[1] It must be added that Darkness symbolizes not only the pre-cosmic "chaos" but also "orgy" (social confusion) and "madness" (disintegra
personality).   tion of the

has a supreme value for human existence. Consider the great importance of initiatory rites involving a *regressus ad uterum*, as a result of which man believes himself able to start a new existence. Remember also the innumerable ceremonies intended periodically to restore the primordial "Chaos" in order to regenerate the World and human society.

(5) Perhaps the most important function of religious symbolism—especially important because of the role it will play in later philosophical speculations—is its *capacity for expressing paradoxical situations or certain patterns of ultimate reality that can be expressed in no other way*. One example will suffice: the symbolism of the Symplegades[1] as it can be deciphered in numerous myths, legends and images presenting the paradox of a passage from one mode of existence to another—transfer from this world to another, from Earth to Heaven or Hell, or passage from a profane, purely carnal existence to a spiritual existence, etc. The following are the most frequent images: to pass between two clashing rocks or icebergs, or between two mountains in perpetual movement, or between two jaws, or to penetrate the *vagina dentata* and come out unharmed, or enter a mountain that reveals no opening, etc. One understands the significance of all these images: if the possibility of a "passage" exists, it can only be effectuated "in the spirit"—giving the word all the meanings that it is capable of carrying in archaic societies: a discarnate being, the imaginary world and the world of ideas. One can pass through a Symplegades in so far as one behaves "as a spirit", that is to say shows imagination and intelligence and so proves oneself capable of detaching oneself from immediate reality.[2] No other symbol of the "difficult passage"—not even the celebrated motif of the bridge filed to the sharpness of a sword-edge, or the razor mentioned in the *Katha Upanishad* (III, 14)—reveals more clearly than the Symplegades that there is a way

[1] See Ananda K. Coomaraswamy, *Symplegades*, Homage to George Sarton, edited M. F. Ashley Montagu, New York, 1947, pp. 463-88. See also Carl Hentze, *Tod, Auferstehung, Weltordnung*, Zurich, 1955, especially pp. 45ff.

[2] See *Birth and Rebirth*, pp. 64ff.

of being inaccessible to immediate experience, and that this way of being can only be attained by renouncing a crude belief in the impregnability of matter.

One could make similar observations concerning the capacity of symbols to express the contradictory aspects of ultimate reality. Nicolas Cusanus considered the *coincidentia oppositorum* as the most suitable definition of God's nature (see supra, chapter II). Now, this symbol had long ago been used to signify not only what we call the "totality" or the "absolute" but paradoxical coexistence in the divinity of the opposite and antagonistic principles. The conjunction of the Serpent (or another symbol of the chthonic and unmanifested darkness) and the Eagle (symbol of the solar and unmanifested light) expresses, in iconography or in myth, the mystery of the totality and the cosmic unity.[1] To repeat, although the concepts of polarity and the *coincidentia oppositorum* have been used systematically since the beginnings of philosophical speculation, the symbols which have obscurely revealed them have not been the product of critical reflection but the result of an existential tension. Assuming its presence in the World, man found himself facing the "cipher" or "word" of the World and this led him to confront the mystery of the contradictory aspects of a reality or sacrality which he was tempted to consider as single and homogeneous. One of the greatest discoveries of the human spirit was naïvely anticipated on the day when, by certain religious symbols, man guessed that oppositions and antagonisms can be fitted and integrated into a unity. From then onwards the negative and sinister aspects of the Cosmos and the Gods not only found a justification but revealed themselves as an integral part of all reality or sacrality.

(6) Finally, we must stress the *existential value of religious symbolism*, that is to say the fact that a symbol *always points to a reality or a situation concerning human existence*. It is above all this existential dimension that distinguishes and divides symbols from concepts. Symbols preserve contact with the deep sources

[1] See *Traité*, pp. 357ff.

of life; they express, one might say, "the spiritual as life experience". This is why symbols have a kind of "numinous" aura: they reveal that the *modalities of the spirit are at the same time manifestations of Life*, and that consequently, they *directly concern human existence*. A religious symbol not only reveals a pattern of reality or a dimension of existence, it brings at the same time a *meaning to human existence*. This is why even symbols concerning ultimate reality also afford existential revelations to the man who deciphers their message.

A religious symbol translates a human situation into cosmological terms, and vice versa; to be more precise, it reveals the unity between human existence and the structure of the Cosmos. Man does not feel himself "isolated" in the Cosmos, he is open to a World which, thanks to the symbol, becomes "familiar". On the other hand the cosmological significances of a symbolism allow him to escape from a subjective situation and recognize the objectivity of his personal experiences.

It follows that the *man who understands a symbol not only "opens himself" to the objective world, but at the same time succeeds in emerging from his personal situation and reaching a comprehension of the universal*. This is to be explained by the fact that symbols "explode" immediate reality as well as particular situations. When some tree or other incarnates the World Tree, or when the spade is assimilated to the phallus and agricultural labour to the act of generation, etc., one may say that the immediate reality of these objects or activities "explodes" beneath the irruptive force of a deeper reality. The same thing takes place in an individual situation, for example that of the neophyte shut in the initiatory hut: the symbolism "explodes" this particular situation by revealing it as exemplary, that is to say endlessly repeatable in many different contexts (for the initiatory hut is approximated to the mother's womb, and also to the belly of a Monster and to Hell, and the darkness symbolizes, as we have seen, cosmic Night, the pre-formal, the foetal state of the World, etc.). *Thanks to the symbol, the individual experience is "awoken" and transmuted into a spiritual act.* To "live" a symbol and correctly decipher its message implies an opening towards the Spirit and finally access to the universal.

THE "HISTORY" OF SYMBOLS

These few general remarks about religious symbolism would certainly require elaboration and finer definition. Being unable to undertake so vast a labour here, let us be content to add some observations. The first concerns what might be called the "history" of a symbol. We have already alluded to the difficulty that a historian of religions meets when, in order to isolate the structure of a symbol, he has to study and compare documents belonging to different cultures and historical eras. To say that a symbol has a "history" may mean two things: (a) that this symbol was formed at a certain historical moment and consequently could not have existed *before* that moment; (b) that this symbol spread from a precise cultural centre and that consequently one must not consider it to have been spontaneously rediscovered in all the other cultures in which it is found.

That there have been many symbols dependant on precise historical situations is beyond doubt. It is clear, for example, that the spade cannot have been assimilated to the phallus or agricultural labour to the sexual act before the discovery of agriculture. Similarly, the symbolic value of the figure 7, and consequently the imagery of the seven-branched Cosmic Tree, did not seize men's minds before the discovery of the seven planets, which led, in Mesopotamia, to the conception of the seven planetary heavens. And very many symbols attached themselves to particular socio-political and local situations, and took form at a precise historical moment: the symbols of royalty and matriarchy, for instance, or systems implying the division of a society into two halves, at the same time antagonistic and complementary, etc.

All this being known, it follows that the second possible meaning of the expression "the history of a symbol" is equally right: symbols connected with agriculture, royalty, etc., were very probably diffused with these other cultural elements and their respective ideologies. But to recognize the historical nature of certain religious symbols does not nullify what we have said above concerning the function of religious symbols in general. On the one hand it is important to make clear that, though numerous, these symbols connected with cultural events are sensibly less frequent than the symbols relative to the cosmic structure or the human condition. The majority of religious symbols *point to the world in its totality or one of its structures* (Night, Waters, Sky, Stars, seasons, vegetation, temporal rhythms, animal life, etc.), or *refer to situations that play a part in all human existence*, to the fact that man has sex, is mortal, and in quest of what we call today the "ultimate reality". In certain cases, archaic symbols relating to death, sexuality, hope of an existence beyond the tomb, etc., have been modified, even replaced by similar symbols brought by migrations of higher cultures. But these modifications, whilst complicating the work of the historian of religions, do not change the central problem. To attempt a comparison with the work of the psychologist: when a European dreams of maize leaves, the importance is not that maize was not imported into Europe till the sixteenth century, that it belongs therefore to the history of Europe, but the fact that as a dream *symbol* the maize leaf is only one of the innumerable varieties of *green leaf*—and the psychologist takes account of this symbolic value and not the historical diffusion of maize. The historian of religions finds himself in an analogous situation when dealing with archaic symbols that have been modified as a result of recent cultural influences: for example, the World Tree, which in Siberia and Central Asia received a new value when it assimilated the Mesopotamian idea of the seven planetary heavens.

In brief, symbols attached to recent cultural events, though dating from historical times, *became religious symbols because they contributed to the "foundation of a World"* in the sense that they allowed these new Worlds revealed by agriculture, by the domestication of animals, by kingship, to "speak", to reveal themselves to men by revealing at the same time new human situations. In other words, symbols bound to new, recent phases of culture were formed in the same manner as the more archaic symbols, that is to say as a result of existential tensions and total apprehensions of the World. Whatever the history of a religious symbol, its function remains the same. To study the origin and diffusion of a symbol does not excuse the historian of religions from his obligation to understand it, and to restore to it all the meanings that it could have had in the course of history.

The second observation to some degree continues the first, since it concerns the capacity of symbols to become richer in the course of history. We have just seen how, under the influence of Mesopotamian ideas, the Cosmic Tree comes to symbolize the seven planetary heavens by its seven branches. And in Christian theology and folklore, the Cross is conceived as erected at the Centre of the World, and acting as substitute for the Cosmic Tree. Salvation by the Cross is a new value attached to a precise historical fact—the agony and death of Jesus—but this new idea continues and perfects the idea of the cosmic *renovatio* symbolized by the World Tree.[1]

All this could be formulated in another manner: symbols are capable of being understood on various levels, one "above" the other. The symbolism of darkness can be read not only in its cosmological, initiatory and ritual contexts (Cosmic Night, pre-natal darkness, etc.), but also in the mystical experience of the "dark night of the soul" of Saint John of the Cross. The case of the Symplegades symbolism is even clearer. As for symbols expressing the *coincidentia oppositorum*, one knows the role they have played in philosophical and theological speculation. But then one may ask whether these "higher" meanings were not, in some degree, implied in the others, whether they were not, if imperfectly understood, at least anticipated by men living on archaic levels of culture. Whence arises an important problem which, unfortunately, we cannot discuss here: how to decide to what degree the "higher" meanings of a symbol are fully recognized and presumed by such and such an individual belong-

[1] See *Images and Symbols*, pp. 151ff.

ing to such and such a culture?[1] The difficulty of the problem lies in the fact that the symbol is addressed not only to the waking consciousness, but to the whole psychic life. Consequently, even in a case where, after a rigorous inquiry directed to a certain number of individuals, one succeeds in discovering what they think of a certain symbol belonging to their tradition, one has not the right to conclude that the message of the symbol is confined only to those significances of which these individuals are fully conscious. The depth psychologist has taught us that a symbol delivers its message and fulfils its function even when its meaning escapes the conscious mind.

If we admit this, two important consequences follow:

(1) If, at a certain moment in history, a religious symbol has been able clearly to express a transcendental meaning, one is justified in supposing that at an earlier epoch this meaning might have been obscurely anticipated.

(2) In order to decipher a religious symbol, we must not only take all its contexts into consideration, we must above all consider also the meanings which this symbol possessed in what we call its "maturity". Analysing, in a previous work, the symbolism of the magic flight, we came to the conclusion that it obscurely reveals ideas of liberty and transcendence, but that it is above all on the levels of spiritual activity that the symbolism of flight and ascension becomes completely intelligible.[2] This does not mean that we must place all the meanings of this symbolism on the same level, from the flight of shamans to the mystical ascension. But since the "cipher" constituted by this symbolism carries in its composition all the values that man has progressively discovered in the course of centuries, in deciphering it we must take into account the most "general" significance: the sole significance which can relate all the particular significances one to another, the sole significance which permits us to understand how all these last ended by forming a single structure.

[1] See M. Eliade, *Centre du Monde, Temple, Maison* in "Le Symbolisme cosmique des Monuments religieux", Rome, 1957, pp. 57–82, especially pp. 58ff.
[2] See *Myths, Dreams and Mysteries*, pp. 99ff., especially pp. 110ff.

Bibliographical Note

The first four studies appeared in the *Eranos-Jahrbüch*, vol. XXVI, XXVII, XXVIII, and XXIX, Zurich, 1958, 1959, 1960 and 1961. The fourth unites texts which appeared respectively in the *Nouvelle Revue Française*, April, 1960; *Paideuma*, VII, July, 1960 (Festschrift für Hermann Lommel) and *Culture in History. Essays in Honour of Paul Radin* (New York, 1960). An English version of the last study was published in the volume, *History of Religions. Essays in Methodology* edited Mircea Eliade and Joseph Kitagawa (Chicago University Press, 1959) and a shortened German translation in the review *Antaios*, II, no. 1, May, 1960.

Index

217

72 73   12 11 10 9 8 7 6 5 4 3

MIRCEA ELIADE

*The Two and
the One*

"Mircea Eliade has achieved world renown through his many writings in the wide fields of the comparative study of religions. He might be called a modern Frazer. . . . In *The Two and the One,* Eliade attempts two tasks. The major part of the book is concerned with comparisons of religious experiences and beliefs, beginning with a modern vision of mystic light in America, and ranging thence to Palestine, India and Tibet. Discussion of the mystery of the whole reveals the opposition of light and dark, gods and demons, the *coincidentia oppositorum*, a favourite symbol of Eliade. There follow descriptions of myths of the destruction of the world and eschatological renewal in a golden age, and notes on cosmic ropes and webs. The second task appears in observations on religious symbolism and the work of the modern historian of religion. . . . The task of historians of religion is 'to assimilate culturally the spiritual universes' of Africa and Asia before they disappear as spiritual universes and are 'reduced to *facts* about social organizations' and colonial history. In this prophetic interpretation there is no more outstanding writer than Mircea Eliade."—*Times Literary Supplement*

"Every so often one comes upon a book which points to an age beyond the horizon of contemporary culture. Such a work is *The Two and the One* by Mircea Eliade, a stimulating synthesis of psychology, anthropology, and religion."—*Catholic Herald*

"Mircea Eliade is the most informative guide to the modern mythologies. Having de-sacralised the world, we yearn for the myths from which we have disassociated ourselves. Eliade is alert to this situation. He gives the whole subject a valuable and comprehensiv new look."—*New Statesman*

MIRCEA ELIADE is the Sewell L. Avery Distinguished Service Professor at the University of Chicago. Among the many books he has written are *A History of Religious Ideas; The Quest: History and Meaning in Religion; The Forge and the Crucible;* and *Occultism, Witchcraft, and Cultural Fashions,* all published by the University of Chicago Press.

A **Phoenix Book** published by the University of Chicago Press

Paper   ISBN: 0-226-20389-1